The Insight of Unbelievers

The Insight of Unbelievers

Nicholas of Lyra and Christian Reading of Jewish Text in the Later Middle Ages

Deeana Copeland Klepper

PENN

University of Pennsylvania Press
Philadelphia

10   9   8   7   6   5   4   3   2   1

Published by
University of Pennsylvania Press
Philadelphia, Pennsylvania 19104-4112

A Cataloging-in-Publication record is available from the Library of Congress

ISBN: 978-0-8122-3991-1

For Patricia and Kent Shifferd, my teachers

Contents

Introduction

In the year 1309, three years after the French king Philip the Fair had expelled the Jews from royal France, in a year that saw the burning of three wagonloads of Hebrew books at the Place de Grève in Paris, Nicholas of Lyra (c. 1270–1349), an important Franciscan Hebraist and Bible scholar, determined a quodlibetal question at the University of Paris asking whether it was possible to prove the advent of Christ from Scriptures received by the Jews. If this essence of Christian truth could be proved by Jewish sacred text, Nicholas wrote, then it seemed "unlikely that the Jews, with so many clever men, exceptionally learned in Scripture among them, would have remained so long in their error."[1] Nicholas's response rehearsed traditional Christian prooftexts but also incorporated extensive engagement with alternative Jewish interpretations of those texts. He ended the question by offering a trio of explanations for persistent Jewish unbelief in the face of what he had presented as overwhelming evidence.[2] Destined to become one of the most widely circulated scholastic questions of thousands determined at the university—the text eventually found its way into hundreds of manuscript copies in a variety of textual settings and later came into print in well over two dozen editions—Nicholas's question reflected the challenges he faced as a Christian Bible scholar determined to exploit rabbinic literature during an era of increasing suspicion of and hostility toward Jews and Jewish texts in western Europe. Nicholas drew from Jewish traditions in his biblical exegesis more systematically than any Latin Christian scholar since Jerome, and he did so at a time when Christian patience with Jewish resistance to Christianity was waning.[3] Hebrew text (and ancient and modern rabbinic interpretation of it) stood at the heart of Nicholas's commentaries in both the Old and New Testaments. In order for his exegetical program to work, Nicholas had to assert the validity of rabbinic interpretation of Scripture as a means of understanding the Christian literal sense while at the same time addressing the error of those rabbis whose insight he so clearly admired. Taken in its entirety, Nicholas of Lyra's work represents both the culmination of a two centuries-long tradition of medieval Christian Hebrew study and an attempt to resolve new difficulties inherent in Christian recourse to rabbinic text.

Nicholas of Lyra came of age in the late thirteenth century, a time when pressures on Jewish economic, religious, and intellectual life were intensifying, leading up to eventual expulsion from many western European lands.[4] The canons of the Fourth Lateran Council attempted to separate Jews from their Christian neighbors, and secular rulers were pressured into compliance by a strong papacy.[5] Concern over usury in Christian society often found an outlet in anti-Jewish rhetoric.[6] Increasingly harsh policies regarding Jewish moneylending restricted the Jews' ability to earn a livelihood, as many other economic pursuits had already been closed off to them.[7] Popular animosity was periodically vented in accusations of ritual murder followed by riots. On the religious front, a new Christian anxiety about perceived errors and blasphemies preserved in the Talmud, Jewish oral law, was equally devastating to Jewish communities.[8] Through the intensive efforts of a small group of clerics, the Talmud was increasingly perceived by Christians as a blasphemous deviation from the Jews' legitimate biblical covenant and served as a focal point for the most serious assault on Jewish religious practice and intellectual life in European history, initiated by the Church and carried out by secular rulers. Although restrictions on synagogue building and "loud chanting" had been common for centuries, never before had Christian authorities intervened so directly in the actual practice of the Jewish faith.

In 1239, at the instigation of Nicholas Donin, a French convert from Judaism, Pope Gregory IX ordered the confiscation and examination of Jewish literature, which led to the infamous trial of the Talmud in Paris in 1240.[9] Although the Jewish community launched a desperate defense, in the end the Talmud was declared heretical and twenty-four wagonloads of Jewish books were consigned to the flames in June 1242. In 1244, the first year of his pontificate, Innocent IV reiterated the condemnation, urging the king of France to remain diligent in the search for copies of the Talmud and to burn the books whenever they were found.[10] When Innocent responded sympathetically some years later to Jewish pleas that their communities could not function without books of the Talmud, Odo of Châteauroux, an active participant in the trial of 1240, arranged for yet another trial in the court of the papal legate in Paris (1248), which resulted in a second condemnation followed by more book collection and burning.[11] Royal ordinances reinforcing the decision were issued by Louis IX in 1257 and Philip III in 1283;[12] the censorship of Jewish books remained a priority for the kings of France as long as Jews were present in their lands. As a result of this interference, the formerly flourishing Jewish academies of France began to fold, the communities unable to sustain significant intellectual and literary pursuits without their books. As late as 1315, in the charter readmitting limited numbers of Jews to specific locations within France (following their expulsion in 1306),[13] Louis X made provision for the return of Jewish books still in royal possession to these communities with the exception of copies of the Talmud, which remained condemned and prohibited.[14]

Although the Talmud was formally put on trial only in France, it was subject to an attack of a different sort in other lands through the preaching activities of Dominican friars.[15] Through their involvement in the Talmud trials, Nicholas Donin and a Dominican prior of Paris, Theobald de Sézanne, brought postbiblical Jewish tradition, and particularly the Talmud, to the attention of a broad range of Christians. Theobald incorporated portions of Peter Alfonse's twelfth-century *Dialogi contra Iudaeos* and Nicholas Donin's initial thirty-five charges against the Talmud into his own *Extractiones de Talmut*. The work of Theobald was, in turn, given a wide circulation across western and central Europe in the late thirteenth century through its inclusion in an anonymous Dominican treatise, the *Pharetra fidei contra Iudaeos*.[16] Numerous other authors borrowed from one or more of the above works, creating in short order a large body of anti-Talmudic literature that was deployed in disputation with or preaching to Jews. The Iberian Peninsula saw an independent effort to expose so-called errors of the Talmud by the students of Raymond Peñaforte, O.P. Led by the Jewish convert Paul Christian, who engaged in a public disputation in James II of Aragon's court with the great Rabbi Moses ben Nahman of Gerona[17] and Raymond Martini, author of two important polemical treatises, the *Capistrum Iudaeorum* and the encyclopedic *Pugio fidei contra Mauros et Iudaeos*, the Iberian approach combined attacks on Jewish blasphemy and error in the Talmud with an attempt to demonstrate that many Talmudic texts could be used to confirm Christian truth, emphasizing a distinction between earlier (*antiqui*) and later (*moderni*) rabbinic traditions.[18] Unlike most earlier Christian polemics, which were generally aimed at a Christian audience, this new approach targeted actual Jewish communities with the goal of achieving large scale conversion of Jews. Forced sermons and disputations were therefore an important corollary to the composition of polemical tracts.[19]

Although it is difficult to discern a causal relationship between new intervention in Jewish religious life and increasing intolerance toward Jewish communities generally, the sum total of secular and ecclesiastical policies in the thirteenth and early fourteenth centuries was an increasing isolation of the Jews from Christian society, perhaps helping to pave the way for the complete removal of Jewish communities through expulsion.[20] There had been brief expulsions of limited numbers of Jews from various regions of France, along with confiscation of Jewish property, dating back to Philip Augustus's expulsion decree of 1182. But with the exception of the complete removal of Brittany's Jews in 1240, significant expulsions of large numbers of Jews from western lands did not begin until roughly the last decade of the thirteenth century—from Gascony in 1288, from Anjou and Maine in 1289, from England in 1290, and from the county of Nevers in 1294.[21] The most frequent justification given by rulers was the Jews' refusal to abstain from usurious activity. Since these rulers could claim to be taking a personal loss of revenue by banishing Jewish communities, they often levied a tax on the inhabitants of their lands to make up for this.[22] Such profits were almost always more lucrative than the profits obtainable outright from the departing Jewish communities.

Expulsions of Jews from one region invariably placed new pressures on Jewish communities—and therefore on Jewish-Christian relations—in other regions. Many of the Jews expelled from England and western lands in France, for example, found their way to Paris, exacerbating the already heightened tensions between the Jewish community and authorities there. The immigrants arrived stripped of most possessions in an already impoverished community severely strained by economic restrictions. The financial difficulties for the Jewish community in assimilating large numbers of new Jews were compounded by a generally hostile attitude on the part of the Christian community toward their increasing numbers in the city. These tensions erupted in the form of the Rue de Billettes host desecration accusation, the first of a new genre of accusations that came to plague the Jewish communities of Europe in the next century.[23] The incident certainly did not help the cause of the Jews in Paris. Mistrust on both sides ran higher than ever, and Philip IV responded by attempting to cut off further immigration of Jews into France.[24] The Crown continued to place new restrictions on Jewish economic and communal life, as well as religious practice, eventually expelling all of the Jews from French royal lands in 1306.

Very few Jews chose conversion as a means of remaining in Paris; among those few who did convert, there were several cases of reversion in the years immediately following the expulsion, indicating some sort of continued Jewish presence, at least in Paris. The continuation of the chronicle of Guillaume de Nangis mentions two separate instances of converts tried for reverting to Judaism in the year 1307, and another relapsed Jew was burned in the Place de Grève in 1310, alongside the beguine mystic Marguerite Porete.[25]

Twelfth-century Christian exegetes like Andrew of St. Victor and Herbert Bosham had been able to incorporate Jewish material into their literal Bible commentaries with a kind of naïve enthusiasm. Certainly charges of Judaizing were possible, as Andrew discovered when Richard of St. Victor chastised him for being too uncritical in his application of Jewish interpretations.[26] Still, a relative openness characterized twelfth-century Christian-Jewish intellectual exchange,[27] and that was replaced with suspicion and condemnation in the thirteenth century. The direct Christian-Jewish intellectual encounter that marked twelfth-century literal exegesis, especially in northern France, had become unthinkable by the turn of the fourteenth century not only because of the increasingly hostile climate just outlined, but also because of the absolute absence of a Jewish community with which to dialogue. Where earlier Hebraists like Andrew and Herbert credited living rabbis in their commentaries, real men with whom they sat in conversation, later Hebraists like Nicholas worked with rabbis only through the texts they left behind.

Over the course of his long and brilliant career, Nicholas of Lyra both utilized and Christianized these rabbinic texts through an interplay of exegesis and anti-Jewish polemic.[28] By the mid-fourteenth century, he had come to serve as the Christian Bible commentator of first resort, based in large part on his perceived mastery of the Hebrew Bible and postbiblical Jewish traditions. Nicholas's extensive writings suggest an ambivalence toward Jews as stubborn unbelievers who nonetheless held indispensable keys to understanding Christian Scripture. The wide, enthusiastic reception his work enjoyed in his own day and for centuries afterward demonstrates an appreciation for Nicholas's use of Hebrew and rabbinic tradition in pursuit of Christian truth and, given the context of later medieval Christian-Jewish relations, reflects Nicholas's successful separation of Jewish literature and tradition from the Jewish community itself. While twelfth- and thirteenth-century scholars looking to find what the Jews had to say about a particular Old Testament passage had turned to neighboring rabbis for help with the Hebrew text, by the end of the fourteenth century, Christian scholars looking for such information were simply turning to Nicholas of Lyra. At just the moment when Jews were being pushed farther and farther to the margins of western European society and were facing increasing harassment in central Europe, Jewish commentary was more widely read in Latin Christendom than ever before, thanks to Lyra's mediation. Nicholas's *Postilla litteralis super Bibliam* became, after the *Glossa ordinaria*, the most widely copied and disseminated of all medieval Bible commentaries, finding its way into hundreds of libraries across the Continent in scholastic, monastic, cathedral, and courtly settings.

In addition to this wide dissemination of Nicholas's commentaries and treatises, his work was also routinely plundered by others, repackaged in new texts either intact or in pieces.[29] Later, with the advent of printing, his commentary came to circulate along with the *Glossa ordinaria*, ensuring his place as the standard Christian resource on biblical interpretation well into the seventeenth century, in Protestant as well as Catholic circles. Although Nicholas's "plain and useful" exegetical style was an obvious component of his success in speaking to so many generations of Christian readers, clerical and lay,[30] his use of Hebrew and Jewish tradition was central. As will be seen, Nicholas's use of Jewish tradition lent an aura of authority to his commentary and contributed to its enormous popularity.

Nicholas of Lyra stands at the center of my book as the figure most responsible for the incorporation of Jewish exegetical traditions into Christian Bible study; his work served to transmit rabbinic traditions to generations of Christian students in a way that coopted Jewish insight into Scripture while dismissing Jewish error. Nicholas's engagement with the Hebrew Bible and Rashi's (Rabbi Solomon ben Isaac, d. 1105) commentary in pursuit of the literal sense of Scripture came at a time when the heyday of medieval Christian Hebraism was past and the Hebraism of the humanists and reformers was yet to begin, and he stands as an important bridge between the two epochs.[31] However central Hebrew learning and Jewish traditions were to his own work, it might be possible to dismiss his interest as anomalous were it not for the overwhelming popularity of his writing. To rephrase Philip Krey's observation on the reception of Nicholas's Apocalypse commentary, Nicholas as a rule may have had few followers in his exegetical program, but he had a great many readers.[32] Nicholas's prominence in the Christian community demands that we give his work, including his use of Hebrew and Jewish source material, serious consideration.

Although Nicholas of Lyra's early life and education remain obscure, we do know that he was born sometime around the year 1270 in Lyre, Normandy,[33] and that he entered the Franciscan order at the convent of Verneuil, Normandy, sometime around 1300.[34] From that point on he appears fairly regularly in various documents, enough for us to be able to follow his career with relatively few gaps. He was sent to the university in Paris almost immediately upon taking his vows, probably beginning his theological studies there in 1301 and attaining the rank of master in 1308.[35] His talents were noted early on, and while still a bachelor he participated in the important and controversial trial of the Knights Templar in 1307.[36] He became the Franciscan regent master in Paris for the year 1308–9, following Alexander of Alexandria in the Franciscan Chair.[37] Nicholas's name next appears among a group of theology masters who condemned the writing of the beguine mystic Marguerite Porete on April 11, 1310.[38] It is possible that Nicholas served a second year as regent in 1309–10, and participated in Marguerite's trial in connection with his teaching position at the university, but it is also possible that he was asked to participate in the proceedings not as regent but because of his already established reputation and because he was still living in Paris at the Couvent de Cordeliers, the Franciscan convent there.[39] He may well have participated during this same period in the trial that resulted in a relapsed Jew being burned alongside Marguerite in the Place de Grève, although we have no trial records to confirm this.[40]

Contrary to contemporary norms within the mendicant orders, after completing his regency he remained in Paris where he spent the rest of his life. Nicholas was named Franciscan provincial minister of France by 1319 at the latest and of Burgundy in 1324.[41] He took part in the Franciscan general chapter meeting in Perugia in 1322 and was an original signatory to two important letters on the poverty of Christ and the apostles that were composed there.[42] Although Nicholas remained personally distant from the political turmoil surrounding the poverty issue, evidence from his *Postilla* suggests that he actively supported the position of the Perugia chapter meeting that Christ and the apostles held no possessions either individually or in common.[43] Nicholas was not only involved in Franciscan affairs but continued to play an active role in the Paris university community throughout his life. Denifle and Chatelain identified him as the "Nicolaus cordifer" who was one of two members of the theology faculty present at a meeting on September 3, 1328, at which the university faculty issued a new statute regulating the conferral of letters of schooling.[44] He was among the twenty-nine Paris theology masters who took part in the debate sponsored by Philip VI of France surrounding Pope John XXII's Beatific Vision position in December of 1333, and he subsequently wrote a treatise consistent with the university faculty's position in *De visione divinae essentiae*.[45]

Nicholas maintained close relations with the royal court in Paris throughout his life, although he does not appear to have been confessor to any members of the royal family. Still, he was clearly a respected presence, and his influence was undoubtedly beneficial to his order.[46] King Philip V's wife, Jeanne of Burgundy, named Nicholas to be executor of her will in 1325, and after her death he helped establish the College of Burgundy at Paris in 1330 with resources Jeanne had bequeathed for that purpose.[47] Nicholas died in the fall of 1349 and was buried in the Couvent de Cordeliers where he had lived for so many years.[48]

We have no way of knowing where and from whom Nicholas obtained his knowledge of Hebrew. As Judith Olszowy-Schlanger has pointed out with respect to the English context, Christian study of Hebrew seems to have been entirely ad hoc without benefit of grammar texts or a formal curriculum of any kind.[49] There are no obvious language schools in which to place him, as we have for Iberian figures like Raymond Martini. Rumors dating from the fifteenth century that Nicholas was born a Jew have been universally discounted by modern historians—as his fifteenth-century critic, Bishop Paul of Burgos (a converted Jew himself) noted, Nicholas's knowledge of Hebrew and rabbinic interpretation was too limited to reflect a Jewish upbringing.[50] Still more unlikely is the claim, first found in a brief biography of Nicholas written in 1406 by the Carthusian monk Henry of Kalkar, that growing up in a poor Christian family, as a boy Nicholas was sent to study in a nearby Jewish school, where he learned Hebrew alongside his Jewish peers.[51] Growing up in Normandy, there would have been no shortage of learned Jews with whom he might have studied. Until the expulsion of the Jews from royal France in 1306, there were a number of important centers of Jewish learning in Normandy, including the town of Evreux, a short distance from Lyre.[52]

Alternatively, Nicholas may have found a Jewish convert to serve as teacher, although he makes no mention of such an aide. It is equally possible that Nicholas worked alongside one of the now-anonymous Christian Hebraists who seem to have flourished in English and French circles in the late thirteenth century.[53] One thing is virtually certain: Nicholas must have studied Hebrew and rabbinic Bible commentary sometime prior to his arrival in Paris in 1301. His earliest exegetical work probably dates to the years 1301–3[54] and was already influenced by the work of Rashi. By the time Nicholas wrote his *Quaestio de adventu Christi* in 1309, he possessed a fairly extensive knowledge of Jewish teaching gleaned from a variety of sources. An appreciation of his skill was undoubtedly in large part responsible for his rapid rise to prominence in the highly competitive atmosphere at the university in Paris.

Nicholas was an extremely prolific writer as well as an active partici-pant in contemporary political and theological affairs.[55] Of his extant works, four were clearly connected with his study of Hebrew and rabbinic text: the quodlibetal question mentioned above (1309); the *Postilla litteralis super Bibliam* (1322–32); the *De differentia nostrae translationis ab Hebraica littera Veteris Testamentis* (1333); and the *Responsio ad quendam Iudaeum ex verbis evangelii secundum Matthaeum contra Christum nequiter arguentem* (1334), written in response to book 11 of the twelfth-century polemical tract *Milha-mot ha-Shem*, by Jacob ben Ruben.[56] The remaining works, his *De visione divinae essentiae*, composed following the Vincennes assembly called in 1333 by Philip VI to consider Pope John XXII's position on the Beatific Vision; the *Oratio ad honorem S. Francisci* (completed sometime after 1332), a set of ten psalms arranged so as to spell out St. Francis's name with accompanying literal commentary;[57] and his brief *Postilla moralis super Bibliam* (completed 1339)[58] remind us that Nicholas's interests were broad and grounded in the larger spiritual concerns of his day.[59]

The earliest of Nicholas's extant works, excluding the fragments of his *Sentences* commentary, is the quodlibetal question in which the *Quaestio de adventu Christi* appeared. The question's dating to 1309 demonstrates that all of the pieces of Nicholas's distinctive exegetical personality were in place by then. Two other questions from the same quodlibet—one asking whether the Jews recognized Christ as the messiah at the time of his coming and the other whether one could prove from Jewish Scripture that King Solomon was saved—still exist in manuscript as well.[60] They, too, are char-acterized by Nicholas's trademark engagement with rabbinic interpretation. As Nicholas incorporated all of these into his *Postilla litteralis*, it is likely that some of the other questions found in that massive work may have had their origins in the same disputation, but we cannot know with certainty. Franz Pelster once suggested that Nicholas held a second series of quodlibe-tal disputations in 1310 in which a number of controversial topics were dis-cussed, including *usus pauper* and whether the time of Antichrist's arrival could be known. However, the attribution of these questions to Nicholas is speculative, and current scholarship is generally against the attribution.[61] Nicholas's earliest exegetical efforts probably date to the years 1301–3, when he would have lectured as a *cursor biblicus* at the university.[62] In his 1309 quodlibet he made references to previous writings on both Daniel and He-brews, suggesting these two books as the likely candidates for his first com-mentaries. By the time he began compiling his definitive version of the *Post-illa litteralis super Bibliam* in 1322, he had already worked out earlier versions of commentary on a number of books, which helps to explain how he was able to complete such a monumental task single-handedly in the span of ten years.

The *Postilla litteralis super Bibliam* formed the core of Nicholas's life's work. Nicholas referred to Jewish scholars on almost every page of the Old Testament and with great frequency in commentaries on books of the New Testament as well. Rashi was by far the most often cited (as Ra. Sa.).[63] Herman Hailperin long ago established Nicholas's textual dependence on Rashi's commentary, but the influence of Rashi on Nicholas extended even beyond the written text. The illustrations of temple implements, maps, and so on that accompany Nicholas's *Postilla litteralis* came from Rashi, who inserted such illustrations in his own commentary.[64] As I will discuss in Chapter 2, Nicholas used Jewish authorities not simply as a source of reliable information on the literal sense of Scripture but also as a tool in challenging traditional Christian interpretation. Just as Rashi had addressed and then moved beyond traditional *derash* toward his own *peshat* interpretation, Nicholas reiterated and moved beyond Christian authorities toward his own Rashi-inspired literal interpretation.[65]

Once Nicholas had completed his literal commentary, he turned his attention to an abridgement of the work called *De differentia nostrae translationis ab Hebraica littera Veteris Testamentis*. In his preface to the treatise Nicholas explained that, being aware that most young scholars could not afford to own the entire *Postilla*, he decided to publish a small volume, accessible to all, that would clarify biblical passages in which the Latin Vulgate version of the Bible differed from the Hebrew. This treatise demonstrates clearly the extent to which recourse to Hebrew text and interpretation defined Nicholas's understanding of effective Christian Bible study.[66] Unlike Robert Grosseteste or Roger Bacon, Nicholas seems not to have agitated for greater attention to language study in western Christendom. He seems not to have been concerned about his own ignorance of Greek or to have considered what a study of Greek-language Scripture might contribute to an accurate reading of the Latin New Testament. But he was determined to provide young Franciscans and Christian scholars generally with a concise tool for incorporating Hebrew Scripture and Jewish interpretation of it into their study of the Old Testament.

This book explores the distinctive concerns of thirteenth- and fourteenth-century Christian scholars with respect to Jewish text and considers how Nicholas of Lyra addressed and resolved those concerns, serving as a pivotal transition in terms of Christian relationship with rabbinic traditions. In the first chapter, I explore medieval Christian Hebrew study, looking particularly at the development over the course of the thirteenth century of two distinct traditions, one aimed at Christian Bible study and the other at converting Jews. I argue that the former category was overwhelmingly represented by Franciscans and the latter by Dominicans and that, eventually, the work of the latter school, highlighting error and absurdity in Jewish text, made the work of the former school more difficult to sustain. The second chapter looks at Nicholas of Lyra's biblical exegesis, particularly his presentation of Hebrew texts for a Christian audience. I examine the precise ways that Nicholas employed Hebrew and rabbinic text in his commentary, working toward an understanding of the importance of Jewish interpretation in his work, including the way that mastery of Hebrew language traditions allowed him to assert his own opinions over traditional Christian authorities. Nicholas fit Jewish texts into a Christian framework through an interplay of direct borrowing, transformation of Jewish teachings, and anti-Jewish polemic.

The third chapter steps back from Nicholas's appeal to Jewish tradition in his exegesis to examine the context of contemporary Christian concern with Jewish unbelief, a concern that had a significant impact on Nicholas's work. How could one profitably use the insights of Jewish rabbis into the Bible, after all, if those same rabbis failed to see the most basic truths present in their own texts? Christian theology dating back to the Church Fathers presumed that prophecy of Christ's advent existed in the Scripture of the Jews even if the Jews themselves failed to see it. In the late thirteenth century, a loosely connected group of Christian scholars—Franciscans all—considered in a series of quodlibetal questions whether one could, in fact, prove Christian truth from Jewish Scripture alone. As the questions utilize the same sort of discourse employed in the debate over cognitive processes by scholars like Henry of Ghent, John Duns Scotus, and, eventually, William Ockham, I link this new, or renewed, concern with Jewish unbelief with contemporary discussion of cognition and knowing.

Nicholas, too, addressed the problem of Jewish unbelief, and Chapter 4 returns to this key figure, exploring his quodlibetal question asking whether Christ's advent and dual nature could be proved by Jewish Scripture and the related question on whether the Jews recognized Christ at the time of his advent. The questions provide an important key to understanding Nicholas's concerns about using Jewish exegesis in Christian study, a practice he clearly found necessary but also potentially dangerous. Through a close reading of the texts, I illuminate Nicholas's careful approach to Jewish tradition, his appeal to the insights of "Hebrews" and Hebrew traditions, and his identification of the errors of "Jews" and "Judaizers." Nicholas's question is remarkable for its time in seeking rational explanations (turning, for example, to Aristotle's *Nichomachean Ethics* on habituation) for the Jews' continued failure to see the Christian truth implicit in their insightful reading of Scripture. I argue that this attempt to isolate the source of Jewish unbelief reflects Nicholas's concern with preserving the value of Jewish biblical interpretation for Christians.

One could hardly find a more widely read medieval exegete than Nicholas, and yet few scholars followed in Nicholas's exegetical footsteps, either in his approach to the literal/historical sense or in his extensive appeal to Hebrew text. It seems that this was the case because of changing circumstances, including increasing frustration with Jewish resistance to Christianity and the expulsion of Jewish communities from England and France, the center of exegetically oriented Christian Hebrew scholarship; because of changing definitions of the literal sense of Scripture in Christian scholarship; and because Nicholas's thorough exploitation of Jewish sources made it unnecessary for Christian exegetes to go to the *Hebraica veritas* or rabbinic texts directly. In the final chapter, I examine the way Nicholas's corpus circulated and was utilized. I also present some fourteenth- and fifteenth-century images of Nicholas for what they tell us about perceptions of him and his Hebrew learning. In one illuminated initial, for example, Nicholas sits directly at the feet of Jerome, the disciple of that master of the biblical letter in Hebrew and Latin. In another, he sits in the scriptorium writing his commentary with Moses and Aaron at his side; Moses holds out to him the scroll of Torah, which he copies into his codex and presents in turn to a royal couple standing before him. The immediacy of Nicholas's connection with the revelation at Sinai is unmistakable, as is his transfer of that revelation to his Christian audience. Nicholas was portrayed as a teacher of noble patrons, poor student friars, even female students. By exploring the many ways in which Nicholas's work was received, in his own day and by later generations, I hope to add another layer to our understanding of the often ambivalent Christian encounter with Jewish tradition in the Middle Ages.

Chapter 1

Medieval Christian Use of Hebrew and Postbiblical Jewish Texts

The incorporation of the Hebrew Bible within the Christian canon established an ongoing connection between Christian and Jewish Scripture, a connection that was sometimes ignored, sometimes engaged, but that effectively bound biblical exegesis with polemic for Jews and Christians alike.[1] At various times, some within the Christian community found themselves drawn to rabbinic teaching as a source for understanding the Christian Old Testament, but such exploitation of Jewish sources could be met with suspicion or hostility, and Christian exegetes who employed Jewish teachers or texts could easily find themselves accused of "Judaizing," or slipping back into a Jewish understanding of the text.

Christian interest in the Hebrew version of the Bible itself was rare in late antiquity and the early Middle Ages. After all, the early Church embraced the Greek Septuagint translation rather than the Hebrew for its Old Testament, and the Church Fathers considered the Greek authoritative. Since the master narrative of Christian Scripture differed from that of Jewish Scripture, the Christian Old Testament quickly took on a character and identity quite independent of its Jewish source. When in the course of producing his own Latin translation of the Christian Bible in the late fourth and early fifth centuries Jerome came to insist on the authority of the Hebrew, the *Hebraica veritas*, over the later Greek, he was roundly criticized.[2] The idea that the older, "original" text was more valid was not self-evident, and prominent contemporaries like Augustine attacked Jerome's Hebraism as Judaizing. Jerome's Vulgate Bible eventually became the standard Latin text of the Bible and his Hebrew etymologies were preserved and read for centuries, but Augustine's allegorizing, spiritual approach to exegesis captivated early medieval Christians in a way that Jerome's literal-historical method did not.[3] The letter was important insofar as it held the spiritual sense but was little valued for its own sake. The nature of early medieval exegesis, focused as it was on the spirit and theology over the letter, demanded no serious reconsideration of inherited Latin texts, and the study of Hebrew in Latin Christendom lapsed.

When a new interest in the literal-historical sense of Scripture emerged at the school of St. Victor in northern France some six centuries after Jerome's death, once again its pursuit was linked with Hebrew study and rabbinic exegesis. The dramatic transformation of intellectual culture under way in the late eleventh and early twelfth centuries led the influential Augustinian canon Hugh of St. Victor (d. 1141) to rethink traditional Latin hermeneutics, focusing much greater attention on the foundation, or the letter of the text.[4] Beryl Smalley in her groundbreaking *Study of the Bible in the Middle Ages* highlighted the relationship between the Victorines' new focus on the literal sense of Scripture and their appeal to Jews in establishing it.[5] Since Hugh was not able to read Hebrew on his own, he turned to Jewish neighbors (or perhaps just one Jew; the number of his consultants is unclear) to help clarify the literal meaning of Old Testament text.[6]

Hugh's student Andrew of St. Victor (d. 1175) developed this approach still further, relying heavily on Jewish interpretations throughout his literal exegesis. It was through Andrew that most thirteenth-century scholars would get their knowledge of Jewish interpretations of Scripture. Like Hugh, Andrew appears not to have had a personal knowledge of Hebrew; he, too, relied on neighboring Jewish rabbis to provide him with information on the Hebrew text and rabbinic interpretation.[7] Herbert of Bosham, another Englishman and likely a student of Andrew's, was remarkable in his day in that he brought a personal knowledge of Hebrew and Greek to his literal exposition of the Bible. Raphael Loewe thought him to be the most accomplished Christian Hebraist after Jerome until Pico della Mirandola and Johannes Reuchlin began working in the late fifteenth century.[8] Although Herbert, too, cited oral communications with a Jewish teacher, he also was able to read Hebrew books on his own and made use particularly of Rashi's commentaries, as evidenced in his Psalm commentary, written after he had retired from Archbishop Thomas Becket's service to the Cistercian monastery at Ourscamp. Herbert was never a teacher in the schools, and his work never found the kind of readership that Hugh's and Andrew's did. The Psalm commentary is his only extant work. Although he stands out as an exceptional Hebraist and exegete, he appears not to have transferred his skill and interest in the use of languages for the study of the Bible to any followers.[9]

The three Parisian masters of what John Baldwin called the "Biblical moral school," Peter Comestor, Peter the Chanter, and Stephen Langton, bridge the gap between the Victorines and thirteenth-century scholars. All three show the influence of the school of St. Victor, and all three used Andrew's writings extensively.[10] Gilbert Dahan found that both Peter Comestor and Peter the Chanter must have consulted with Jews, as they utilized Jewish exegesis in their writing (citing *Hebraei*) that was not to be found in Andrew or other earlier Christian sources. Of the three, the Englishman Stephen Langton was the only one to live into the thirteenth century. He may not have worked with Jews himself, but he definitely used the commentaries of both Peter Comestor and Peter the Chanter, as well as Andrew and Jerome, to introduce Jewish opinions into his teaching and writing.[11] At least two other twelfth-century scholars, including two more Englishmen, Ralph Niger and Alexander Neckam, also introduced Hebrew into their work and consulted with Jews on the literal interpretation of Scripture.[12]

In the thirteenth century, a small but important group of scholars picked up the thread, utilizing Hebrew and Aramaic in their efforts to correct problems in the transmission of the Latin Old Testament—to develop new translations of various Old Testament books or to devise new literal-historical readings of Scripture. This tradition of Hebrew scholarship continued through the middle of the fourteenth century, after which point Nicholas of Lyra's writings, with their extensive presentation of alternate readings from the *Hebraica veritas* and rabbinic tradition, came to serve as the primary source of information on Jewish exegetical traditions in Latin Christendom.[13]

In the second half of the thirteenth century, some Christians began studying Hebrew for other, less benign purposes, namely in the creation of anti-Jewish polemic for use in preaching to or disputing with Jews. Prior to this time, most anti-Jewish literature had been directed at an internal Christian audience; even supposed disputational exchanges, like that of Gilbert Crispin, were generally rhetorical.[14] With the notable exception of the convert Peter Alfonse's dialogue with his former (Jewish) self, which brought a wealth of rabbinic teaching to Latin eyes, references to postbiblical Jewish traditions were rare.[15] Polemicists instead drew on centuries-old proofs of Christianity drawn from the Old Testament, as invoked by the Church Fathers. Treatises addressed Christian self-doubt through the refutation of Jewish error; as Amos Funkenstein, David Berger, and others have suggested, the intellectual revival of the twelfth century opened up potentially dangerous questions of faith, which required firm Christian resolution and led to a dramatic increase in the composition of anti-Jewish polemic.[16] The rise in anti-Jewish polemic evident during the twelfth century thus was reflective of the increasingly open interaction between Christian scholars and their Jewish counterparts, part of the same trend that had facilitated the work of the early Hebraists.

The Paris Talmud trial of 1240–42, and especially the Latin translation of Talmudic material that circulated after the trial, made more Christian scholars aware of more Talmudic traditions than ever before.[17] Shortly after the event, the list of accusations drawn up by Nicholas Donin, the converted Jew who first brought the "errors and blasphemies" of the Talmud to the attention of Pope Gregory IX and who represented the Church during the proceedings, was appended to another selection of excerpts from the Talmud and Rashi's commentary translated into Latin by the Dominican prior of Paris, Theobald de Sézanne. These *Extractiones de Talmut* were disseminated throughout Europe and incorporated into new anti-Jewish treatises, including the very widely circulated *Pharetra fidei contra Iudaeos*.[18]

A circle of Dominican friars under the leadership of Raymond Peñaforte (1180?–1275) came to view postbiblical Jewish texts as a valuable tool in their efforts to convert Jews to Christianity.[19] Just as the Dominicans saw learning and rational argumentation as the key to bringing heretics back to orthodox belief and practice, so they believed they could bring Jews and Muslims to Christianity by developing rational arguments against those religions and in support of the Christian faith. Raymond recognized that such arguments would only be effective if Christian preachers utilized texts accepted as authoritative by Jews and Muslims themselves as a starting point. With this goal in mind, Raymond worked hard to establish language schools throughout the Iberian Peninsula to train preachers in Arabic, Hebrew, and Aramaic so that the friars could master Jewish and Muslim texts for such a purpose. His two most important disciples were Paul Christian, a convert from Judaism, and Raymond Martini, another Iberian friar. Paul's well-documented public disputation with Rabbi Moses ben Nahman of Gerona (Nahmanides) at the court of James II of Aragon in 1263 focused on an engagement with Talmudic sources, highlighting so-called absurdities and errors in rabbinic text while utilizing other rabbinic traditions as proofs of Christian doctrine.[20] The disputation provided an important venue for testing and refining the new polemic. Shortly after the dispute, Raymond Martini edited two different collections of anti-Talmudic argumentation, the *Capistrum Iudaeorum* (1267) and about a decade later (1278) the more encyclopedic *Pugio fidei contra Mauros et Iudaeos*.[21]

Raymond Martini demonstrates in the *Pugio fidei* what was arguably the most thoroughgoing mastery of Hebrew and Aramaic of any medieval Christian Hebraist. The language skills of most exegete-Hebraists, even by the end of the thirteenth century, tended to be rudimentary. The study of Hebrew among the Bible scholars seems to have been entirely informal and individual and focused on practical translation with no systematic study of grammar or style.[22] Bible scholars studied Hebrew for a limited, practical purpose: to be able to employ it in clarifying the text of the Latin Bible, devising new translations of biblical books or, in some cases, to make use of rabbinic insight in their own Bible commentaries. The needs of the Dominican friars were different: preachers needed a much more sophisticated and complete mastery of Hebrew and Aramaic in order to develop arguments against the Jews that would sound plausible to Jews themselves. The Dominican language schools, and later the chairs of Hebrew at the universities, were aimed at inculcating a knowledge of Hebrew sufficient to carry out the tasks of the missionary.[23] It is not surprising that those dedicated to challenging Jews by means of Jewish texts demonstrated a greater mastery of the language and a greater breadth in reading Jewish texts than those who worked within the Christian schools, but judging the relative skill of various Christian Hebraists misses the point that the language was studied to a specific purpose. Over the course of the twelfth through fourteenth centuries, more Christians developed the ability to consult independently the Hebrew Bible and rabbinic commentary and to evaluate this material for incorporation into their Christian study of the Bible, even if the level of their skill was rudimentary when compared to converts like Paul of Burgos or dedicated missionaries like Raymond Martini.

While Dominicans formed the overwhelming majority of missionizing Hebraists, Franciscans, especially those with English connections, were clearly the driving force behind the use of Hebrew for Bible scholarship in the thirteenth century. Noting this interest within the Franciscan order led the English scholar Charles Singer to go so far as to say that "when in a thirteenth- or fourteenth-century manuscript we find any evidence of Hebrew knowledge, we may suspect a Franciscan origin."[24] This exegetically motivated strain of Hebraism, like that of the Victorines, was linked with an emphasis on the letter of the Bible, the historical narrative within the text. Joachim of Fiore's interpretation of the historical ages of the Church inspired many Franciscans to read contemporary events historically and apocalyptically, but even at a more basic level the Franciscan emphasis on imitation of Christ and the apostles heightened interest in history.[25] English scholarship, in turn, continued to be influenced by a longstanding emphasis on the natural sciences and history. A fascination with the flow of history brought members of these two overlapping groups to explore the literal or historical sense of Scripture and led them to employ Hebrew texts in its pursuit.

Franciscans clearly were not the only thirteenth-century scholars with a renewed interest in literal exegesis—the phenomenon extended to other mendicants and seculars as well. The Dominican general chapter meetings in Padua (1308) and Turin (1309) decreed, for example, that every province should set up at least one house for teaching exposition of the literal sense.[26] Yet even when Dominicans became involved in literal exegesis, they rarely turned to the Hebrew Bible or to Jewish sources to aid their efforts.[27] Perhaps the Dominican missionaries' antirabbinic polemic in the later thirteenth century made it increasingly awkward for Dominican Bible scholars to justify the appeal to rabbinic authority that had always been a part of Christian Hebraism. In any case, among Franciscans, the desire to achieve an understanding of the literal sense led them to pursue the study of Hebrew in greater numbers than elsewhere.

In order to understand the particular emphasis on Hebrew, we need to turn to the English context. The preponderance of English Bible scholars with a knowledge of Hebrew in the thirteenth and early fourteenth centuries indicates that the tradition of such language study was strongest there. An emphasis on history, language, and science in the English schools made the study of Hebrew a natural component of biblical scholarship. Close links between England and northern Europe during this period insured the diffusion of such learning to the Continent, where Paris, with its strong Franciscan presence and school of theology, became a center of Hebraism.

English interest in Hebrew may have come from a general historical, linguistic, and scientific orientation, but Hebraism took root particularly among the Franciscans there because of the powerful personality of Robert Grosseteste, who was as important for the growth of thirteenth-century Hebraism as Hugh of St. Victor had been for the twelfth, as well as the efforts of a string of influential English Franciscans, including Adam Marsh and Roger Bacon.

Robert Grosseteste (1175–1253) was not himself a Franciscan, but he was lecturer to the Franciscans at Oxford from 1230 until he was appointed bishop of Lincoln in 1235.[28] Grosseteste's affiliation with the Franciscans was close and it lasted beyond his years as the Oxford lector. As bishop of Lincoln, he maintained Franciscan friars within his household, and upon his death in 1253, he left his library to the Franciscan friars at Oxford.[29] R. W. Southern attributes Grosseteste's commitment to the Franciscans to the influence of Jordan of Saxony, St. Dominic's successor to the Dominican order, who visited Oxford in 1229–30 preaching against the dangers of academic pride. The message apparently had a profound impact on Grosseteste, who shortly left off teaching at Oxford University in order to work with the Oxford Franciscans. In the following year, he renounced almost all of his revenues, devoting himself to following the more spiritual path of his Franciscan students.[30]

Grosseteste was an extraordinarily popular lecturer, and as such he helped shape the direction of Franciscan scholarship in Oxford and beyond. Adam Marsh was probably the most famous of his pupils, but his influence can also be seen in the work of William de la Mare, Roger Bacon, and other, anonymous Franciscan linguists working in England and France in the thirteenth century.[31] Grosseteste insisted on teaching theology from the Bible itself rather than from the *Sentences* of Peter Lombard.[32] He also encouraged the study of Greek and Hebrew, the original languages of the Bible. He learned Greek toward the end of his life and assembled teams of translators to work on a number of translation projects, mainly of Greek texts, but also including an interlinear translation of the Psalms from the Hebrew.[33] Beryl Smalley, pursuing a suggestion by Samuel A. Hirsch, linked Grosseteste with a collection of thirteenth-century Hebrew-Latin psalters from England. The prototype of these psalters, known as the *Superscriptio Lincolniensis*, was commissioned by Grosseteste and contains a prologue thought to have been written by him, although he did not compose the translation himself.[34]

Although he insisted on the integrity of the biblical letter, Grosseteste emphasized the spiritual rather than the literal/historical sense of Scripture in his exegesis. In his *Hexameron* (Genesis 1:4, *He divided the light from the darkness*) Grosseteste described how "light comes when [the darkness of] the carnal sense of Scripture bursts forth into the spiritual sense."[35] Smalley considered Grosseteste to be out of step with his times in his loyalty to the spiritual sense. She supposed that it was for this reason that his works, in spite of their presence in the Oxford Franciscan library, were not often used until John Wyclif revived interest in them roughly a century after Grosseteste's death. Southern, making a similar observation, held that Grosseteste had virtually no influence on scholarship until the late fourteenth century.[36]

This assessment of Grosseteste's influence is not altogether accurate; Roger Marston, for one, was not only a great admirer of Grosseteste's work but also borrowed directly from it.[37] In addition, it seems clear that Grosseteste did exert a considerable influence on others, even if his writings were not used directly and his advice on teaching methods not altogether heeded. Certainly not all scholars have believed Grosseteste's immediate influence to have been so slight as did Smalley and Southern. Andrew G. Little expressed the opinion that "a special tradition of learning was founded by Grosseteste and prevailed through several generations of masters in the Franciscan school."[38] This tradition was based on a study of the Bible (rather than the *Sentences*), the study of languages, and the study of mathematics and physical science. And Daniel Callus noted that Grosseteste represented precisely those things that set thirteenth-century Oxford apart from Paris: "a preference for Augustinian-Platonism; a bent for mathematics and the natural sciences; and a study of languages."[39] While Grosseteste's emphasis on the spiritual sense of Scripture may have been abandoned in pursuit of the literal and his antipathy toward teaching from the *Sentences* disregarded, given that Richard Rufus of Cornwall began lecturing on them little more than a decade after Grosseteste left off teaching, other aspects of his approach to learning continued to hold sway. For Franciscan Hebraists of the thirteenth century, Grosseteste's influence was profound.

Adam Marsh, O.F.M. (d. 1258), a devoted friend and student of Grosseteste,[40] served as a link between Grosseteste and Roger Bacon. He pursued Grosseteste's program of study in which Christian scholars were to learn the languages of the Bible and was mentioned with respect by Bacon as one of only a few scholars of his day who had such a mastery. Prior to his inception as a theology master, Adam seems to have collaborated with Robert Grosseteste on some of the latter's philosophical works. Adam probably incepted at Oxford around 1245, after his return from the general council at Lyon, to which he had accompanied Grosseteste. He served as the Franciscan lector in Oxford from around 1247 until 1250. He then spent much of his later years engaged in political and ecclesiastical affairs until his death around 1258. Adam left in his correspondence a great deal of information on his public activities but little insight into his scholarly pursuits.[41] Our knowledge of Adam's work has come down to us via the praise of medieval authors such as Roger Bacon, Salimbene, and Nicholas Trevet. Roger Bacon indicated that Adam wrote works on philosophy and the natural sciences. From Roger we also know that Adam, like Robert Grosseteste, preferred to lecture on the Bible itself rather than Peter Lombard's *Sentences*.[42] Salimbene states that Adam was the author of many works on the Bible, mentioning particularly Adam's commentary on Genesis, from which Salimbene says he heard a brother Stephen of England lecture.[43]

With Adam we also have the first clear introduction of Joachite apocalypticism into the mix—Adam had an interest in the writing of Joachim of Fiore and sent copies of the Calabrian abbot's work to Grosseteste.[44] Although Adam's works are for the most part lost to us, we know that he was widely respected by his contemporaries as a great scholar and that he held a prominent place in Oxford for a good number of years; his interest in the study of biblical languages and the prominence of biblical texts in the study of theology must surely have had some influence on Franciscan students there during that time.

Roger Bacon (d. 1292) saw himself as a disciple and a staunch advocate of Grosseteste's method of theological study.[45] Grosseteste and Adam Marsh may have inspired Bacon to enter the Franciscan order in 1252. Both men are mentioned with great respect in Bacon's writings, and Bacon's attitude toward the text of the Bible clearly shows their influence. Bacon appears to have developed an abiding interest in apocalypticism, which may have played a part in his sudden conversion into the Franciscan order many years into his academic career.[46]

Bacon's *Opus maius*, *Opus minus*, *Opus tertium*, and *Compendium studii philosophiae* all contain discussions of philology, his basic premise being that the pursuit of knowledge must begin with words themselves. Bacon cautioned against the use of translations, warning that many translated texts, particularly the Vulgate version of the Bible, had become corrupt. He also suggested that Christians were sometimes intentionally given corrupt copies of Hebrew and Arabic texts by Jews and Muslims who did not want Christians to have access to the true text, a charge almost as old as Christian scholarship itself. Although Bacon, like Grosseteste, wrote on more than one occasion that a knowledge of Hebrew, as well as Arabic, would be invaluable in attempting to convert nonbelievers,[47] he also had a more scholarly interest in the language.

Bacon himself knew some Hebrew as well as Greek. He boasted that he could teach any intelligent individual Hebrew in three days. Bacon supposedly composed a Hebrew grammar in addition to his Greek grammar, but no copies have been found to this date. Samuel A. Hirsch, upon studying the fragment of a Hebrew grammar found in a Cambridge manuscript, determined that it must have been written by Bacon. However, Hirsch believed the fragment to be a draft of the grammatical notes later placed in

Bacon's *Opus maius* rather than an independent grammar.[48] If, in fact, Bacon did compose a complete Hebrew grammar, it remains to be found.

Roger Bacon had a great deal to say about attempts to "correct" the Latin Bible in the thirteenth century. As Bible studies advanced in the late twelfth and early thirteenth centuries, there were various attempts to develop a standard Bible text for use in the schools. Stephen Langton's new chapter divisions were part of the process, as was the "edition" of the Paris Bible, or Vulgate, which was a synthesis of existing textual variations and which became the model for all new Bibles in use at the university in the early thirteenth century. Roger Bacon complained about the sorry state of the Paris Bible, charging that it deviated in many places from older Bibles and Jerome's original translation, that the process of copying Bibles for use in the schools, done largely by ignorant scribes, contributed to the decline of an already seriously corrupt text, and that layers of gloss only added to the confusion.[49]

There was a general recognition among thirteenth-century scholars of the need for a better version of the Bible, and so began numerous efforts, led by Dominican and Franciscan friars, to correct obvious errors.[50] One of Bacon's complaints was that the correctors made changes without a proper understanding of the history of the Latin Bible or a knowledge of biblical languages. In the early *correctoria*, such as that of Hugh of St. Cher, the correctors somewhat indiscriminately revised the Vulgate text through comparison with older Bibles and patristic glosses and with Greek, Hebrew, and other Latin versions. Bacon urged a more scientific approach, emphasizing recourse to ancient Bibles and Jerome's Latin translation with the use of Hebrew and Greek versions of the Bible to ascertain difficult meanings.[51]

At least two later Franciscan *correctoria* met the criteria laid out in Bacon's writing, beginning with a knowledge of biblical languages. William de la Mare, O.F.M., was the author of what Heinrich Denifle thought to be the most sound of the *correctoria* he studied for his work on the subject, *correctorium* D. Denifle noted how closely this author followed the approach to correction of the Bible outlined in Bacon's writings; Samuel Berger went on to identify William as the author of *correctorium* D and also saw in him a disciple of Bacon.[52] The English friar displays a solid understanding of Hebrew grammar in his *Correctorium* and his *De Hebraeis et Graecis vocabulis glossarum Bibliae*. He used Rashi's commentary, in addition to the *Hebraica veritas*, to clarify difficult passages of the Bible.[53] As is the case for most Christian Hebraists, we do not know where or when he learned the language. Because of his English origins, many scholars, including Andrew G. Little, have suggested that he may have studied in Oxford before going to Paris, where he became a student of Bonaventure.[54] However, there is no evidence of his ever having studied or taught at Oxford.[55] He was regent master in theology at the Franciscan convent in Paris in the year 1274–75 and probably remained there as a teacher throughout his career.[56]

Gerard de Huy, O.F.M., also made extensive use of Hebrew sources in his biblical scholarship. Little is known about him, except that he apparently was from Belgium, was well versed in Greek and Hebrew, and was author of the *correctorium* labeled E in Denifle's study, and also the *Liber triglossos*, a glossary of biblical words in Hebrew, Greek, and Latin.[57] Berger thought that he was associated with the same school as William de la Mare and saw their work as connected.[58] Gerard was a contemporary of Roger Bacon and may have met him in Paris. Arduin Kleinhans identifies him as the *homo sapientissimus* of Roger Bacon's *Opus tertium*,[59] based on Gerard's adherence to Bacon's principles and the fact that his age would place him into the correct time frame. Roger Bacon, writing in 1267, speaks of a man who has already spent forty years in correcting texts, which could have been true of Gerard.[60]

As is clear in the case of the *correctoria*, attitudes toward Hebrew study and Scripture that may have been shaped in part in England quickly filtered into the Franciscan order as a whole. Throughout the thirteenth century, Englishmen who had the money and connections to do so would follow what Richard W. Southern has called "the continental road to success," traveling to Paris or another foreign school for an arts education, returning to England to work for a few years, then going back to Paris for theology study, and finally returning to England, ideally to a high position.[61] Until the second quarter of the fourteenth century, a great many Englishmen continued to go to Paris for at least part of their theological studies, and there was an ongoing exchange of ideas as a result. A Franciscan interest in new translations of Scripture from the Hebrew, for example, extended beyond England's borders. An early fourteenth-century Franciscan Bible from Italy contains a fresh translation of the Book of Psalms from the Hebrew in what is otherwise a standard Vulgate version of the Bible.[62]

Franciscan scholars used their Hebrew skills not only in writing corrections of the Paris Bible and working out new translations of biblical texts, but also in some cases adduced passages from the *Hebraica veritas* and Jewish commentary in their exegesis. These commentators considered the rabbis to be authoritative explicators of the literal sense of the text.[63] The

Expositio hystorica Cantici Canticorum secundum Salomonem, a literal commentary on the Song of Songs by an anonymous Franciscan author, stands
out in contrast to the usual interpretations of the Song as spiritual allegory.
Focusing on the letter of the text (in the sense of the letter as the historical
representation), the commentary treats the Song of Songs as an allegory for
the history of biblical Israel from the Exodus from Egypt to the time of the
Romans. The author follows Rashi's commentary on the Song of Songs so
closely that Sarah Kamin and Avrom Saltman referred to it as "a Latin version of Rashi's commentary" in their edition of the work.[64] The commentary makes frequent reference to differences between the Vulgate and the
Hebrew text, with the introduction "hebreus habet." Rashi is not named as
a source of information, nor is the common twelfth-century formula "hebreus dicit" utilized. The sole manuscript containing the commentary
(along with almost the complete work of Andrew of St. Victor) belonged to
the Franciscan cardinal John de Murro (d. 1312) and passed upon his death
to the Franciscans of Fabriano in the March of Ancona.[65]

John de Murro first comes to our attention as one of three theology
bachelors assigned along with three masters from the Paris university to
examine the writings of Peter Olivi in 1283.[66] Originally from the March of
Ancona, he must have arrived in Paris sometime between 1278 and 1282. He
incepted as a master in theology and was regent in 1289–90, and possibly
also the following year.[67] He had close relations with Pope Nicholas IV, who
intervened on his behalf so that he might incept as master in Paris in 1289
and then appointed him lector at the papal curia in 1291. John later served
as the Franciscan minister general from 1296 to 1304 and was named cardinal of Porto by Boniface VIII in 1302. Although not a Hebraist himself, his
possession of a manuscript containing the works described above demonstrates how an interest in literal exegesis based on the use of Hebrew sources
reached to all levels within the order. A general agreement on the value of
Hebrew as a tool for the Christian student is evident in Franciscan circles
of the late thirteenth and early fourteenth centuries.

A lack of personal knowledge of Hebrew did not prevent some scholars from incorporating Hebrew or Jewish scholarship in their work. William Brito, an English Franciscan living in Paris, composed (sometime between 1250 and 1272) a popular vocabulary of biblical words from the
Hebrew and Greek with very little knowledge of either language. William
drew his information from Latin sources as diverse as Jerome, Bede, Isidore
of Seville, Peter Comestor and Alexander Neckam.[68] The *Vocabularium* was
widely used by scholars who themselves had no knowledge of biblical lan-

guages; it was one of three books that Archbishop John Pecham (d. 1292) ordered to be purchased and kept chained to a table at the library of Merton College, Oxford, so as to be readily available for use by all members of the college.[69] Just as William relied upon Latin sources to write his *Vocabularium*, Christian scholars were able to make use of Rashi and other rabbinic material through Latin translations[70] and through the secondhand reporting of others, such as Peter Alfonse[71] and Andrew of St. Victor. The circle of scholars who made use of Hebrew or Jewish material in their writing was much wider than the circle of those who actually read Hebrew themselves.

English scholars clearly played a disproportionate role in Christian Hebraic scholarship and the pursuit of literal exegesis based on biblical languages and Jewish traditions. Among the twelfth-century pioneers, Andrew of St. Victor and Herbert of Bosham were Englishmen. Stephen Langton, Ralph Niger, Alexander Neckam, Robert Grosseteste, Adam Marsh, Roger Bacon, William de la Mare, and William Brito are some of the most important of known English scholars, in addition to all of the anonymous English Hebraists whose work we find in Hebrew-Latin psalters, among other places.[72]

Richard Southern's essay on the place of England in the twelfth-century renaissance provides some clues as to why Englishmen in particular may have been attracted to a type of biblical exegesis that led them to look at the Hebrew Bible and to turn to Jewish exegetes for clarification of Old Testament texts.[73] Of the four areas that Southern outlines as fields in which Englishmen excelled in the twelfth century, two of them, history and science, help to explain the English propensity for literal exegesis and Hebraism.

Southern describes a uniquely English tradition of historical writing that may have left English scholars particularly disposed to the study of the historical letter of the Bible. Dating back to the age of Bede, English monasteries were actively involved in the writing of histories; prior to the Norman Conquest, the Anglo-Saxon Chronicle provided a national history. But it is after the Conquest, in the first half of the twelfth century, that Southern sees the creative flowering of English history. In places such as Canterbury, Worcester, Malmesbury, Evesham, Ely, Rochester, Abingdon and Durham, survivors of the Conquest took to assembling the information that would protect their properties, establish the history of valuable religious relics, and preserve the memory of England's now-fallen aristocratic houses for posterity.[74]

Along with the renewed interest in history came a corresponding interest in earlier English monastic intellectual traditions in the sciences. New tools imported from the Continent following the Conquest fueled a scientific curiosity that, in a limited form, had remained a part of the English monastic inheritance since the days of Bede. By the second quarter of the twelfth century, the pursuit of scientific learning had become the domain of secular clerics, who began traveling abroad not only to the schools of France and Italy but also to faraway Spain to learn about science from the Muslims.[75] Southern draws a direct line from the monastic writers of the pre-Conquest period to Robert Grosseteste and his students at Oxford.

Connections between England and Paris continued to be strong throughout the thirteenth century, leading such modern experts as William Courtenay to caution against the attempt to consider the history of one during this period apart from the other.[76] It wasn't until around the beginning of the third decade of the fourteenth century that English schools began to come into their own as an alternative to a Continental education. The lines of influence ran in both directions. We learn from Salimbene that Robert Grosseteste and Adam Marsh were good friends of Alexander of Hales, who, along with William of Middleton, O.F.M., was Bonaventure's teacher in Paris.[77] Throughout the thirteenth and early fourteenth centuries, virtually all advanced students spent at least some time in Paris studying, and English scholars including John of Wales, John Pecham, William de la Mare, and John Duns Scotus were regent masters in theology there.

The mid-thirteenth century saw a conflict at Oxford regarding the teaching of theology at the university, at least for as long as Bishop Robert Grosseteste remained alive. The point of contention was the extent to which philosophical methods and the disputation of speculative questions ought to apply to theology. The disagreements centered particularly on the use of Peter Lombard's *Sentences* in the schools. The Oxford Franciscans, still under the influence of Grosseteste and Adam Marsh, favored the use of the Bible as the only legitimate textbook for the study of theology. Others were anxious to follow the lead of Parisian scholars in using Peter Lombard's *Sentences* in ordinary lectures in theology.[78] The differing positions were articulated in the writings of two Oxford masters, Richard Fishacre, O.P., and Richard Rufus of Cornwall, O.F.M.[79]

The Dominican scholar Richard Fishacre favored the Parisian model and was the first Oxford master to comment on the *Sentences* during ordinary lectures, sometime between 1241 and 1245.[80] In the prologue to his commentary, Fishacre expressed his view that philosophical/scientific methods of study in theology were essential to understanding Sacred Scripture. Peter Lombard's *Sentences*, exploring doctrinal questions implicit in the Bible, was, in his view, really a form of biblical exegesis.[81] By introducing the study of the *Sentences* within the context of biblical lectures, Fishacre believed that he was rejoining two essential components of the study of Scripture: traditional moral instruction, *lectio*, and the exploration of doctrinal questions, *disputatio*.[82]

Richard Rufus of Cornwall was the first Franciscan to lecture on the *Sentences*, sometime around 1250.[83] Richard's lectures on the *Sentences* were the object of some of Roger Bacon's most virulent criticism: Roger charged Richard with having invented and promulgated errors, calling him "the worst and most foolish author of these errors."[84] Richard Rufus was in a difficult position, caught between the mode of theological study then in vogue at Paris, based on the use of the *Sentences*, and the clear position of a powerful friend to the Franciscans, Bishop Robert Grosseteste, who saw such a move as a threat to the primacy of Sacred Scripture in theology.[85]

Richard entered into his lectures cautiously, acknowledging the danger of treating Peter Lombard's work as if it were on a par with the Bible or patristic authorities. His solution was to lecture on the *Sentences* while denying their place in theology per se. In his prologue, which is in large part an answer to Richard Fishacre's position on theology in his *Sentences* commentary, Richard Rufus writes what amounts to an apology for his lectures. According to Rufus, the *Sentences* may provide assistance to scholars in making clear things intentionally left obscure in Sacred Scripture. However, the *summae* are not to be confused with theology, which consists of the study of Sacred Scripture itself, complete without need of any *summa*. Richard repeats this position several times in his *Sentences* commentary, as well as in his commentary on Mark, where he defines the work of the theologian as fourfold: the praise of God in the divine office; the exposition of the Bible; the teaching of morals; and the attempt to explain the difficult, clarify the ambiguous, and, insofar as is possible, elucidate the obscure. The *Sentences* provides a useful, but essentially unnecessary, set of footnotes in this effort.[86]

Peter Raedts questions Richard Rufus's sincerity in taking this position, seeing it as a politically expedient effort to appease the bishop of Lincoln. While defending Grosseteste's traditional, allegorical approach to theology, Richard himself made use of the dialectical method rather than a narrative, allegorical one. Raedts further notes that Richard went on to write a summary of Bonaventure's *Sentences* commentary around 1256, not long after Bonaventure composed the work in Paris. Richard interjects many comments and opinions into this faithful summary of Bonaventure's commentary, and nowhere does the question of the place of the *Sentences* in theology come up. Raedts attributes this to the fact that by the time Richard composed this work, Grosseteste was no longer alive, and so there was no need for him to distance himself from the work at hand. Raedts suspects that while Richard was respectful of Grosseteste's feelings on the place of the Bible in theological study, he personally was as devoted to the new method of speculative theology as was Richard Fishacre.[87] Comparing the work of Richard and Grosseteste on points where they overlap, Raedts finds that Richard was very much the product of his Parisian training; only the power of Grosseteste's personality kept Richard a defender of the earlier approach to theology.

Raedts's interpretation would seem to open the question of whether the death of Grosseteste signaled the end of any distinction between English Franciscan and Dominican approaches to theology. If that was ever the case, it would have been only for a relatively few years. Roger Bacon's attack on Parisian scholars, including Albert the Great; the Paris and Oxford condemnations of 1277; and the anti-Thomist activity of scholars such as William de la Mare and Roger Marston point to a shift and geographical expansion of the conflict rather than an end to it.[88]

John Pecham, archbishop of Canterbury, representative of a significant group within the Franciscan order, saw himself as the defender of an authentic Augustinian Christian tradition against the corrupting influence of Thomistic Aristotelianism.[89] As an arts student, John Pecham may have counted Roger Bacon among his teachers. Pecham studied theology in Paris at a time when Bonaventure was still the dominant force in the Franciscan order. Pecham's pupils included Peter Olivi, Matthew of Aquasparta, Roger Marston, and John de Murro, all of whom saw themselves as part of an Augustinian tradition. In Oxford in 1284, John Pecham renewed the prohibitions of 1277 against a number of teachings, including a number related to some of Aquinas's controversial positions. Tensions were high as the Dominicans quickly appealed to the pope, viewing the move as a direct attack on their order by the Franciscan archbishop. Although the Dominicans made their peace with Pecham within a few years, the intellectual divergence between members of the two orders, which had become evident during the conflict, remained.

True, the writing of the anti-Thomistic Augustinians was itself infused with Aristotelian philosophy. Bonnie Kent explains the apparent contradiction, arguing convincingly that when Augustinian thinkers opposed the "Thomistic synthesis" they did so not because they feared the encroachment of Aristotelian thought but because they were themselves "attempting a synthesis of Augustine's teachings and Aristotle's. Far from calling attention to conflicts between the greatest philosopher and the greatest Church father, they tended to claim Aristotle's authority for their own views, working to reconcile his teachings with those of Augustine and other Christian authorities, but warping his meaning in the process."[90] Pecham's faithfulness to a distinctive Augustinian intellectual tradition was characteristic of the Franciscan order in general.

The controversy over the influence of Aristotelianism and Averroism in theology coincided with the controversy over apostolic poverty and helped to fuel an already well-established Joachimism within the Franciscan order. Joachim's typological exegesis had found its way into Franciscan commentaries as early as the 1240s, when Alexander Minorita worked the Calabrian abbot's prophecies into his Apocalypse commentary.[91] Even earlier, Adam Marsh was impressed enough with Joachim's work to have sent copies to Robert Grosseteste.[92] Although we have no record of Grosseteste's personal response to the writing of Joachim of Fiore, the Franciscan chronicler Salimbene tied Grosseteste to the Franciscan Joachite Hugh of Digne, saying that Hugh counted Grosseteste among his four closest friends.[93] Interest in Joachim's thought continued to grow within the order, and the most influential Franciscan theologian of the thirteenth century, Bonaventure, developed a theology of history with strong Joachimist leanings. Viewing the influence of Aristotelian philosophy on theology as a real danger, concerned as well with the conflict over poverty with seculars, Bonaventure interpreted the events of his day apocalyptically. The most telling evil signal of the coming crisis was "the adulteration of the wine of revelation by the water of pagan philosophy," while the coming of St. Francis, "the angel of the sixth seal," was the most important positive sign.[94] A similar apocalyptic understanding of Church history is evident in the work of other mainstream Franciscan theologians, including Bonaventure's disciple John Pecham.[95]

Joachite readings of the Old and New Testaments clearly penetrated beyond the circle of radical Joachites. If the actual incorporation of Joachite typologies into Franciscan commentary was relatively rare, using Joachim's ideas as "a general source of inspiration" was common.[96] The Franciscans' interest in history, like their twin interests in science and the letter of the Bible, contributed to a distinctively Franciscan interest in the uses of Hebrew Bible and rabbinic commentary. It is worth noting that Henry of Cossey, O.F.M., an Englishman who was one of the last medieval exegetes to introduce significant rabbinic material into his commentary, has been labeled by David Burr as "next to Olivi, the most Joachite Franciscan commentator whose works have survived."[97]

The Christian use of Hebrew in biblical scholarship reached its apex in the early fourteenth century with Nicholas of Lyra, whose literal commentary on the entire Christian Bible made extensive use of the Hebrew Bible, Rashi's commentaries, and other rabbinic texts. Nicholas continued and expanded upon the tradition of the Victorines and earlier generations of Franciscans; almost every page of his Old Testament commentary and substantial portions of his New Testament commentary made some reference to the Hebrew Bible or postbiblical Jewish literature, especially Rashi. Nicholas, like the Victorines before him, was convinced that Christian truth could be found in the letter of the Hebrew Bible and that rabbinic learning was an indispensable tool for drawing it out. Neither an Englishman, a Joachite, nor an anti-Thomist,[98] Nicholas nonetheless inherited a fascination with the historical sense of the Bible and a dedication to the use of Hebrew text as a window into Christian truth.

Nicholas entered the Franciscan convent at Verneuil around 1300 and was sent on to Paris for theological study almost immediately after. A significant portion of Nicholas's education remains a mystery; in order to complete his theological studies in 1308, he must have spent time in study before 1300. Working backward from his theological regency in 1308–9, we can assume that he lectured on the Bible as a *baccalaureus biblicus* around 1301–3.[99] In his *Quaestio de adventu Christi* (1309), Nicholas referred to his commentaries on the biblical books of Daniel and Hebrews, which he composed between 1301 and 1303 and in which he already demonstrated significant knowledge of Hebrew and familiarity with a number of postbiblical Jewish texts, including Rashi's commentary.[100]

When Nicholas first arrived in Paris around 1301, John de Murro was minister general of the order. John's ownership of a manuscript containing the literal commentaries of Andrew of St. Victor, along with the anonymous literal reading of the Song of Songs, suggests an interest in literal/historical approaches to the Bible, and he may well have offered encouragement to a talented young scholar with the ability and inclination to incorporate Jewish texts into his study of the Christian Bible. We know that Nicholas was familiar with at least some of John's work. Mark Zier has found that Nicholas's commentary on Daniel, one of the first books the young Franciscan commented on as a theology student, was influenced by the minister general's own Daniel commentary.[101] Since Nicholas found himself sitting as a bachelor on the same panel as John de Murro, by then

Cardinal de Murro, in the trial of the Templars in 1307, the two men clearly knew each other more than just in passing.

In his appeal to Hebrew texts, Nicholas was following a path well trod by fellow Franciscans. Like Grosseteste, Nicholas placed the direct study of the Bible ahead of Peter Lombard's *Sentences* or the integration of Aristotelian philosophy into theology. We find several of Roger Bacon's themes echoed in Nicholas's work, indicating more than just a passing familiarity with Bacon's writing.[102] Like William de la Mare, Nicholas used Hebrew grammar and vocabulary to establish the letter of Old Testament text. As the anonymous Franciscan commentator on the Canticle used the biblical letter and Hebrew precedent to produce a historical reading of a text traditionally read spiritually, so Nicholas subjected all of the Old Testament and much of the New to such treatment.

The study of Hebrew among Bible scholars was exceedingly rare in the century after Nicholas: with the expulsions from western European lands, few Jews and no Jewish schools remained near the centers at Oxford and Paris, and with no systematic curriculum in Hebrew grammar for Christian Bible study, there was little support for the pursuit. Although the Council of Vienne mandated the establishment of chairs of Hebrew, Aramaic, and Arabic, the mandate was only minimally effected. In any case, such schools were clearly aimed at mission rather than biblical exegesis. The Dominican preachers' attack on rabbinic texts must have served as a further obstacle to Hebrew learning among fourteenth-century Christian Bible scholars, as Jewish texts were increasingly suspect and increasingly difficult to find.[103] In addition, the practice of literal exegesis changed over the course of the late thirteenth and early fourteenth centuries, and eventually the literal/historical approach established by the Victorines began to give way to a more expansive hermeneutic in which much of the spiritual sense was understood to be situated within the literal. In essence, Nicholas's work, popular though it remained, was marked by an approach to the literal sense that was rapidly falling out of fashion.[104] Though Nicholas's work won quick and overwhelming acceptance as an invaluable guide to understanding the Bible, largely on the basis of his presentation of Hebrew and Jewish tradition, he was not widely imitated.[105] Nevertheless, the nearly universal availability of his *Postilla litteralis super Bibliam* meant that a vast body of Jewish interpretation, already integrated into a Christian context, was accessible to generations of Christian readers, clerical and lay alike. Nicholas of Lyra, through his Bible commentary, came to serve as the most important mediator of Hebrew traditions for late medieval Christians.

Nicholas of Lyra, O.F.M.: Mediating Hebrew Traditions for a Christian Audience

Nicholas of Lyra's renown as a Hebraist surpassed that of virtually all of his predecessors and contemporaries. By the time of the Reformation, Nicholas, "the second Jerome," was one of the very few medieval Hebraists whose name was still familiar.[1] When sixteenth-century reformers called for a return to the sources, it was his example that they cited. Nicholas's achievement was not, of course, as singular as his admirers seemed to think; his biblical scholarship represented the culmination of over a century and a half of Christian Hebrew study and the development of literal exegesis. But Nicholas brought these interests to bear on his Bible commentary in a more rigorous, systematic way than had previously been done, and his interest in postbiblical Jewish writing gave all of his work a distinctive character.

In pursuit of the literal sense, Nicholas turned regularly to the Hebrew Bible and postbiblical Jewish sources, citing Rashi or other rabbinic authorities extensively in his commentary on the Old Testament and very frequently in his New Testament commentary as well. Nicholas's *Postilla litteralis* quickly became the most widely read Latin commentary after the *Glossa ordinaria*, alongside which it was most often used. The widespread diffusion of the *Postilla litteralis*, in many hundreds of manuscript copies and later in over a hundred printed editions from the fifteenth through the seventeenth centuries, kept his memory alive long after the work of other medieval Hebraists had slipped into obscurity.[2] And so thorough was Nicholas's integration of the Hebrew Bible and Jewish tradition into his commentary and related works that his writing quickly came to serve in place of firsthand recourse to Hebrew texts for Christian commentators.[3]

Nicholas's immersion in rabbinic interpretation was, as it had been for the Victorines, linked with his determination to highlight the literal sense of

Scripture, although his understanding of that sense was somewhat different. While fourteenth-century exegetes continued to utilize the traditional rubrics of the fourfold sense of Scripture when discussing hermeneutics (the letter teaches events; allegory, what you should believe; tropology, what you should do; anagogy, where you should aim),[4] in actual practice the definition of and relationship among the four senses had changed dramatically over the course of the thirteenth century. Commentators increasingly introduced material into literal exegesis that would have been understood earlier as spiritual or allegorical. A. J. Minnis understood this phenomenon to result from the application of an essentially Aristotelian theory of literary authorship to the biblical letter, according to which the human author was the efficient cause of the biblical text. For later medieval exegetes, he argued, the literal sense reflected the intention of that human author, whatever that may have been.[5] While affirming the importance of Minnis' observations on the scholastic application of Aristotelian causal categories for understanding biblical text, Christopher Ocker rejects the notion that Nicholas ("or anyone else")[6] understood the efficient cause to be limited to the intention of the human author and suggests instead that the increasing integration of spiritual/theological material into the literal sense depended not on new theories of authorship but on a new understanding of natural and verbal signification in the text. Ocker argues that "the fading distinction between the literal and spiritual in the late Middle Ages"[7] reflected a new theory of verbal signification with respect to sacred text in which "the external world, and the literal text with it, was seamlessly joined to internal and divine truths in a late medieval reader's experience. . . . The late medieval biblical poetic located divine truth in the text and in the world."[8] According to Ocker, medieval exegetes increasingly introduced substantial metaphorical and mystical material into their literal commentaries because the meaning of the letter itself had been opened to include theological presuppositions and dialogue with the whole of Christian tradition. Nicholas, for the most part, resisted this maneuver even while he acknowledged its legitimacy, which makes the popularity of his commentary all the more interesting.

Where Bonaventure and Thomas Aquinas allowed for metaphorical layers of meaning (Christological or soteriological) routinely embedded within the literal sense itself, Nicholas was inclined toward a much more restrictive literal/historical reading.[9] Like exegetes of an earlier generation, he avoided recourse to theological interpretations and future significations in the literal sense whenever possible. In his reading of Isaiah 66:9, *Shall I who give generation to others be barren? says the Lord your God*, for example, he cautioned that while some Christian doctors read the letter as a reference to the eternal generation of the Son by the Father, such interpretation belonged more properly to the mystical sense than the literal.[10] In an essay on Nicholas's psalm commentary, Theresa Gross-Diaz notes how rarely Nicholas strayed from a strictly historical reading of the text.[11] On those occasions when his historical reading (or Rashi's *peshat* interpretation, which he typically presented as the historical reading) was completely irreconcilable with an essential Christological reading, Nicholas turned either to a univocal parabolic sense or to what he called the "double literal sense" (*duplex sensus litteralis*).[12]

Nicholas invoked a parabolic literal interpretation when he felt there was no other reasonable option. As he explained in his prologue to the *Postilla moralis*, some texts were exclusively metaphorical in their primary intention. Like Thomas Aquinas and other contemporaries, he turned to Judges 9:8, *The trees went forth to anoint a king to rule over them*, and Matthew 5:30, *If your hand causes you to sin, cut it off and throw it away*, to demonstrate how a text might hold exclusively metaphorical significance in its primary (and hence literal) sense.[13] The Song of Songs presented some exceptional challenges to Nicholas's pursuit of the literal sense since its entirety was understood metaphorically. Most Christian authors focused on the spiritual sense of the Song as an allegory of either the relationship between God and the Church or God and the individual soul, but Nicholas chose to follow Rashi in viewing the literal sense of the book as a parable of the love of God for his people Israel as shown in history, beginning with the Exodus from Egypt.[14] Unlike the anonymous Franciscan author of the *Expositio hystorica Cantici Canticorum* described in Chapter 1, however, Nicholas adopted Rashi's approach then transformed it, explaining that the Song slipped in and out of a literal and mystical signification of the bride alternatively as the Jewish people and the Church. Nicholas read chapters 1 through 6 of the Song as a parable of the redemption of the Israelites out of Egypt, and then switched to a parallel reading for chapters 7 and 8 as prophecy of New Testament history.[15]

Elsewhere, Nicholas argued that some passages could hold two temporally distinct but equally valid literal/historical readings, suggesting that at the same time that the Bible referred literally to David or Solomon, for example, it might also refer literally (rather than allegorically) to Christ. Nicholas brought a number of these passages together in a concise explanation of the double literal sense in Revelation Chapter 11, as he tried to reconcile two different literal interpretations of the text's witnesses as either Enoch and Elijah or Sylvester and Menas. Nicholas presents his concept of the double literal sense so clearly here that it is worth presenting at length:

> This exposition (Enoch and Elijah) harmonizes with the text more than the preceding one (Sylvester and Menas). Both, nevertheless, can be called literal. It should be known that a figure of one thing is necessarily something in itself, since what is nothing cannot figure or signify something else. Therefore a figure can be taken in three ways: in one way, as the thing itself, in another way, as the figure of another thing, and in the third way, both as the thing itself and as the figure of another. This threefold manner is frequently found in Sacred Scripture. For example, that which is said concerning Solomon in 3 Kings (1 Samuel) 11:4, "His heart was turned away by women to follow strange gods" is said only with reference to himself and in no way as the figure of Christ that he was, and thus the literal sense refers to Solomon. And that which is said concerning him in Psalm 71:17 (72:17), "His name remains before the sun," cannot be understood as referring to Solomon himself, but only as he was a figure of Christ, on account of which the literal sense refers only to Christ, as I have explained fully in that passage. That, moreover, which the Lord said concerning him in 2 Kings (2 Samuel) 7:14, "I will be a father to him, and he shall be a son to me," is understood to refer to Solomon himself and also to him as a figure of Christ because he [Solomon] was the son of God through adoption in the beginning of his reign, as is clear in 2 Kings (2 Samuel) and he [Solomon] was a figure of Christ, who is the son of God by nature, which sonship is more perfect than the other. Thus there is a double literal sense in one: one concerning Solomon by reason of his adoptive sonship; the other concerning Christ by reason of his natural sonship figured through this. And the Apostle [Paul] turns to this second sense in Hebrews 1 to prove the divinity of Christ, which proof cannot be made effectively through Scripture except according to the literal sense, as Augustine said against the Donatists. So there is a double literal sense in that which is set here, and one sense was fulfilled in Pope Sylvester and Menas, the servant of God, who were figures of Enoch and Elijah, and the other will be fulfilled in Enoch and Elijah, about whom the letter accords more strongly, as was seen. And the letter will be fulfilled in them more perfectly because the principle intent of the [literal] sense is about them.[16]

Occasional parabolic or double literal interpretations aside, Nicholas chose for the most part to articulate the straightforward historical meaning of the letter. Although Nicholas's conservative exegetical approach may have left him outside the trend toward increasingly "spiritual" literal readings, his embrace of the parabolic and the double literal senses at critical intervals demonstrates that he shared contemporary assumptions about the relationship between theology and the biblical letter.[17] Nicholas's relative neglect of theological concerns in his literal commentary was intentional, done with an awareness that the letter could contain multiple layers of

meaning. He did not deny the theological implications of the letter but preferred to place those theological implications in the spiritual rather than the
literal sense.

Whether it was his predilection for Jewish exegesis that led him to his
essentially conservative approach to exegesis or vice versa must remain an
open question, but the two were clearly related. Further, the tremendous
appeal of Nicholas's literal exegesis, evident in the rapid and wide diffusion
of the *Postilla litteralis* and related treatises into university, school, monastic, and courtly libraries, indicates that interest in a more narrowly defined
literal sense characterized by recourse to Jewish traditions was still strong.
At the very least, as Christopher Ocker suggests, it was still seen to be a
useful tool or resource for application in a more broadly constructed approach.[18]

Nicholas's commitment to the historical sense of the biblical letter was
exceptional in his day, and his exploitation of Hebrew and rabbinic source
material was unparalleled; that he saw the two as intimately connected is
evident in his student text, *De differentia nostrae translationis ab Hebraica
littera Veteris Testamentis,* compiled in 1333. In making an abridgment of the
Postilla litteralis available to young scholars, he chose to highlight specifically those biblical passages in which the Latin Vulgate version of the Bible
differed from the Hebrew.[19] This was in his own eyes, evidently, the heart
and greatest contribution of his literal commentary. In the abridgment, he
did more than simply highlight points of divergence in the biblical text; he
also discussed related points of divergence in exegesis. *De differentia* not
only links his work with thirteenth-century efforts to restore the integrity
of the Vulgate Bible through the Hebrew letter, it also demonstrates the
close relationship between his reading of the biblical letter and his use of
postbiblical Jewish text to establish a Christian understanding of the literal
sense.

Like earlier exegetes, Hugh of St. Victor, for example, he readily acknowledged that the literal sense was to serve as the entry point for understanding the multifaceted mystical sense embedded in Scripture. In his
commentary on Ecclesiastes 12:10, *Quaesivit verba utilia: et conscripsit ser-
mones rectissimos ac veritate plenos,* Nicholas noted that "in the truth of the
letter there are contained many mystical truths."[20] Nevertheless, he preferred to keep the two categories distinct, and he spent very little time expli-
cating the depths of the mystical sense. His *Postilla moralis* was written only
after he had completed not only the literal commentary but also his *Responsio ad quendam Iudaeum* and his abridgment of the literal commentary, *De*

differentia nostrae translationis ab Hebraica littera Veteris Testamentis. And in contrast to his thorough treatment of the literal sense, Nicholas cautioned that he intended not to cover the moral sense exhaustively but to provide brief comments on those aspects that he thought would be of special interest to readers (*lectores*) of the Bible and to preachers.[21]

Paradoxically, the very popularity of Nicholas's *Postilla litteralis* has prevented its thorough treatment in modern scholarship. The commentary is so large and the number of partial and complete manuscript copies so great that, while it serves as a vital point of reference in many studies dealing with late medieval theology, biblical exegesis, or Christian-Jewish encounter, it has not received the sustained, comprehensive study its centrality deserves. In an effort to address this unfortunate gap, Philip Krey and Lesley Smith recently organized and edited a collaborative effort on the *Postilla*, asking a group of scholars of medieval biblical exegesis to turn their eyes to specific books of the commentary.[22]

While the diverse collection of essays supplies a less coherent picture of Nicholas as exegete than a more systematic study of the *Postilla litteralis* might, the essays as a group greatly expand our understanding of how Nicholas functioned as an exegete. Like the Victorines before him, Nicholas was sharply focused on expounding the literal sense of Scripture, although it meant something different to him than it had to his twelfth-century predecessors. As Lesley Smith notes in her essay on Nicholas's *Postilla* on Ruth, Nicholas's commentary is characterized by a "studious interest in the detail of history."[23] He worked through chronologies and genealogies with a passion seldom seen. Although certain Christian texts like Peter Comestor's *Historia scholastica* were helpful to him in this regard, Rashi was more so. Nicholas frequently compared Christian and Jewish traditions concerning the details of history and typically found the Jewish position more convincing. Smith writes, "Most, but not all of the Rashi commentary is utilised; much, but not all, of Nicholas's literal commentary can be seen to depend on him."[24] Smith links Nicholas's appreciation for Jewish interpretation with his desire to set the record straight.

A number of the essays in the Krey and Smith collection address Nicholas's use of the double literal sense and its limits. Influenced by Thomas Aquinas, whom he quoted not infrequently,[25] and new trends in biblical hermeneutics, Nicholas incorporated metaphor and future signification into his exposition of the literal sense, albeit to a lesser degree than most contemporary exegetes. Theresa Gross-Diaz notes with some surprise how rarely Nicholas turned to standard Christological explications of the

Psalms, preferring a restrictively historical interpretation unless pushed by theological necessity to a double literal or parabolic sense.[26]

As interested as he was in the historical meaning of the biblical letter, Nicholas resisted historicizing the present in the way many of his Franciscan colleagues did. Careful to avoid political controversy, he expressed his opinions on matters such as the poverty of Christ and the apostles in a way that could be read with equal satisfaction by parties on either side of the conflict. This ability to tread a middle path was observed years ago by Rega Wood when she demonstrated how useful sixteenth-century Protestant reformers found Nicholas's ecclesiology. While Nicholas clearly assumed the legitimacy of papal authority and expected weaknesses in Church leadership at all levels to be reformable, his commentary could also be readily used by those who sought to emphasize the authority of the community of believers.[27]

Noncontroversial Nicholas may have been, but he was also more willing to break with the authority of the Church Fathers than was typical of medieval exegetes. Kevin Madigan notes that the *Postilla* shows significantly less dependence upon and quotation of Church Fathers than most contemporary writings. Not only did he rely less on patristic authority, Nicholas did not hesitate to deviate from it, regularly arguing against traditional interpretations of the text.[28]

Nicholas's relatively light use of patristic exegesis in his literal commentary was probably related to the way he understood his job in employing the literal sense; he tended to prefer rabbinic exegesis (that is, Rashi's "Hebrew Gloss")[29] as the most immediate or direct connection to the literal sense of the text. His independence of thought with regard to the Fathers was obviously related to his esteem for rabbinic interpretation. When he challenged patristic interpretation, Nicholas almost always did so in the context of competing Jewish interpretations. And just as his most important Jewish source, Rashi, often presented rabbinic *derash* on a verse followed by the comment, "but according to the plain sense it means . . . ," Nicholas generally questioned patristic interpretations only on the basis of the literal sense.[30] In both cases, the application of the literal sense served to convey an alternative to established interpretations; both Rashi and Nicholas challenged traditional authorities—rabbinic or patristic—specifically on the basis of literal rather than allegorical understanding.

Those scholars who have treated Nicholas of Lyra's recourse to Hebrew text in some way, have focused primarily or exclusively on mapping his direct borrowing from Rashi's commentary in Nicholas's Old Testament commentary.[31] While scholars have acknowledged the importance of the Hebrew letter and rabbinic commentary in Nicholas's exegesis, the significance of Jewish tradition for Nicholas and his readers remains to be fully explored.[32] Herman Hailperin suggested that Nicholas was drawn to Rashi because his narrative structure, his "elucidation of the scriptural text in verse succession," was particularly suited to Nicholas's own approach to the text.[33] Minnis argued that Nicholas (and other contemporary scholars who turned extensively to Jewish interpreters as reliable sources of information on the literal sense in spite of their error and unbelief) made use of rabbinic commentary because he believed that Jews were "adept at expounding the words of the human *auctor* even though they fail[ed] to grasp the spiritual significance intended by the divine *auctor*."[34] Rashi's continuous commentary on the Hebrew Bible may have been especially congenial to Nicholas's own continuous commentary, and new theories of authorship may have, in part, allowed Nicholas to separate Jewish wisdom from Jewish error, but these would seem to be at most facilitating factors that still beg the question of why Nicholas was interested in what the Jews had to say about the text in the first place. In part, Nicholas was simply continuing the tradition of Hebraism in Bible study outlined in Chapter 1; he found in Jewish tradition a powerful tool for exploring the biblical letter. Whether Nicholas's fascination with rabbinic exegesis led him to emphasize a historical sense[35] or whether a commitment to that sense led him to rabbinic commentary, Nicholas's successful manipulation of Hebrew and rabbinic interpretation allowed him to forward his own literal interpretations over those of Jerome, Bede, the *Glossa ordinaria*, and other contemporary commentaries. Furthermore, as we will see in Chapter 5, Nicholas's expertise in Hebrew text was largely responsible for the reputation he enjoyed for centuries as an exegete.

Many of the qualities that cause Nicholas's commentary to stand out from those of his contemporaries (in ways both significant and small) can be traced to his encounter with Jewish tradition. In his study of Nicholas's Matthew commentary mentioned above, Madigan noted that, in sharp contrast with other late thirteenth- and early fourteenth-century Franciscan commentaries, the text remained a "highly traditional and conservative effort, one whose similarities with the dominant thirteenth-century, nonparticularizing Parisian tradition are far more numerous than the differences."[36] Madigan found none of the post-Bonaventuran innovations that marked much contemporary Franciscan work: no distinctively Franciscan language or references, no distinctive engagement with poverty, no imprint of Joachimism.

There were three areas, however, in which Madigan did find Nicholas's *Postilla* on Matthew to differ from both particularizing and nonparticularizing Franciscan commentaries. First, where most commentators saw the Gospel According to Matthew as pertaining primarily to Christ's humanity, Nicholas suggested that it pertained more precisely to Christ's dual nature, simultaneously human and divine. Nicholas used the temptation of Christ in Matthew 4:1–11, for example, to insist that "the purpose of the narrative was to demonstrate both the true humanity and the true divinity of Christ."[37] Second, as has already been noted, Nicholas's *Postilla* showed markedly less dependence upon and quotation of the Church Fathers, contributing to its relative brevity when compared to other contemporary efforts. Even more, Nicholas was, as already noted, unusually comfortable breaking with patristic authority, and he encouraged his readers to find comfort along with him. Arguing against Jerome's interpretation of Matthew's genealogy of Jesus, for example, Nicholas took on Jerome directly, reassuring his audience that "no one should be disturbed if I depart in this from the opinion of Jerome."[38] Finally, Madigan noted that the work contained surprisingly few of the theological questions that typically lace late medieval commentary.

Each of these distinguishing characteristics, I would argue, is connected in some way to Nicholas's Hebraism and his involvement with Jewish tradition. Nicholas's emphasis on Matthew's portrayal of Christ's dual nature, for example, reflects a preoccupation from the earliest days of his career with the problem of Jewish unbelief. Nicholas immersed himself in the study of Jewish texts and knew well that one of the most critical issues preventing Jews from accepting Christianity was the theology of the Incarnation and Christ's dual nature. In fact, when Nicholas framed his 1309 quodlibetal question on whether or not one could prove the advent of Christ from Scriptures received by the Jews, he specifically set up the question to prove Christ's full humanity and full divinity.[39] In another question from the same quodlibet, later placed in his commentary on Matthew 21, Nicholas set out to prove that Old Testament prophecy pointed clearly to Jesus not only as the Christ, but also as fully human and divine in his messianic role. Nicholas's distinctive understanding of the "purpose" of Matthew's Gospel as described by Madigan was undoubtedly the result of his engagement with Jewish unbelief in Christ's divinity. Even avid readers of Nicholas's commentary were apparently unswayed by this interpretation of the Gospel's message. The English Carmelite John Baconthorpe, a close follower of Nicholas on Matthew in many regards, pointedly ignored Nicholas's peculiarity here, choosing instead to follow the *Glossa ordinaria* in seeing the Gospel as speaking specifically to Christ's humanity.[40]

Nicholas's minimal use of the Church Fathers was more than likely the result of his preference for Hebrew doctors, who brought him closer, it seems, to the literal sense of the text. When Christian and Jewish interpretations came into conflict, Nicholas generally preferred the rabbinic interpretation, unless, as noted by Gross-Diaz, the text contained a Christological imperative.[41] Even the images with which Nicholas illustrated key points of interpretation show this preference: in quite a number of places, he provided two illustrations, one conveying the interpretation of the Christian doctors and one conveying the opinion of Jewish doctors, or Rabbi Solomon specifically.[42]

That Nicholas had earned a measure of authority in this regard may be seen from an interesting passage in a late fourteenth-century adaptation of Nicholas's work by a Dominican friar named George of Siena. George assembled a collection of 116 prophecies from Hebrew Scripture proving the advent of Christ. In addition to heavy use of Augustine and Jerome, George inserted the entire text of Nicholas's *Quaestio de adventu Christi*, pasting it into the appropriate sections of his own treatise. George never mentioned that he was using Nicholas of Lyra's work but carefully edited Nicholas's self-references to suggest that he himself was writing the arguments. This is not surprising, given what we know about medieval scholarly practices with respect to borrowing from contemporaries. But when George came to a passage where Nicholas overtly disagreed with Bede's conclusions about the seventy weeks prophesied in Daniel, whether those weeks of years ought to be considered as solar or lunar years, George's courage failed him. At the point where Nicholas had stated point-blank that Bede was wrong, George stopped in midsentence and suddenly invoked Nicholas of Lyra as a counterauthority, the very author whose words he has been taking on as his own, writing that "According to Nicholas of Lyra, Bede is wrong here." Clearly George was more comfortable having Nicholas disagree with a Latin authority than taking such a position himself, and clearly he thought that Nicholas, with his command of Hebrew, could stand up against Bede successfully.[43]

The last of Madigan's three observations on distinctive characteristics of Nicholas's Matthew commentary seems also to have a connection with Nicholas's involvement with rabbinic exegesis. Given how few questions

Nicholas incorporated into his commentary, it is worth noting that many of them concerned the problem of identity and Jewish unbelief. Questions asking "whether the Jews knew Jesus of Nazareth to be the messiah promised to them by the prophets," "whether the old law provided justification," and "whether it is true that Christ fulfilled the law and did not abolish it" all followed a similar direction, addressing the problem of persistent Jewish unbelief in the context of an ongoing appeal to the wisdom of the rabbis in reading Scripture. Because his exegesis was so dependent upon Jewish insight into the meaning of Scripture, he paused with some frequency to account for the Jews' failure to follow the logic of their own presentations to their logical Christian conclusion, addressing the problem of persistent Jewish unbelief more regularly than most contemporaries.

There are a number of ways, then, overt and subtle, in which Nicholas's knowledge of Hebrew and attraction to Jewish interpretation shaped his writing. The following discussion addresses five distinctive (interrelated) aspects of his commentary that are related to that experience. The first and most obvious effect of his Hebrew learning was that it allowed him to appeal directly to the *Hebraica veritas* to clarify the literal sense of the Vulgate version of the Bible, following in the footsteps of the Victorines and of thirteenth-century Bible correctors. In some cases, this served as a basis for challenging Christian authorities. Second, his desire to exploit the Hebrew text fully led Nicholas, like Jerome and the Victorines before him, to make direct use of postbiblical Jewish material, including midrashic, Talmudic, and contemporary commentary. The most important source for such material was Rashi, whose commentary Nicholas understood as the Jewish equivalent of the *Glossa ordinaria*.[44] Third, his desire to harmonize the Hebrew text with Christian understanding of the text led him to cite alternative Jewish sources—the Septuagint, the Aramaic Targum, or Josephus—as the language there was often more consonant with Christian understanding in messianic passages. Having established these sources as authoritative, he also used them occasionally to forward a Jewish opinion over a widely accepted Christian one. Fourth, his continual emphasis on the insight of the rabbis led him to wrestle at certain moments with those Jewish interpretations that denied key points of Christian doctrine. Nicholas used polemic with precision, careful not to allow it to create doubt as to the accuracy of the rabbis' other insights. Fifth, as we saw in the Matthew commentary briefly discussed above, there is a preoccupation with matters of Jewish faith and unbelief that runs through the entire *Postilla*. Nicholas may have asked few theological questions relative to contemporary exegetes, but when he did ask them, they most often had to do in some way with ancient or modern Jews' relationship to God, revelation, and salvation. Let us now consider each of these areas in turn with an illustration of how each emerges in Nicholas's commentary.

Appeal to the *Hebraica veritas* or General Hebrew Knowledge

In both the Old and New Testament commentaries, Nicholas often turned directly to the *Hebraica veritas* to ascertain the best literal meaning of a passage. Sometimes Nicholas employed Hebrew to support or to clarify a widely accepted Christian interpretation and sometimes to correct standard interpretations. In some cases Nicholas turned to the *Hebraica veritas* simply to communicate information not evident in the Latin, to highlight the use of the Tetragrammaton, for example.

In a discussion of the important prooftext from Jeremiah 23, he wanted to demonstrate Christ's dual nature by the use of the Tetragrammaton in the reference to the messiah as "our just Lord":

Also in Jeremiah 23, *Behold the days are coming, says the Lord, and I will raise up to David a just branch*, the Aramaic translation, authentic among the Hebrews, reads *I will raise up a just messiah, and he will reign as king and wisdom will be, and he will cause law and justice to reign on earth.* And it follows, *and this is the name that they will call him,* "Our just Lord." By [the first part] his humanity is evident, and by that which follows, *and this is the name that they will call him,* "Our just Lord," his divinity is made clear. Now for this name "Lord" the *Hebraica veritas* has the tetragrammaton, which according to the Hebrews is the highest name of the creator of all things. So says Rabbi Moses in his book, *Guide of the Perplexed*, Part I chapter 60, that this tetragrammaton signifies the perfect and undifferentiated divine essence, while other true names of God are seen to be derived from divine works, so Creator, Lord, Savior, and so on in this manner.[45]

Nicholas went on to provide proof that this name was intended to reflect the divinity of its bearer, the messiah himself, not just as praise to the Lord who would send the messiah, as Rashi and Jewish interpretation insisted.

Other times Nicholas turned to the Hebrew to highlight points of divergence between the Latin text and the Hebrew. At Genesis 16:13, Nicholas presented both Christian and Jewish interpretations of Hagar's encounter with the angel in the wilderness, linking differences in interpretation to differences between the Latin and Hebrew biblical text. After a brief comment on the understanding of "our expositors," according to whom the passage suggested that the angel appeared to Hagar in an assumed form, as if its face were averted so that Hagar could perceive it only indirectly, as Moses was able to see only God's back in Exodus 33:18–23,[46] Nicholas continued, "The Hebrews, however, say something different." He introduced two Jewish readings of the passage, including an almost verbatim account of Rashi's commentary, explaining that the Hebrew word *acharei* was understood here to modify the time and/or place of the vision, not an aspect of the angel. According to this reading, Hagar expressed surprise at encountering the angel out in the wilderness because she was accustomed to seeing him as a visitor at the home of Abraham. Hagar's lack of fear at seeing the angel was held as evidence that it was a familiar experience.[47] Nicholas attributed the difference between Latin and Hebrew readings here to the fact that "the Hebrews do not have a grammar separated and distinguished by means of declensions of nouns and verbs as have the Latins and Greeks. Also there are many equivocal words among them, and on account of this the same letter is taken to have different significations and senses at different times."[48] The Hebrew might be read as the Latin Christian translation had it, but it could also be read as the Jews understood it. The notion of equivocality is important, as it suggested that the choices made by Hebrew interpreters were not necessarily superior to the choices made by Jerome in composing his translation.

Nicholas elaborated on the problem of equivocality in his treatise *De differentia nostrae translationis ab Hebraica littera Veteris Testamentis*, which dealt extensively with precisely these sorts of situations:

Know also that among the Hebrews there are many equivocal nouns and sometimes our translation holds to one sense and the Hebrew to another, as was shown in many places in this work. Also various Hebrew doctors on account of these differences vary from one another on their interpretation of the Old Testament. In such cases I have followed Rabbi Solomon, whose teaching among modern Jews is respected as most authoritative.[49]

Although Nicholas conceded that Jerome's translations conveyed plausible readings of equivocal text, in practice, Nicholas almost always favored a Jewish understanding over the Latin in such cases. In the opening verse of the Song of Songs, for example, Nicholas took issue with Jerome's translation, complaining that the Vulgate had improperly fixed the meaning of an equivocal Hebrew word, choosing the inferior meaning. Nicholas determined to set the record straight, explaining that where the Latin text has the Song's bride saying to the bridegroom, *Kiss me with the kisses of your mouth, for your breasts are sweeter than wine*, the Hebrew actually reads *for your love is sweeter than wine*. Nicholas explained that the Hebrew word *dodekha* might mean either breasts or love but suggested that the voice of the bride here makes the latter reading a better choice, since it would be odd for the bride to be praising the bridegroom's breasts.

While it is self-evident that clarifying the Latin text by comparison with the Hebrew might be effective with respect to those Old Testament books taken from the Hebrew Bible, Nicholas found many opportunities to invoke Hebrew text in his treatment of books from the Apocrypha and the New Testament as well, even though there was no Hebrew version of those books. The frequent quotation of Old Testament text within the New Testament allowed many openings, as did references to Old Testament figures, places, prophecies, and so on. In the very beginning of the Matthew commentary, for example, Nicholas turned to the *Hebraica veritas* to challenge Jerome on an interpretation of the genealogy of Jesus. Jerome had highlighted the blameworthiness of Jesus' human ancestors, arguing that the genealogy intentionally named only sinful women so as to emphasize both Christ's humanity and the promise he held out to repentant sinners. Jerome's position was almost universally accepted, but as Nicholas was aware, it left room for Jews (like the eleventh-century polemicist Jacob ben Ruben, for example)[50] to attack the Christian faith on this point. A number of Jewish traditions mocked the Virgin Birth and dismissed the alleged nobility of Jesus' blood. Nicholas may have feared that holding forth a family tree populated by sinful women might alienate Jews further from Christianity. Or he may simply have been responding in defense of Jesus' ancestors. Nicholas acknowledged Jerome's position but argued that he was wrong in his interpretation. Nicholas defended each of the women in turn, and when he arrived at Rahab, he invoked the *Hebraica veritas* to prove that she was not a sinner but a virtuous woman and a true hero of the Israelite people. Following Josephus, the Targum, and Rashi, Nicholas explained that where the Latin identified Rahab as a *meretrix*, a harlot, the Hebrew word *zonah* could also be understood to mean *hospita*, an innkeeper. That was the sense, he argued, in which it ought to be applied to Rahab.[51]

And Judah begot Phares and Zara of Tamar. Jerome, moreover, responding to how this Tamar ought to be understood says thus, "Note that in the genealogy of the Savior there are no holy women present, but [instead] those whom Scripture reproves, as he came on account of sinners, that, concerning these sinners, being born he might erase the sin of all. And so in consequence Rahab was a harlot, Ruth a Moabite and Bathsheba the wife of Uriah. But it is evident that this position is not credible. . . . That which he says about there being no holy women in the genealogy of Christ is clearly false concerning Mary, the mother of Christ, who was and is the holiest of women. Also that which he says about Rahab and Ruth being there specifically on account of their sin does not appear to be true, but rather [they are there] on account of their virtuous acts. About Rahab it is written that on account of her virtue, she aided the Israelite spies and saved them, as is clear in Joshua 2, on account of which she was placed in the ranks of those who by faith performed courageous acts, as is explained in the Epistle to the Hebrews 11. Moreover "meretrix" here is nothing more than her last name, and therefore it should not be taken as having significance according to an actual thing, just as some poor rustic may have the last name of "King," as in "Peter Rex." And in this manner the Hebrews say "innkeeper" where we have "harlot," as I have already discussed fully in Joshua chapter 2.

In Joshua 2, Nicholas was more explicit about the equivocality of the Hebrew word for harlot. A summary of the argument appears in *De differentia nostrae translationis ab Hebraica littera Veteris Testamentis* at Joshua 2:

Latin: They went into the home of a harlot. Hebrew: They went into the home of an innkeeper. The words are alike, but because a prince of the most noble tribe of Judah accepted her as a wife (Matthew Chapter 1), it therefore follows that where Rahab is named "harlot" it ought to be understood as "innkeeper." Another reason is that the word [*zonah*] in the Hebrew letter differs from ours, and the name found in the Hebrew is equivocal, meaning either harlot or innkeeper. The Hebrew interpretation (innkeeper) is better here for the above named reason.[52]

This passage finds Nicholas invoking the *Hebraica veritas* to forward his Rashi-inspired interpretation over a traditional Christian authority. Nicholas recognized his debt to the Fathers, especially to Jerome, but he also felt little fear in challenging their interpretations, particularly when the matter at hand touched on Jewish texts or Jewish traditions. In this case, a concern with Jewish unbelief seems to have moved the direction of his exegesis. Archbishop Paul of Burgos, the fifteenth-century Jewish convert and author of an extensive set of corrections to Nicholas's literal commentary,[53] objected to Nicholas's interpretation of the women in the genealogy, taking Jerome's position that the women were sinners all, though penitent rather than impenitent ones. Given his own status as a convert, it is not surprising that Paul chose to focus on the conversion to righteousness of these women. But Nicholas's primary interest in providing a respectable human lineage for Jesus is evident not only in his treatment of the women, including Rahab, but also in the care with which he attempted to reconcile the genealogies of Matthew and Luke, including a genealogical diagram (Figure 1).[54]

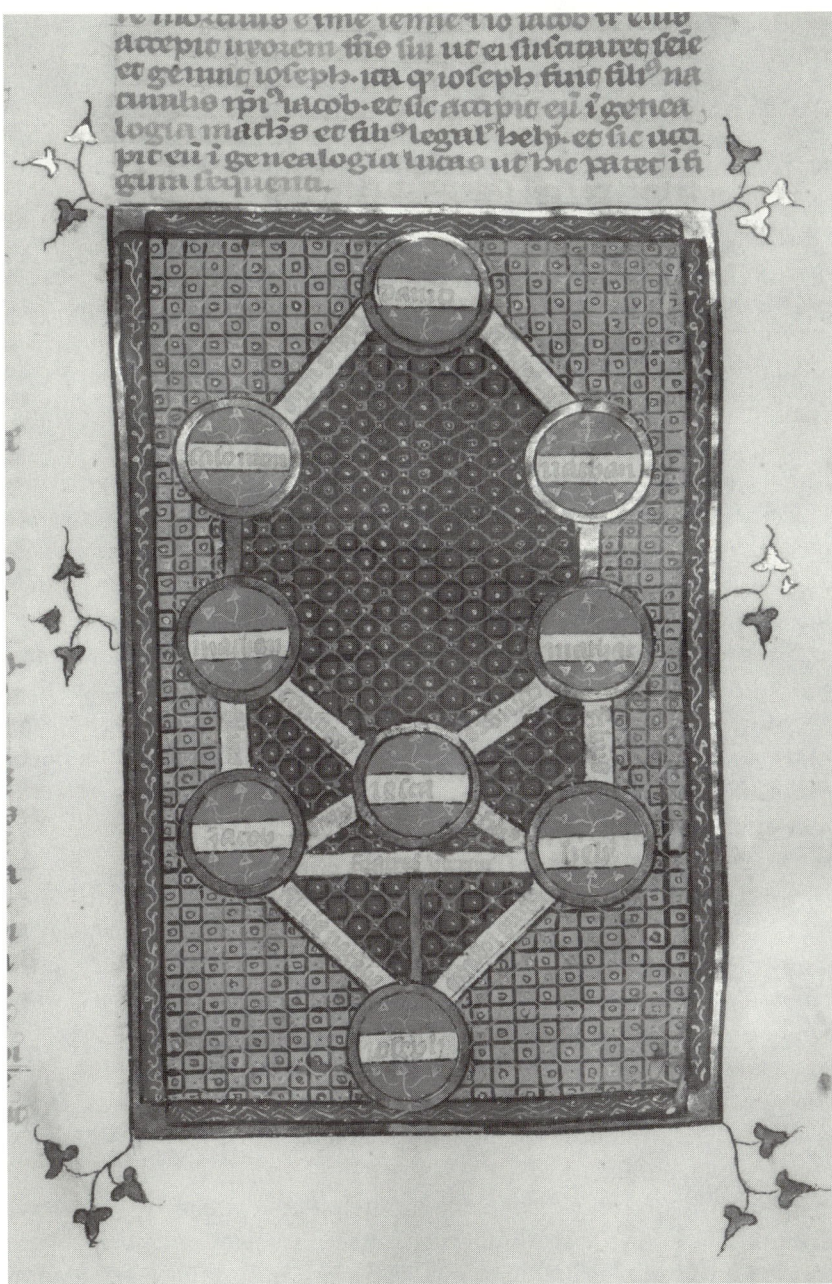

Figure 1. The Genealogy of Jesus, Reconciling Matthew and Luke. *Postilla litteralis super Bibliam*. Princeton University Art Museum. Museum Purchase, Carl Otto von Kienbusch, Jr. Memorial Fund. MS y1937-266, fol. 122r. Photograph by John Blazejewski.

Appeal to Jewish Exegesis

Nicholas turned in many different situations to the *Hebraica veritas*, but he also turned frequently to Jewish interpretation of the Hebrew text to gain a sense of its true literal meaning. He identified these interpretations unapologetically as authoritative. Nicholas, like many other Christian exegetes, tended to make a distinction between Hebrews and Jews in his writing, preferring in general to call Jewish expositors of Hebrew text, whether ancient or modern, *Hebraei*, while reserving the term *Iudaei* to reflect the Jewish community. In the *Postilla* we see *Hebraei*, both *antiqui* and *moderni*, thinking, explaining, saying, holding, even differing in opinions. *Iudaei*, in contrast, tend to be a collective whether in a positive, negative, or neutral way. *Iudaei* act in covenant with God, hold a kingdom, err, are blind, suffer dispersion, or await the arrival of the messiah in the future. The same individual may be identified as *Hebraeus* in one context and as *Iudaeus* in another. It would be a mistake to see the distinction simplistically as approbation and disapprobation. In Romans 2:17 Nicholas explained that the Jews in the time of Abraham were known by the name "Hebrew" in reference to their ancestor Heber, that the people subsequently came to be known as Israelites in reference to Jacob and that they were eventually called "Jews" in honor of the nobility of the tribe of Judah. Rashi is a *Hebraeus* when Nicholas cites him in his introduction to Psalm 49 *Deus Deorum Dominus locutus est* in support of a messianic reading of the psalm, saying, "Rabbi Solomon the Hebrew says that this Psalm speaks according to the letter about the king messiah." But Rashi is no less *Hebraeus* when, according to Nicholas, he erroneously reads the line *Congregate illi sanctos eius* as a reference to the return of the dispersed Jews to Jerusalem upon the messiah's arrival at some future time. Nicholas simply asks his readers to accept the truth of Rashi's messianic interpretation while dismissing the falsity contained in the next passage. As *Hebrew* is used to refer to Rashi's hermeneutical status, so *Jew* is used to refer without judgment to a communal entity; it is the *Iudaei* who are dispersed and *Iudaei* who will return.[55]

Nicholas's favorite *Hebraeus* was surely Rashi, whom he cited more often than any other Jewish authority, but he cited quite a number of other Jewish sources too, including Talmudic, midrashic, Targumic, and a number of other medieval commentators. A close examination of those citations, however, indicates that he probably found the overwhelming majority of them within the pages of Rashi's own commentary. For example, regarding Genesis 7:11, Nicholas noted that the Jews held two different opinions about which month saw the beginning of the rains that brought the Flood. Nicholas presented the opinions of both Rabbi Joshua and Rabbi Eliezer, citing the rabbinic material as if he were looking at it firsthand. A look at Rashi on this passage, however, shows that the material was available to Nicholas there. Nicholas's citation of Rabbi Symeon on the transgression of Nadab and Abihu similarly may be found in Rashi at Leviticus 10. His citation of the Targum's translation of Genesis 49, "the sceptre will not fall away from Judah until the messiah comes," is also found in the relevant section of Rashi's commentary. In dozens of places, Nicholas's apparently independent citation of rabbinic texts can be traced back to Rashi's commentary. Nicholas's citation of other medieval commentators likewise seems often to have come through Rashi's filter. Where Nicholas cited Moses ha-Darshan, an eleventh-century commentator from Narbonne, for example, Rashi had done so first.

Although Rashi's commentary provided Nicholas with a wide range of sources, he also seems to have drawn from Raymond Martini's *Pugio fidei contra Mauros et Iudaeos* and perhaps an additional Latin source for Maimonides. Görge Hasselhoff doubts that Nicholas read Maimonides on his own, as he cites so few of his teachings and all of the citations of Maimonides' *Guide of the Perplexed* and *Mishneh Torah* used by Nicholas were available in Latin in the work of Thomas Aquinas or Raymond Martini.[56] We have already seen that Nicholas seems to have known the *Pugio fidei* by the time he began to publish his *Postilla*, and his primary use of Maimonides in polemic, to support Christian interpretation of Scripture, suggests a source in Raymond's work. Nicholas does not treat Maimonides as a superior authority the way that Thomas Aquinas did or the way that he himself did with respect to Rashi. In fact, he does not even distinguish in his text between Moses ben Maimon and Moses ha-Darshan, referring to them both simply as "Rabbi Moyses." It is left to the reader to determine by context which Moses Nicholas has in mind in any particular passage. There are only a handful of ways that Nicholas uses Maimonides as an authority: for evidence on the significance of the Tetragrammaton (three times), for Jewish corroboration that Jesus performed miracles (twice), and to articulate Jewish messianic doctrine in support of a Christian interpretation of Jewish prophecy.

Although a large number of Hebrew manuscripts would have been available to Nicholas, since confiscated Hebrew manuscripts were given in large numbers to the Dominicans and Franciscans in Paris both before and after the 1306 expulsion, it does not seem that Nicholas read widely in Hebrew material outside of Rashi. It does seem that he may have read Rashi in more than one manuscript context, however. Responding to Nicholas's misattribution of a teaching of Joseph Kara to Rashi, for example, Michael Signer has speculated that Nicholas may have been working, at that point, with a manuscript containing the commentaries of both men.[57]

Signer's observation corroborates other evidence that, in spite of the fact that various pieces of Rashi's commentary on the Bible and the Talmud were available in Latin translation in Nicholas's day, Nicholas worked from Rashi's Hebrew text. Nicholas quoted faithfully from a vast number of passages and, in the absence of a complete Latin translation of Rashi's commentary on the Hebrew Bible, he could only have done this from a Hebrew version or versions of the text. The only known selection of Rashi's Bible commentary in Latin is the excerpts of errors that circulated along with Theobald de Sézanne's *Extractiones de Talmut,* as found in BNF lat. 16558 under the rubric *De glossis Salomonis Trecensis.*[58] As Gilbert Dahan has pointed out in his partial edition of *De glossis Salomonis Trecensis,* the excerpts from Rashi were chosen specifically to highlight the error of the Jews. That being the case, most of the excerpts dealt with rabbinic midrash rather than the *peshat* interpretations that most interested Nicholas. Raymond Martini's *Capistrum Iudaeorum* and *Pugio fidei* are similarly limited in the range of Rashi material they present; while many of Nicholas's polemical engagements with rabbinic traditions seem to have a source in Raymond's text, the range of material available was limited by Raymond's purpose in marshaling "weapons" against Jewish error.[59]

Beyond the voluminous textual parallels with Rashi's Hebrew text, further evidence for Nicholas's direct use of Rashi rather than an intermediate Latin source comes from the cycle of illustrations found in Nicholas's commentary. These illustrations, approximately thirty in number, parallel those that Mayer Gruber has determined Rashi placed in his own commentary and include subjects like the Temple implements in Exodus 25 and Ezechiel's vision of the Temple in Ezechiel 40.[60] Often doubled to highlight differences between Jewish and Christian readings of the text, the images work well with Nicholas's literal exegetical program, but there was no Christian precedent for such didactic imagery.[61]

If Nicholas could read enough Hebrew to make his way through a Hebrew text, why did he not seek out more Hebrew sources beyond Rashi? One cannot presume he had such a naïve understanding of Jewish interpretation that he believed it to be univocal in its literalism, since Nicholas made clear on a number of occasions that he was aware of divergent opinions within the Jewish world.[62] Rather, it seems that Nicholas approached Rashi's commentary as the equivalent of the Latin *Glossa ordinaria*, as a compilation of the most important Jewish perspectives on the Torah. Puzzling over a reference to a Jewish interpretation by a Christian author, Nicholas complained, "Where this tradition comes from I do not know, especially because Rabbi Solomon, who arranged the Hebrew glosses, says something different here."[63] Nicholas believed that in utilizing Rashi's commentary, he was consulting a diversity of Jewish opinions much as one might in reading the Christian *Glossa ordinaria*, and he cited various contributing sources by name just as he would have Augustine or Bede if he cited them from the *Glossa*. Nicholas appears to have been confident in his own mastery, through Rashi, of what Hebrew tradition had to teach him about Christian Scripture.

Nicholas was often quite creative in his application of Jewish tradition. Certainly, as Herman Hailperin demonstrated, he often repeated Rashi's interpretations verbatim at the precise locations in text where Rashi discussed a particular matter.[64] But Nicholas made Jewish traditions his own, and he often employed them in places of his own devising. The first chapter of Matthew provides a wonderful example of Nicholas's comfort with Jewish midrash and his skill in deploying it to achieve a desired end. We have already seen Nicholas turning to the *Hebraica veritas* to restore Rahab's reputation as part of a larger attempt to rehabilitate all of the ancestral women presented there. Just as Nicholas was loath to concede the sinfulness of Jesus' ancestors, he was eager to emphasize the nobility of those recognized by tradition. When he came to the names of Amminadab and Nahshon he paused, eager to sing their praise. This Nahshon, Nicholas said, was the very one who left with his father, Amminadab, out of Egypt with Moses. Nicholas played on the use of "Aminadab" in the Vulgate version of Songs 6:12, *Before I was aware, my soul set me in a chariot beside Aminadab* (the two words of the masoretic Hebrew text, "ami nadiv," appear as one word, the name Aminadab, in the Vulgate), to make a connection with Exodus and the crossing of the sea by following the Jewish interpretation of the Song of Songs as a narrative of the love between God and Israel as demonstrated through the Exodus from Egypt. He then commented that the tribe of Judah earned rulership over Israel through this Amminadab. Citing *doctores Hebreos* on the Song of Songs, Nicholas commented on the role played by Amminadab and Nahshon in crossing the sea. As the Israelites' fear (lack of faith) prevented the waters from parting, Amminadab and his son, Nahshon, followed by the entire tribe of Judah, rushed into the waters and the

children of Israel all followed him to safety, Judah thereby earning rulership:

Phares begot Esrom. This Phares descended into Egypt with Judah his father and
Jacob his grandfather. And there he begot Esrom, and Esrom Aram, and Aram Amminadab and Amminadab Nahshon. And this Nahshon left Egypt with his father,
and therefore he was prince of the tribe of Judah in the desert, after his father. That
this Amminadab was the prince of the tribe of Judah in the exodus from Egypt we
have from Song of Songs 6, where it is said, *My spirit was disturbed on account of
the chariots of Amminadab.* About whom consider the evidence that the book of
Songs, according to the Hebrew doctors, is about God and the community of Israel
led by Him out of Egypt. And in the exodus of Israel from Egypt, the Lord dried a
path through the middle of the Red Sea, and the water parted into high walls as is
found in Exodus 14. And the children of Israel were afraid to enter. This Amminadab, prince of the tribe of Judah, entered first after Moses, and from this the tribe
of Judah earned the dignity of kingship, and therefore it is said, *my spirit was disturbed,* etc. because the children of Israel, seeing Amminadab with his chariot ahead
of them, were awed by his bravery and they followed after him. Therefore, after this
Amminadab, his son Nahshon was prince of the tribe of Judah in the desert, as is
described in the first chapter of Numbers.[65]

This is a particularly good example of how Nicholas deployed rabbinic
midrash with precision and purpose. Nicholas accorded Nahshon's role in
the midrash to his father, Amminadab, in order to make the connection
between the Song of Songs and the Exodus more forcefully while still cele-
brating the tribe of Judah. Since the story of Nahshon (or Amminadab) at
the sea played specifically on the concept of faith and its rewards, it was
especially useful to invoke in Christ's genealogy, given the concern we
have already seen to demonstrate the virtue and nobility of Jesus' human
ancestors.

Appeal to Alternative Jewish Sources

Nicholas appealed with some frequency to alternative Jewish texts—the
Greek Septuagint or the Aramaic Targum or Josephus (*Antiquities* and *The
Jewish War*)—to make the case for a particular historical reading. In a reprise at Hebrews 11:31 of his position on the worthiness of Rahab in Joshua
chapter 2 and Matthew chapter 1, Nicholas reminded his readers that the
Hebrew word for "harlot" could also mean "innkeeper." Here he brought
the point home more forcefully by introducing the Aramaic Targum, saying
that "where our translation has 'they came to the home of a woman prosti-

tute' the Aramaic translation has 'the home of a woman innkeeper.' "[66] In other cases, Nicholas used the Targum to demonstrate a messianic intention not evident in the Hebrew and, more importantly, denied by Rashi and other Jewish expositors. At Genesis 49:10, *The sceptre shall not fall away from Judah nor the ruler's staff from his thigh until he comes who is to be sent,* for example, Nicholas followed Raymond Martini's example in using the Targum to strengthen the traditional Christian messianic reading of the passage. Since where the Hebrew reads "until he comes who is to be sent" the Targum reads "until the messiah comes," he argued, the rabbis must concede the Christian position that the messiah arrived during the reign of Herod the Idumean. The passage on Jeremiah 23 discussed above in the section on Nicholas's use of the *Hebraica veritas* likewise was strengthened by recourse to the Aramaic translation as well as the Hebrew Tetragrammaton. The Septuagint, too, could serve Nicholas as an authentic rendering of ancient biblical text. In the same discussion of Jeremiah 23, Nicholas used the Septuagint for further corroboration of the text's intention.[67]

Nicholas utilized Josephus as a reliable source of information on historical Israel and the Roman-Judaean landscape in which Jesus functioned. At Matthew 22:23, *In illo die accesserunt ad eum Sadducaei qui dicunt non esse resurrectionem et interrogaverunt eum,* Josephus's *Antiquities* served as a source of information on the controversy over resurrection in Second Temple Judaism. At Matthew 24:4, *Et respondens Iesus dixit eis videte ne quis vos seducat,* Nicholas used Josephus's *Jewish War* as proof that the text prophesied the pestilence and suffering that would come with the destruction of Jerusalem. Nicholas cited Josephus fairly extensively as an authority on the Second Temple and its implements as well. At Exodus 25:10–22, Nicholas turned to Josephus in conjunction with Rashi to develop a proper description of the ark of the covenant. As he so often did, Nicholas sided with Rashi's understanding of the text over Christian interpretations, in this case utilizing Josephus as confirmation of Rashi's opinion:

According to Josephus, the rings were arranged in the four corners so that they were near the upper part of the ark under the moulding, and so that the shafts passing through the rings went along the length of the ark. In this the text seems to concur because there it is said, *Let there be two rings on one side and two rings on the other.* However, the side of the ark is generally interpreted as referring to its length, and according to this the space between the two shafts was one and one-half cubits referring to the width of the ark which was between the two shafts. Rabbi Solomon says that the rings were arranged in the corners so that the shafts passed through along the width of the ark. So between the two shafts there was a space of two and one half cubits along the length of the ark which was contained between the two shafts. This seems more rational, because the shafts were put there for this purpose: that when the camps were moved the priests might carry the ark by using them. It was necessary that the priests carry it on their own shoulders, and on account of the weight of the ark and its contents at least four men would be required, two in front and two in back. However two men next to each other are more suited to bearing the shafts in a space of two and one half cubits than in a space of one and one half cubits which would seem too small for two men walking side by side to carry the ark. Nothing in the text stands in the way of this interpretation.[68]

A few verses later, Nicholas addressed different conceptualizations of the cover and cherubim that were placed over the ark.

You shall make a propitiatory of the finest gold: Rabbi Solomon and the Hebrews say that this propitiatory was the cover of the ark, since there is no mention of any other cover, and its length and width are described as being the same as the ark. Certain other doctors say that it was not the cover of the ark, but a table of gold raised above it, carried by the cherubim themselves who were at the ends of the ark, and it was as a chair for God and the ark's cover was as a footstool for that chair, according to Psalm 79 *You who sit above the cherubim*, that is, above the propitiatory. . . . *And in the middle of the two cherubim who were placed above the ark*: From this Rabbi Solomon says that the two cherubim stood above the table of the ark on its edge. Other doctors, however, as has already been mentioned, say that those [cherubim] were placed on the floor of the tabernacle at the end of the ark. They are said here to be above the ark because they were raised high above the height of the ark. So that the above said things can be understood more easily I have described it in a figure.[69]

The figure that follows demonstrates Rashi's presentation of rings and staves running along the short sides of the ark so as to allow more room for two carriers standing side by side and depicts the cherubim standing on top of the cover as well. In the image attributed to "other doctors," the rings and staves run along the long side of the ark, allowing much less room for carriers and the cherubim are depicted standing on the floor raising the cover high above the ark (Figure 2).

Although Nicholas did not side with one position or another in the second instance, concerning the cherubim, he had already aligned with Rashi with respect to the rings and staves, and one might argue that this lent a higher degree of authenticity to the first image, the Jewish interpretation. Nicholas did not identify these "other doctors" on Exodus 25 by name in the text, but many of the early fourteenth-century manuscripts make a link explicitly with Thomas Aquinas, and this may represent Nicholas's own in-

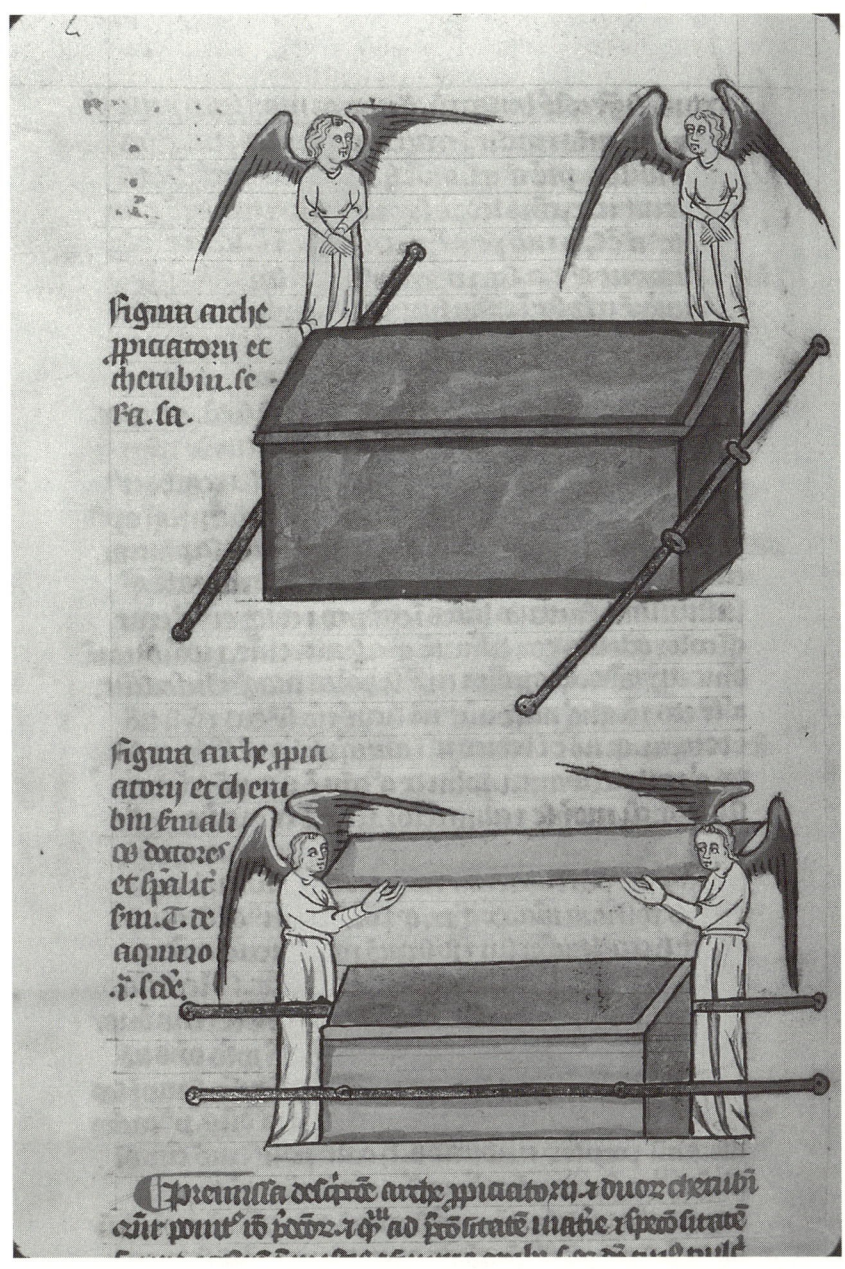

Figure 2. The Ark of the Covenant According to Rabbi Solomon and According to Other Doctors, Especially Thomas Aquinas. *Postilla litteralis super Bibliam*. Bibl. Mun. Reims MS 178, fol. 52v.

structions. Where some manuscript copies simply present "the figure of Rabbi Solomon" with "the figure of others" or "the figure of other doctors," other early manuscripts are more specific, contrasting Rashi's image with "the ark cover and cherubim according to other doctors, and specifically Thomas Aquinas."[70] There is no extant Exodus commentary by Thomas, but he did discuss the tabernacle at some length in his commentary on the Epistle to the Hebrews at 9:5, where the text refers back to the tabernacle, describing how above the ark *were the cherubim of glory overshadowing the propitiatory.*

Thomas wrote:

[The Apostle] describes here those things that were in the second tabernacle, namely, the ark of the covenant, made of incorruptible sethin wood, covered in every part, that is, within and without, with gold. In the ark, moreover, were three things, namely, a golden urn holding manna, in memory of the blessings given to them (Ex. 16:32); the rod of Aaron that had blossomed (Num. 17:8), in memory of the priesthood of Aaron, so that no outsider would presume to approach; and the tablets of the covenant (Ex. 25), in memory of the Law. Also, above the ark were two cherubim who touched each other with two wings and touched the sides of the tabernacle with the other two wings. Between the two wings with which they touched each other, there was a golden table of the same length and width as the ark, namely, two cubits in length and a cubit and a half in width, and there was raised above [it] that which is called the propitiatory. From which it was a sort of throne from which God would listen for repropitiating the people (Ps. 79:2, *You who sit upon the cherubim, etc.*). The ark was truly as a footstsool. Those two cherubim, their faces toward each other, looked upon the mercy seat.[71]

In this case, Nicholas's familiarity with both the Hebrew original and Jewish apparatus for understanding the original allowed him to deviate from a respected Christian position on the literal sense of the text. And citing Josephus—a long-recognized authority in Christian tradition—lent additional strength to his acceptance of Rashi's interpretation.

Polemical Engagement with Rabbinic Traditions

Many examples of polemical engagement may be found in the *Postilla*, most of them either traditional or part of the increasing corpus of anti-Talmudic argumentation that began circulating after the Paris Talmud trial and the Barcelona disputation between Paul Christian and Nahmanides in the thirteenth century. Many of these arguments had been organized and presented by Nicholas in his 1309 question on whether the Advent and dual nature of Christ could be proved by means of Jewish Scripture.[72] Nicholas inserted most of the arguments raised in that question at appropriate points in his Bible commentary. In several places, he rehearsed the range of material he brought into the question, as at the end of Ezechiel and in John 5:39. His citation in Ezechiel is one of several places where he not only mentions the question but seems to acknowledge its continued circulation and relevance in academic circles. At the end of Ezechiel he claims that modern Jews misunderstand the vision in part because they deny that "the messiah promised to them in the law and the prophets was to be God." He continues, "As much as their anticipation of his advent in the future I have extensively disproved by the Scriptures of the Old Testament in a certain quodlibetal question written many years ago, nevertheless, I will repeat a bit of that here," and he goes on to do so. John 5:39, *Search the Scriptures in which you think to find eternal life* was a particularly important text for the Christian belief in Jesus as messiah, as it quite clearly indicated that evidence for Christian truth was, indeed, to be found in the Scriptures of the Jews.

Nicholas quickly ran through a laundry list of classic prophetic passages that offered proof of Jesus' messiahship, to which Jesus must have been referring here: Genesis 49:10 (*The sceptre will not fall away from Judah . . .*), Daniel 9:24 (*Seventy weeks will be shortened upon your people . . .*), Micah 5:2 (*And you, Bethlehem Ephrata, you are little among the tribes of Judah . . .*) Isaiah 7:14 (*And a virgin will conceive and bear a child*), Zacharia 9:9 (*Behold your king comes to you*), Isaiah 53:7 (*As a lamb to slaughter he will be led*), and finally wrote, "And in brief, all mysteries of Christ are to be found clearly in the Old Testament and fulfilled in Christ and therefore it is possible truly to know from the Scriptures of the Old Testament that he was the Christ promised in the law, as I have extensively discussed in a certain question in which I determined this." Nicholas referred to his 1309 question dozens of times in the course of the *Postilla*, at the many points in which he returned to the arguments he had presented in that scholastic disputation.

Although his polemic, when it appears, is typically detailed and precise, occasionally he makes a quick aside or alludes to a problematic element of Jewish unbelief without engaging it extensively, as in John 5:43–44, when he noted that Jesus' words *I come in my father's name and you do not accept me, but if another will come in his own name only, you will accept that one* were left unfulfilled "until the time of Ben Cozeba," whom the Jews received "as if he were the messiah," even though he clearly fulfilled none of the scriptural prophecies.[73]

Preoccupation with Matters of Jewish Faith and Unbelief

One of the most important ways in which Nicholas's involvement with Jewish exegesis affected his *Postilla* was in a general preoccupation with matters of Jewish faith and unbelief; he often wrestled with the problem of the Jews' covenantal relationship with God in light of their failure to accept Christ. Given how few theological questions he presented, relative to other late thirteenth- and early fourteenth-century commentators, it is noteworthy that so many had to do with Israel, the Jews, and Jewish salvation and unbelief. He seems to have felt that the most valuable expertise he had to share with his readers concerned questions regarding the Jews (rather than matters of more general theological or philosophical concern). At Matthew 5:17, for example, *Do not think that I have come to abolish the Law and the Prophets; I have come not to abolish but to fulfill,* Nicholas took the opportunity to ask "whether this question may be true, that Christ fulfilled the Law and did not abolish it." This allowed him to conduct an extensive discussion of Mosaic precepts and Christian law and exterior versus interior restraint. Hebrews 10:37 provided an opportunity to ask "whether the sacraments and sacrifices of the Old Law justify." Nicholas came to the unsurprising conclusion that the Old Law had no salvific value in itself, except insofar as dedication to it inspired and demonstrated faith in God and, even if innocently, in the true sacrifice that was to come with the incarnation of Jesus.[74] Any grace conferred by the Old Law thus functioned only in response to faith and in the promise of Christ to come. Although Nicholas clearly was challenging the Jews here, he did not explicitly engage in polemic with the Jewish position. The only proofs introduced in favor of the proposition were Leviticus 8:31, where Moses instructed Aaron and his sons in the proper performance of sacrifice, and the opinion of unnamed "holy doctors" that circumcision conferred grace. Nicholas dismissed both proofs with the assertion that any grace obtained by adherence to the Law was grace obtained through faith (not action). At least two of Nicholas's 1309 quodlibetal questions found their way into the *Postilla litteralis: Whether the Jews perceived Jesus to be the Christ promised to them, which does not appear to be the case* at Matthew 21:38 and *Whether the final salvation of Solomon can be proved by Scripture* at 2 Kings 7:15 and 22:51. In addition, most of the text of Nicholas's *Quaestio de adventu Christi* from the same quodlibet was worked into the *Postilla litteralis* at appropriate places in the text. The overall effect is to see Nicholas continuously engaging with Jewish resistance to Christian truth.[75]

The *Postilla litteralis* in the Context of Late Medieval Bible Study and Christian-Jewish Encounter

To assert that Nicholas's Bible commentary was shaped by his encounter with Jewish tradition is one thing, but to assert an impact on the broader Christian tradition is another. However, with hundreds of manuscript copies in circulation by the end of the fourteenth century and continuing circulation in manuscript and print right up until its final edition in the seventeenth century, the popularity of Nicholas's commentary can hardly be denied and, in that sense, whatever he did within the pages of the work must be seen as important for the Christian tradition as a whole. Whether or not those aspects of his Bible commentary inspired by his encounter with Jewish exegesis were specifically taken up by followers may not be as important as the fact that they were so widely studied and absorbed. I will discuss the reception of Nicholas's commentary at some length in Chapter 5. For now, it may suffice to note that Nicholas served as a highly effective conduit for Jewish traditions into Christian exegesis and awareness, and that he simultaneously played a vital role in shaping Christian responses—both positive and negative—to those traditions.

Nicholas's encounter with Jewish tradition came at a critical moment in medieval European Christian-Jewish relations, a time when Jews were beginning to experience an increasingly harsh climate marked by the seizure of their books, a new missionizing effort spearheaded by the Dominican order and supported by the papacy, and numerous expulsions. As a young scholar immersed in both Christian and Jewish Bible commentary, Nicholas lived through the expulsion of the Jews from France, watched Hebrew books go up in flames at the Place de Grève, and witnessed the trial of a relapsed Jewish convert. He must have been deeply aware of the challenges confronting him as he sought to follow an exegetical path established by Rashi and the rabbis. But there was yet another challenge to Nicholas's desire to follow the insight of Jewish rabbis with respect to sacred text that we have yet to consider. From the second half of the thirteenth century, scholars in Paris and elsewhere, influenced by the reading of Aristotle, had been paying a great deal of attention to epistemology and the acquisition of knowledge through the processes of natural cognition and spiritual grace. These phenomena were a subject of particular interest within his own Franciscan order, and Nicholas's writing shows their influence. In order to understand the impact this had on Nicholas's use of Jewish text in his exegesis

and his audience's reception of his work, we must turn back to that epistemological discussion, particularly as it was applied to questions of Jewish
unbelief and the reading of Hebrew Scripture. How could one justify the
use of rabbinic teaching on Scripture, after all, if the rabbis themselves
failed to follow it to Christian truth?

Chapter 3

The Challenge of Unbelief: Knowing Christian Truth Through Jewish Scripture

Aptly borrowing from Claude Lévi-Strauss's structuralist theory of myth, Miri Rubin observed that medieval Christians found Jews to be "very good to think with."[1] Jews served as an important symbolic construct for medieval Christian writers and so appeared in all sorts of contexts, some of which had little or nothing to do with concerns about real Jews. Jewish unbelief was a serious problem for Christians, not only in a real sense, but also in a theoretical one. While Dominican friars gave themselves over to an effort to conquer real Jewish unbelief and to bring contemporary Jews into the Christian fold, others found Jewish unbelief in itself to present a philosophical as well as a theological problem. Ongoing Jewish unbelief was a puzzle particularly for those exegetes who accepted that Hebrew Scripture was key to an understanding of God's Word and that the Jews held critical insights into Scripture's literal sense. It was difficult to reconcile persistent Jewish unbelief with the notion that Jewish Scripture, properly read, pointed the way to Christian truth.

That Christian truth could be proved through Jewish Scripture was self-evident to most Christian theologians in the Middle Ages. Medieval Christian theology assumed an inherent, unbreakable connection between the Old and New Testaments, as everything promised in the Old Testament was held to have been fulfilled in the New. Christian Hebraism was predicated upon the notion that a better, fuller understanding of Old Testament Scripture would necessarily lead to a better, fuller understanding of the entire history of salvation. When the language of reason entered the schools in the twelfth and thirteenth centuries with its emphasis on rational foundations of belief, theologians embraced the language of philosophy and proclaimed the essential rationality of Christian faith.[2] The Dominican mission to the Jews was built upon the assumption that the Hebrew Bible and even postbiblical rabbinic interpretations of the Bible could be used as proof to demonstrate rationally and conclusively the Christian faith. Persistent Jewish unbelief in the face of such compelling evidence was especially troubling, according to Jeremy Cohen, who has argued that the early medieval conception of the Jew as blinded from truth shifted over the course of the thirteenth century to a conception of the Jew as a deliberate disbeliever, rejecting clear evidence that should have led any rational mind to Christian truth.[3]

During the latter part of the thirteenth century, however, a philosophical challenge to such confidence arose in the schools, particularly in Franciscan circles, as new epistemological theories, launched in large part by Robert Grosseteste and Roger Bacon and then transformed by the secular theologian Henry of Ghent (d. 1293) and the Franciscans Peter Olivi (1248–98) and John Duns Scotus (1266–1308), led scholars to a vigorous debate over knowledge, cognition, and the attainment of certitude.[4] Roger Bacon's widely disseminated cognitive theory, influenced by Aristotle, Avicenna, Averroës, Alhazan, and Grosseteste and based upon the notion of multiplication of species, provided an alternative to Augustine's emphasis on the role of divine light in the attainment of knowledge, an idea embraced and incorporated into a scholastic framework by Bonaventure and his followers John Pecham, Matthew of Aquasparta, and Roger Marston. Steven Marrone argues that the doctrine of divine illumination in the attainment of ordinary knowledge was already on the wane when Henry of Ghent developed its fullest expression in a series of writings between 1276 and 1285.[5] In any case, Henry's position sparked further debate by a number of Franciscan thinkers, most notably Olivi, Duns Scotus, and, eventually, William of Ockham.

As Robert Pasnau explains, "Medieval theologians took particular interest in human cognition both as a way of establishing the epistemological foundations of theology and as a way of coming to know and to understand God."[6] Cognition was the concern of the theology faculty because it dealt with the human ability to experience God in the natural world (God's revelation in material creation) as well as in Scripture (God's revelation in the Word). The intensity of interest in cognition theory among Franciscans is not surprising, given the order's emphasis on knowing God through God's footprint in the natural world.

The Franciscan circles where the discussion was most lively included many of the same figures who were prominent in the Christian study of Hebrew and the use of Jewish exegesis outlined in Chapter 1. Nicholas of

Lyra came along late in the debate—he arrived in Paris around the same time as Duns Scotus in the first years of the fourteenth century—but his application of the language of medieval epistemology directly to the problem of Jewish unbelief is telling. In a quodlibetal question asking whether the Jews knew Christ at the time of his advent, Nicholas wondered how literate Jews could have missed the signs of the messiah's coming if it could have been read accurately from their own prophetic texts. His response concluded that recognizing the fulfillment of prophecy was no simple matter because scriptural prophecy could be variously interpreted and certitude is attainable only when established through demonstration and perception. Since certain proof was lacking here, knowledge of the Advent could be divined only "with difficulty as probable and verisimilar."[7]

Nicholas employed the language of broader epistemological discourse when he spoke in terms of certitude, proof, and verisimilitude. When he concluded that the reality of Christ's appearance would have been known only as a verisimilitude (rather than a verity), he reflected more than half a century of discussion about the process of cognition and the nature of demonstrable proof in discerning natural and divine truths.[8]

Nicholas's question on whether the Jews recognized Christ at the time of his advent was considered in the same quodlibetal disputation as his much more widely disseminated and better-known question on the advent of Christ. Modern scholars have treated the *Quaestio de adventu Christi* as a work in the medieval *adversus Iudaeos* tradition.[9] Yet while its arguments certainly draw from that tradition, the question is more closely related to broader theological concerns than has generally been understood. The same concerns about truth and certainty raised in Nicholas's question on recognizing Christ are evident also in the much longer *Quaestio de adventu Christi*. Although this question took on a life of its own outside the schools, it was developed in the context of scholastic debate and followed on the heels of other questions of a similar nature.

Quite a number of Franciscan scholars in the late thirteenth and early fourteenth centuries began to ask questions concerning the possibility of proving Christ's advent, or similar theological truths, by means of Jewish Scripture or prophetic texts. These questions have received little scholarly attention; most remain buried in scholastic manuscripts.[10] While not every question was framed in explicitly epistemological terms, the interest in epistemology, along with increasing tension between Franciscan interest in rabbinic interpretations of Scripture and the problem of Jewish unbelief, is abundantly evident.[11] From Roger Marston's 1283 question, "Whether it is possible to prove by prophecies that Christ has already been incarnated," to Nicholas of Lyra's "Whether the Jews knew Jesus of Nazareth to be the Christ promised to them" and "Whether from Scriptures received by the Jews it is possible to prove effectively that our savior was both God and man," both disputed in 1309, the questions to be considered here demonstrate a concern with the nature of prophecy as evidence, or proof, of religious truth.[12] They tend to acknowledge the difficulty of attaining certain knowledge of divine truths while insisting nevertheless that Old Testament prophecy is a legitimate source of evidence for such truths.

Some of the questions were specifically concerned with the possibility of proving Christ's advent to the Jews, while others were simply concerned with the possibility of proving Christian doctrine on the basis of prophecy. Some of them suggested that a reasoned consideration of historical circumstances was sufficient to attain and affirm such knowledge, while others suggested that it was impossible without the light of faith. In each case, however, we can see the shadow of a broader discussion about intellect and religious knowledge. The authors of these questions were all Franciscans, and all took part in the discussion of epistemology in the late thirteenth century. All of the men wrote their questions in the context of quodlibetal disputations, where the problem was placed alongside other questions concerning faith and the acquisition of knowledge and understanding. The authors also all made use of traditional Old Testament proofs of Christianity and engaged, to a greater or lesser degree, in polemic, but such polemic was incidental to the internal Christian negotiation over how one might come to knowledge of religious truth.[13]

The first question in the group dates to 1283 or 1284, when Roger Marston, O.F.M. (d. 1303), determined in a quodlibetal disputation "whether it is possible to prove by prophecies that Christ has already been incarnated" or, alternatively, "whether it is possible to prove by the writing of the Old Testament that the one about whom the Law and Scripture speaks has already come, against the Jews."[14] Roger left his native England in order to study in Paris around 1270, where he counted among his teachers the English Franciscan John Pecham and most likely the Hebraist William de la Mare as well.[15] While there, Roger would have certainly encountered Bonaventure and probably also Roger Bacon.[16] He may have incepted at Cambridge upon his return from Paris in 1275, but if so, nothing remains of his work there. He went to Oxford in 1280 and was the Franciscan lector from 1282 to 1284. He remained an important figure among English Franciscans to the end of his life, serving as provincial minister from 1292 until 1298. All of his extant questions were disputed during his time in Oxford, including the question on the incarnation of Christ.[17]

Roger Marston was part of the Augustinian school back in Oxford. Bonaventure was an important influence, although he turned most frequently in his quodlibeta to fellow Bonaventure disciples John Pecham, William de la Mare, and Matthew of Aquasparta. Roger also engaged with the work of Thomas Aquinas and Henry of Ghent, with whom he often disagreed.[18] In the question on prophecy, he borrowed extensively from Robert Grosseteste's "On the Cessation of the Old Law" (c. 1230–35). The incorporation of such extensive argumentation from Grosseteste and the apologetic tradition makes Roger's treatment of the question, around forty pages in its modern edition, far longer than the other questions in the quodlibet.[19]

Roger began by answering the question in the negative, citing Genesis 49:10, *The sceptre shall not be taken away from Judah, nor a ruler from his thigh, till he come that is to be sent, and he shall be the expectation of nations.* He presented a Jewish view of the scepter as referring loosely to law, ruling, and governing rather than absolute dominion, acknowledging that the Jews read this passage differently than did Christians. According to this interpretation, even when the Jews had lost dominion, as during the Babylonian Captivity and in the time of the Maccabees, this scepter of semiautonomy had never fallen away completely. Even though the Jews were now living under the dominion of Rome, the scepter had not completely fallen away and so the messiah was yet to come.[20] In favor of the proposition, Roger argued simply that the tenets of the Christian faith and the words of the Gospels and apostles made it evident that the promises made in Old Testament prophecies were fulfilled in Christ.

Roger used his response to address, and dismiss, Jewish unbelief by explaining that just as it is impossible to acquire natural knowledge (*naturalis scientia*) through instruction if a man remains turned toward phantasm and away from natural light,[21] when men are deprived of the light of faith, and worse, deformed by depraved error, they cannot be persuaded of articles of Christian faith, especially the greatest of sacraments, the incarnation of Christ. He compared the attempt to attain religious knowledge without the light of faith to the attempt of simple men to comprehend mathematical proofs without the requisite intellectual tools—they would not be able to attain certitude, even though the truth was demonstrable. His message was clear: the limitations of the recipient did not diminish the validity of the proof. Drawing from the words of 2 Corinthians 10:5, Roger insisted that "all common understanding toward those things that are true, I believe can be captured in obedience to Christ sufficiently through Scripture."[22]

Having thus accounted for the fact that the Jews' reading of prophecy did not lead them to Christian understanding while preserving the legitimacy of the effort, Roger stated his intention to pursue a three-pronged approach to his proof: first, from the decline of the synagogue; second, from the event of the Advent itself; and third, from the success of the Church.[23] Roger divided each of the three main sections of the question into four subsections. Concerning the first subject, Roger discussed "the abolition of legal sacrifice, the removal of priests of the Law, the innovation of expression of the Law, and the banishment of a legal nation."[24] Roger devoted his second section to prophetic descriptions of "the truth of Christ's humanity, the height of His divinity, the holiness of His conduct, and the bitterness of His passion."[25] The final section on the progress of the Church he divided into the categories of "the universality of religious faith, the concord of conformity, the success of prophecy, and the vigor of teaching."[26]

Many, if not most, of Roger's arguments originated with Augustine,[27] who, with Jerome a distant second, is the most frequently cited authority in the work.[28] Roger used Bede's *De temporum ratione* for the calculation of relevant dates and cited him also by name.[29] A dependence on Augustine is quite typical of Roger's work as a whole, and so it is no surprise to find such dependence here as well. Like many of his Franciscan contemporaries, Roger clearly saw himself as a defender of an Augustinian tradition against Thomism, even while integrating Aristotelian thought into his own work. Franz Pelster attributed to Roger a knowledge of Augustine's writing "such as one finds only among the best theologians of his school."[30] In an article illustrating the work of Roger Marston as an example of "Avicennized Augustinism," Gilson noted that within the realm of philosophy, Roger's point of departure was always Augustine. Insofar as Roger had an interest in Avicenna's Aristotelianism, it was to bring Avicenna (and Aristotle) in line with Augustine, not the other way around.[31] It is no surprise to see Roger turning here to the most important authority he knew after Scripture.

Of course, Roger's reliance on Augustine also reflects the influence of Robert Grosseteste's *On the Cessation of the Old Law*, from which Roger borrowed liberally. Grosseteste's lengthy treatise was one of a number of similar works on the Old Law composed in the late twelfth and early thirteenth centuries.[32] Roger had access to Grosseteste's writings in the Franciscan library at Oxford, where he lived at the time he disputed this question. We know that he admired Robert's work because he cited him fairly frequently in his quodlibeta; he explicitly indicated his admiration for the bishop in one question, calling him a "great teacher" with "ingenious talent."[33] Grosseteste's influence on Roger's question on the advent of Christ is evident not only in his appeal to Augustine as an authority but also in the nature of his discussion, a third of which is framed in terms of the termination or transformation of Jewish law and legal standing (Roger's "decline of the synagogue"). Roger's use of the term "infidel" with respect to Jews in this question, though apparently not as unusual as James Muldoon has argued, also mimics Grosseteste's use of the term with respect to Jews in his *On the Cessation of the Old Law*.[34]

Roger borrowed directly from Grosseteste in a number of places, such as in his treatment of Daniel 9:24–27 *Seventy weeks are shortened upon thy people, and upon thy holy city, that transgression may be finished . . . And a people with their leader that shall come, shall destroy the city and the sanctuary: and the end thereof shall be waste, and after the end of the war the appointed desolation* and in the somewhat odd placement of Augustine's story of the Erythraean Sibyl. In the midst of an extensive argument about Old Testament prophecy of the Passion, Roger abruptly turned and suggested that if the Jews were not satisfied with the warnings of their own prophets, perhaps they would believe the prediction of a gentile, the Erythraean Sibyl. Roger then provided a summary of book 18, chapter 23 of Augustine's *City of God*, in which Augustine described an apocalyptic poem purported to have been written by a sibyl around the time of the Trojan War and which he claimed prophesied the passion of Christ. Though obviously a well-known text, the prophecy of the Sibyl was not typically used in Christian apologetic or anti-Jewish polemic in this period, even by those authors who relied heavily on Augustine. Roger's dependence upon Grosseteste is clearly in evidence here.[35]

Because Roger aimed to defend the legitimacy of using Old Testament prophecy to attain Christian understanding in the face of Jewish rejection, he regularly introduced and refuted Jewish errors in the interpretation of the prophets. He perceived himself as working with sources that should have been acceptable to the Jews, and at one point noted that while he could easily prove the advent of Christ from Gospel sources to believers, since he was concerned with proving the Advent to unbelieving Jews, he would use the words of their own historian, Josephus, instead.[36] Roger did not know Hebrew and worked exclusively with the Latin Vulgate, with an occasional turn to individual Hebrew words as found in Jerome. In contrast to his regular citation of Christian authorities by name, Roger never identified his sources when presenting Jewish opinions, stating only vaguely that *Iudaei dicunt, Iudaei consideraverunt,* or *ut volunt Iudaei.* These most often came right out of Jerome or other readily available Christian sources.

Sometimes Roger attempted to dismantle Jewish "misinterpretations" of prophetic texts with rational refutation,[37] but more often he simply invoked Augustine's authority. In spite of his claim to be proving the Advent to unbelievers, Roger was clearly aiming his arguments at an audience of theology students and masters. The kinds of arguments Roger borrowed from Augustine, based upon Christian interpretations of prophecy and allegorical readings of Scripture, would hardly have convinced a Jewish doubter. For example, in the second part of the first section, proving the Advent by the transfer or removal of the priesthood, Roger proved the Christian priesthood to be the superior successor to the old priesthood of Aaron by quoting from *The City of God* at length, pointing to Augustine's argument that the "man of God" who prophesied to Eli about the future fall of his house in 1 Kings 2:27–36 was really talking about the fall of the entire line of Aaron.[38]

While Roger made extensive use of Augustine's spiritual readings of Scripture, Jerome was his source for literal interpretation and Hebraic information. For example, Roger quoted from Jerome's commentary on Isaiah to explain why the Hebrew in Isaiah 7:14, *Behold a virgin shall conceive, and bear a son, and his name shall be called Emmanuel* contains the word *alma,* meaning a young woman, rather than *betula,* which specifically means virgin. Roger repeated Jerome's argument that the word *alma* was used to indicate that she was "not only a girl, or a virgin, but a virgin hidden and protected, whom no man had looked at, but whose parents had protected her with great care."[39] Jerome's authority, and especially his mastery of Hebrew, enabled Roger to defend the validity of Christian interpretation of this important prophetic passage in the face of a Jewish challenge.

Indeed, at the end of Roger's twelve proofs, after dismissing numerous such Jewish objections by introducing Christian authorities, he finally concluded, "I firmly believe, therefore, beyond any doubt, that the advent of Christ can be proved—not only with probability, but most sufficiently—by means of Scripture."[40] As for the primary objection against the proposition—that Genesis 49:10 proves that Christ has not yet come—Roger dismissed that, too, as failing to hold up to scrutiny. Drawing on long-established Christian arguments, he insisted that from the Babylonian Captivity until the time of the Romans, descendants of the tribe of Judah remained in control over the Jews until the placement of Herod on the throne fifteen years before the birth of Christ, when the Jews were directly controlled by a foreigner for the first time. Furthermore, since Herod murdered all of the descendants of the previous rulers, that assured that no one of the tribe of Judah would ever again be able to rule. Therefore, the messiah must have come during the reign of Herod, and Jesus must have been that messiah.[41] Since Christian, Roman, and even Jewish sources[42] all concurred on Herod's misdeeds, no one could legitimately argue against the Advent on the basis of Genesis 49. As far as Roger was concerned, the evidence of Scripture, read carefully with the appropriate light of faith, necessarily led the mind to the truth of Christ's advent.

In contrast to Roger's extensive treatment of the subject, Raymond Rigauld, O.F.M. (d. 1296), wrote just one paragraph on "whether it is possible to prove by the Old Testament the incarnation of Christ."[43] Raymond was probably the Franciscan regent master at Paris in 1287–88, between Richard of Middleton and John de Murro. His question on the incarnation of Christ was disputed in Paris at that time.[44] Raymond was twice elected provincial minister of Aquitaine, first in 1279 and again in 1295. Ferdinand Delorme suggested that in between, from around 1280 until 1295, Raymond occupied himself with teaching and writing.[45] Raymond was a teacher of Vital de Furno, O.F.M., later cardinal, who borrowed on more than one occasion from Raymond's work.[46] Perhaps Vital's own interest in divine illumination was inspired by Raymond, whom Steven Marrone names as "yet another Franciscan calling for reconsideration of the classic illuminationist position" on cognition.[47]

Raymond's question, the thirty-seventh of his fourth quodlibet, appears alongside a number of other questions on the perception of divine things; immediately after the question on the Incarnation, Raymond asked several related questions about Christ's nature, the presence of Jesus in the Eucharist, and the nature of the Sacrament. Rather than marshaling specific prooftexts as Roger did in his question, Raymond focused directly on the problem of proving the Advent through Scripture. In favor of the proposition, Raymond cited John 5:39, *Search the Scriptures*, in which Jesus rebuked the Pharisees, complaining that the very books that they revered testified to his coming, and yet they did not believe in him. Against the proposition, Raymond followed Roger Marston's lead, introducing Genesis 49:10, *The sceptre shall not be taken away from Judah* and stating very briefly that "it is not withdrawn because the sceptre was at first idle in captivity."[48] This highly abbreviated reference clearly refers to the same Jewish position described in Roger's question above. Unlike Roger, Raymond did not refute the interpretation. Instead, in his response, Raymond acknowledged the impossibility of proving by reason religious truths that ultimately required faith for their acceptance. Although the incarnation of Christ is a truth (*veritas*), it, like creation and other aspects of God's work, exceeded the natural perfection of the universe and cannot be grasped by natural light (*lumen naturalis*). An understanding of the Incarnation, therefore, can only be fully attained by means of faith.[49] In a conclusion that would obviously have been problematic for those friars actively working to convince Jews of Christian truth, Raymond argued that, given the necessity of a preexisting faith to make sense of it, the Old Testament could not on its own provide proof of the Incarnation. Nevertheless, Raymond conceded that Old Testament prophecy *could* be used to prove the Incarnation to Christians, since the Old and New Testaments were bound up together, the New contained within the Old like a wheel within a wheel.[50] And so, "just as by the New are proved things fulfilled, so from the Old truly are proved things predicted."[51]

Questions seven and eight of Peter Olivi's second quodlibet asked "Whether from the Old Testament it is possible to prove the Jews to have been blinded in the advent of Christ and truly excluded from the condition of faith" and "Whether it is possible to prove the time of the advent of the messiah by the Old Testament." The collection of quodlibeta in which these questions appear is found only in an unmarked sixteenth-century edition, which J. H. Sbaralea and Franz Ehrle agree must have been published by Lazarus Soardus in Venice in the year 1509.[52]

Although Olivi remained a bachelor in theology, his place in medieval Christian theology was such that Glorieux felt bound to include him in his survey of Parisian theology masters.[53] Sometime prior to 1268 Olivi was sent to study theology in Paris; he heard Bonaventure preach his *Collationes de septem donis Spiritus Sancti* there in 1268. Ehrle believed him to have followed Bonaventure's spirit more closely than did any of his Franciscan contemporaries. Bonnie Kent argues that of all the late thirteenth-century Franciscans who saw themselves as anti-Thomistic Augustinians, Olivi, "more than any other writer of the period, could appropriately be described as anti-Aristotelian."[54] Not only did he criticize the ubiquitous appeal to Aristotle and other pagan philosophers in the schools, he also challenged various theological opinions that he found problematic, including Henry of Ghent's doctrine of divine illumination, which was popular among other neo-Augustinians.[55] Olivi's career was marked by a series of censures and defenses, as he continually skirted the edge of accepted theology. However, in spite of his popularity among some Spirituals who stepped beyond the bounds of Church authority, Olivi himself remained an obedient, if troublesome, member of the Franciscan order.[56] Olivi was quiet for a few years after his censure in 1283, returning to the classroom in 1287 when he was sent by Matthew of Aquasparta to lecture in the Franciscan studium at Santa Croce in Florence.[57] He was there for just two years when the sympathetic Raymond Gaufridi, elected minister in 1289, sent him to lecture at the Franciscan convent in Montpellier, where he remained until as late as 1295.

Olivi's first question, while similar to those on proving the advent of Christ through Old Testament texts, differs slightly in its focus on the blindness of the Jews to Christ's advent. It looks specifically at unbelief, its source and ramifications, and the position of the Jews in salvation history. Olivi argued in favor of the proposition—that the Jews have lost their state of being within the faith by their blindness to Christ's advent—from Isaiah 49:5–6: *And now says the Lord, that formed me from the womb to be his servant. . . . It is a small thing that you should be my servant to raise up the tribes of Jacob, and to convert the remnant of Israel.* Olivi's only comment on the passage was to point out that God was speaking here about Christ himself. Later in the question, Olivi explained more clearly the Christian interpretation of this text as a prediction of Christ's reaching out to the gentiles and offering salvation to the whole earth. Olivi's argument against the proposition stated that since all of the prophets indicated that upon the advent of the messiah the people of Israel would be restored to glory, and instead the people have been defeated and dispersed and persecuted across the globe, the messiah cannot yet have come.

Olivi quickly dismissed this argument by saying that the current miserable state of the Jews was entirely consistent with Old Testament prophecy that the majority of the Jews would be blinded and rejected at Christ's advent and that only a small portion of Israel was to be saved and raised up, as in Isaiah 10:22, *For if your people, O Israel, shall be as the sand of the sea, a remnant of them shall be converted.*[58] The first, and longest, portion of Olivi's proof expanded on this idea with extensive quotations from Isaiah and other prophets concerning Israel's wickedness and the indication that only a remnant would be brought back to God. In one of many such passages (Isaiah 6:11–13), Isaiah learned that God would "blind the heart of this people." Isaiah asked how long the blindness would endure, and Olivi paraphrased God's answer, "until they are totally destroyed, except for a small remnant of the elect."[59]

Olivi related the fulfillment of these prophecies to the time of Christ, when the blindness of the Jews to the Advent was followed by the gathering of the gentiles under Christ. Olivi wove together passages from the prophets to strengthen the perception that they were predicting the ascendance of a gentile (rather than Jewish) community of believers, as in this passage concerning Isaiah 59 and 60, "and the text follows immediately concerning the general conversion of the nations; accordingly, *all from the west and from the east will fear the name of the Lord and his glory*, and therefore it follows, *Arise and be enlightened, Jerusalem, because your light is come, and the nations will walk in your light, etc.*, where it is most evident that it is speaking here about things that happened under Christ."[60]

Toward the end of the question, Olivi put Jewish unbelief in the context of seven *status* (ages), leading up to the time of Jesus. As David Burr explains, a *status* was for Olivi something both temporal and qualitative; a status was a period of time, but more than that, it referred to a condition of being. In other writings, most importantly his commentary on the Book of Revelation, Olivi used the term with respect to both threefold and sevenfold divisions of history.[61] Here, Olivi described a sevenfold division of the time and status of the people of God (*circumstantia temporis et status populi Dei*) up to the Advent. The first stage saw (1) general iniquity among the people of God, followed by (2) the arrival of prophets who taught and admonished them, followed by (3) the persecution of the prophets, (4) the stubbornness and blindness of the people, (5) the murder or captivity of the people, (6) the return of a portion of the people out from captivity, and finally (7) the last days (*novissimo tempore* and *novissimis diebus*), in which Christ would come. These seven stages had implications for the entire history of salvation, not only leading up to the Advent, but continuing through to the end of days, which Olivi thought were beginning to unfold.

Olivi emphasized Jesus' simultaneous fulfillment of three distinct prophetic designations of the messiah: as prophet, king, and priest. As king, Olivi noted, he triumphed over the forces of evil and introduced wisdom, justice, holiness, grace, and glory finally into the world. In his role as prophet, Christ was poor and a beggar; Olivi noted that Christ was often introduced as *pauper, mendicus, viator, peregrinus, incognitus*, and *despectus*.[62] As priest, Christ put an end to (Jewish) legal rituals, prophetic traditions, and earthly wealth.[63] In part because of his poverty and lowly status, the Jews were blinded to the Advent, and yet as king and priest he overturned the old institutions of wealth and power.

In his conclusion, Olivi had one final word to say about the objection introduced at the beginning of the question: since the Jews were to be redeemed at the time of the messiah but they remain persecuted and dispersed, the messiah must not have come. Olivi drew from a Joachimist framework to argue that when the prophets spoke of the time of the messiah, they were speaking simultaneously of three distinct "times" (*tempores*) of Christ: the first, in which the majority of Jews were blinded and a great number of gentiles were converted; the second, in which the carnal Church (*carnalis ecclesia*), as if another synagogue, would be blinded and in which the whole of the Jews and other infidels would be converted; and finally, the third time, in which everyone would be brought to eternal judgment, either damned to hell or glorified in the heavenly Jerusalem.[64] Olivi emphasized the eventual salvation of the remnant of Israel through their conversion in the second time of the messiah. Of course, just as the blindness of the Jews would be healed in time, so would the blindness of the "carnal Church" of his own day.[65]

The unbelief of the Jews was a simple matter for Olivi here; it was part of the unfolding of salvation history. The Jews' rejection of Jesus at the Advent, as well as the rehabilitation of a small remnant of them at the end of days, had been foreseen by the prophets years before. Because of the concordances between the history of Israel before Christ and the history of the Church after Christ's advent, the fate of the Jews in their relationship with God was particularly important to Olivi. Olivi's conflict with the Church and his reading of contemporary events in apocalyptic terms are evident in both the framing and the execution of the question.[66]

Olivi's second question, by far the longer of the two, built upon the previous one, moving beyond the general phenomenon of Jewish blindness to address specifically whether the time of the Advent could be proved by means of Old Testament prophecy. Again Olivi's eschatological concerns framed the question. It is very clear that he was not asking whether or not one could prove to the Jews the time of the messiah's advent. Rather, he was interested in whether the time could be accurately discerned through a Christian reading of Old Testament prophecy. Not surprisingly given his Joachimist leanings, Olivi determined that with a properly illuminated reading of Scripture, the time of the Advent could easily be discerned from Old Testament texts.

Against the proposition Olivi noted that prophecies could be calculated differently and cited a calculation of the seventy weeks of years prophesied in Daniel 9 that would have misplaced the messiah's advent by about one hundred years. Olivi was working backward here. Since Jesus clearly was the messiah, any inconsistency in dating must pertain to the ability of

Old Testament prophecy to predict accurately the time of the Advent. Olivi argued in favor of the proposition on the basis of Luke 12:56 and 19:44, where Christ rebuked the Jews for not recognizing the time of the advent of the messiah; Olivi says that it would have been irrational for Jesus to have so rebuked them had it not been possible to know with certainty the time from their own sacred writings.[67] According to Olivi, the Jews failed to recognize Christ at the time of his advent because they resisted the spirit of grace and its spiritual illumination by means of which they could have understood (*intellexissent*) the inner virtue of the letter, and so Christ's nature and presence.[68] Because of this primary failure, their reading of prophecy was bound to be flawed.

Just as the previous question, though dealing ostensibly with Jewish blindness, appeared by the end to be aimed at those Christians whose faith had become weak like that of the Jews, so here, too, Olivi seems primarily concerned with the weakness of his Christian audience. Olivi specifically identified those who raised objections to the calculation of the Advent by Daniel's prophecy not just as "Jews" but as "Jews or Judaizers."[69] His response, filled with evidence from Christ's words, Christ's genealogy from the Book of Matthew, and similar New Testament material as proof, certainly would not have served to convince Jews, but he may have hoped it would prove compelling to those unnamed Judaizers who doubted whether Scripture could provide specific information on the timing of landmark events in salvation history.

Olivi proposed three viable methods of proving the time of the Advent by means of the Old Testament. He incorporated the first, a concordance of Christ's deeds as recounted in the New Testament with the prophecy of the Old Testament, as had been suggested by Raymond Rigauld, into the argumentation of the second and third. The second used Daniel's vision of the four kingdoms that would rule the earth before the coming of the messiah's final, eternal kingdom. The four kingdoms, represented both by the statue in Nebuchadnezzar's dream described in chapter 2:31–45 and by Daniel's vision of four beasts described in chapter 7, led eventually to fulfillment under Rome. After describing how the circumstances of the Roman Empire fulfilled Daniel's prophecy, Olivi concluded this fairly brief discussion with corroboration from Zechariah. Olivi connected Zechariah's vision of four horns and four blacksmiths in chapter 1 with the four reigns of Daniel and then took the vision of four chariots in Zechariah 6 to indicate that here, too, the fourth and final reign was "to be the strongest and to spread across the whole globe."[70]

The third method of proof calculated the seventy weeks of years predicted in Daniel 9:24–27 from the return from the Babylonian exile to the coming of Christ: *Seventy weeks are shortened upon your people, and upon your holy city . . . and after the end of the war the appointed desolation.* Like Roger Marston, who addressed the same passage in Daniel, Olivi borrowed extensively from Bede in his calculations, but he incorporated other sources as well. In addition to Jerome's prologues and commentary,[71] he also used the chronology of Julius Africanus, which he used to corroborate Bede's numbers, reconciling the differences between the two where necessary.[72] Olivi used Daniel's prophecies to tie the destruction of Jerusalem and the Temple by Titus and Vespasian (and the current captivity of the Jews) specifically to the Jews' rejection of Christ.[73]

The Jews' inability to see that which was clearly there to be seen served as a warning to Christians. As has already been noted, Olivi seems not to have been concerned with developing arguments that could be used to convince Jews of the truth. But since Christian scholars could be misled by reading "absurd" or "false" Jewish interpretations, whenever necessary he demonstrated the error of Jewish calculations through an appeal to Christian authorities.[74] His knowledge of Jewish interpretation was limited to the sorts of traditions that had already made their way into Christian commentaries, primarily from Victorine exegesis. The single Jewish interpretation brought in as evidence for his Christian position, a Talmudic midrash describing the six thousand years that the world would endure—two thousand years of vanity, two thousand years of the Law, and two thousand years of the messiah—was likewise something widely accessible in Christian sources.[75] Olivi used the midrash to support his calculation of Daniel's prophecy, demonstrating that the two-thousand-year period of the Law ended precisely in the time of Titus and Vespasian with the destruction of the Temple.[76]

Olivi's interest in proving that one could accurately calculate the advent of Christ through prophecy was motivated by an interest in calculating, at least roughly, the end of days for his own time.[77] Like Joachim of Fiore, Olivi saw elaborate concordances between the Old and New Testaments, between the first, second, and third ages of the Church. In order to preserve his apocalyptic framework, Olivi needed to defend the possibility of knowing truths that were of this world through prophetic text. Olivi admitted that such knowledge could be attained only with the light of grace, but he did not present this as problematic, even though elsewhere he described the necessity of conjecture in moving from the "indubitable" insights attained through such light to probable conclusions.[78] Unlike some of the other authors, he was not particularly concerned with whether or not one could use prophecy to demonstrate the Advent to unbelievers. Rather, he was concerned with proving to the Franciscans in front of whom he taught that, imbued with the light of the spirit, they could read the signs of their own times and understand the unfolding of salvation history.

A student of Olivi's, Peter of Trabes, O.F.M., took a very different approach than his master when, returning to the sorts of concerns we saw in earlier quodlibeta, he asked "whether it is possible to prove to the Jews that Christ has already come."[79] The quodlibet, disputed in 1296, is found in a Franciscan manuscript dating from sometime between 1302 and 1304.[80] The attribution of the quodlibetal questions to Peter is in a later hand, but a number of scholars have made compelling arguments for the accuracy of the attribution. Hildebert A. Huning, in a study of Peter's philosophical writing, found that the positions taken in a number of the questions corresponded closely with Peter's subsequent prologue to book 1 of the *Sentences*, albeit sometimes in a less developed form.[81] Sylvain Piron rehearses the debate over attribution and builds on Huning's argument to make an even stronger case for Peter's authorship.[82]

Little is known about Peter, except that he was a member of the Franciscan order, was active in the late thirteenth century, and studied at the Franciscan studium at Santa Croce in Florence during the late thirteenth century, most likely during Peter Olivi's tenure in 1286–87.[83] The ideas expressed in his *Sentences* commentary followed so closely in some respects the opinions of Olivi that Franz Ehrle wondered if perhaps they were one and the same person.[84] Bernhard Jansen put this doubt to rest after examining a *Sentences* commentary by Jacob of Trisantis, O.F.M., who cited Peter of Trabes numerous times. As Jansen stressed, Jacob was far too close to the Spirituals within his own order to have had any confusion as to the identity of Peter Olivi.[85] Huning's subsequent examination of Peter of Trabes's *Sentences* commentary demonstrated that distinctions between the works of the two men abound.[86]

Like the other authors of questions on proving the advent of Christ from Jewish Scripture, Peter saw himself as a defender of traditional Augustinian theology against the encroachment of misguided Aristotelianism. Like others of the "Augustinian school," Peter was not averse to using Aristotelian ideas in his work, but he turned to Augustine's writings more frequently than any other source. In an interesting comparison of citations of Augustine and Aristotle in the third distinction of book 1 of the *Sentences* commentaries of Bonaventure, Thomas Aquinas, and Peter of Trabes, Huning found that Bonaventure cited Augustine 47 times and Aristotle only 3, Thomas cited Augustine 18 times, Aristotle 15, but Peter cited Augustine no less than 115 times and Aristotle 42.[87] Peter had a solid foundation in Aristotelian philosophy, but he also had a clear sense of the place of such knowledge in the scheme of things: philosophy could be a useful tool for the theologian but was to be kept clearly subservient to theology.

Peter's question, like that of Raymond Rigauld, demonstrates concern over the challenge of Jewish unbelief. If Old Testament Scripture could prove Christian truth, then the Jews should be able to see such truth as well. Peter argued first in favor of the proposition—that it is possible to prove the Advent to the Jews by the Old Testament—by turning to a New Testament event. He argued that since St. Peter, according to the Book of Acts, successfully preached articles of faith by rational means, it must be possible to prove the Advent, the greatest principle of faith, by such means. Against the proposition, Peter argued that, since the Incarnation stands beyond reason, the Advent cannot be proved at all.[88] The authority of the New Testament cannot be used because it is not accepted as authoritative by the Jews, nor can the authority of the Old Testament be used because it contains much that is false in the literal sense, and no other sense can be used in rational argumentation.[89] Finally, the Old Testament cannot prove that those things that it predicted for the future had already happened.[90]

Peter responded by introducing Old Testament texts that he insisted did prove the advent, beginning with Psalm 39:7–9, *Sacrifice and oblation you did not desire; but you have pierced ears for me. . . . In the head of the book it is written of me that I should do your will: O my God, I have desired it, and your Law in the midst of my heart.* According to Peter, this passage predicted the advent of Christ at the time when sin offerings and burnt offerings ceased to be made.[91] Since God from the beginning showed that he desired some sort of sacrifice to be made in his honor, it is evident that he must be receiving some type of sacrifice more acceptable than was that of the Law. Only the sacrifice of the Church could possibly be that new sacrifice.[92]

Peter argued that the validity of the Christian sacrifice was further confirmed by Malachi 1:11, in which Malachi prophesied that *from the rising of the sun even to the going down, my name is great among the gentiles, and in every place there is sacrifice, and there is offered to my name a clean oblation: for my name is great among the gentiles, says the Lord of Hosts.* Peter pointed out that this prophecy could not possibly refer to Jewish sacrifice, as the Jews were prohibited in Deuteronomy 12 from establishing sacrifice anywhere except in Jerusalem.[93] However, the spread of the Christian sacrifice far and wide represented a clear fulfillment of the prophecy. Later he mentioned, as did Roger Marston, the claim made by Paul in Hebrews 7 and expanded upon by Augustine that the Christian priesthood represented the line of Melchisedech, which superseded the priestly line of Aaron.[94]

Peter argued that the dispersion of the Jews following the destruction of Jerusalem by Titus and Vespasian was further evidence for the advent of Christ. Echoing an old Christian proof, Peter argued that the current exile had lasted so much longer than had the Babylonian exile that the sin that sparked the dispersion must have been much greater. There can have been no sin greater than the idolatry that prompted the first exile except for the hateful and malicious sin of Christ's death.[95] Peter introduced the prophecy from Daniel 9 about the seventy weeks until the destruction of Jerusalem, which appeared in so many other places, but he gave only a cursory explanation of how it was fulfilled, and he deviated from his teacher Olivi in calculating the seventy weeks to end at the time of Christ's death under the emperor Tiberius, rather than with the destruction of Jerusalem by Titus and Vespasian. Like Roger Marston and Olivi, Peter accepted the notion put forward by Bede that the prophecy must be interpreted in terms of lunar rather than solar years.

Peter's final proof came from Genesis 49:10: *The sceptre shall not be taken away from Judah* which he identified as "that most famous of prophecies" (*illa prophetia famosissima*). He noted that no foreigner ruled directly in Judea until five years before the birth of Christ, when Herod was placed on the throne by the Romans, thus fulfilling Jacob's prophecy that the tribe of Judah would rule until the coming of the messiah.[96]

Peter had argued against the proposition that the Advent, being a matter of faith, necessarily stood beyond reason. Without really addressing the problem of proving articles of faith or using prophecy to do so, he simply dismissed the objection by stating that it was weak; despite the apparent objections, one could nevertheless effectively prove the Advent from Old Testament sources because such proof did not depend upon one piece of evidence but could be demonstrated by many different approaches. If one argument failed, another might well convince.[97]

Each of these figures took Augustine's reading of Isaiah's words, "unless you believe, you shall not understand," as a point of departure for the reading of Scripture.[98] Some specifically contrasted the "light of faith" with "natural light" in the process of understanding religious truth, but with or without the language of epistemology, each scholar acknowledged the challenge that Jewish unbelief presented to the Christian conviction that the advent of Christ was knowable through prophetic text. With the exception of Raymond Rigauld, each of the authors discussed here answered in the end that, yes, one could prove the advent of Christ through Old Testament prophecy. Yet none was able to construct proofs that could stand outside a Christian context. In the end, their proofs remained fixed in the realm of traditional Christian apologetic. They used the Latin Vulgate Bible for proofs, with the introduction of an occasional Hebrew word or phrase from St. Jerome or other commentators. They relied heavily on patristic sources and drew from the same well of oft-cited prophecies. When Jewish interpretations were cited for refutation (and only once was a Jewish position introduced to prove a point, by Peter Olivi), the source of the teaching was vague and almost certainly came from Jerome, Peter Alfonse, Andrew of St. Victor, or a similar Christian source.

Roger Marston cited Augustine's *City of God* throughout his question, and the scribe of the Peter of Trabes manuscript noted in the margin that many items relevant to the question could be found in Augustine's work,[99] but for the most part, the spiritual interpretations of Scripture developed by Augustine were difficult to integrate into these questions. The commentaries of Jerome were of more practical use; Jerome highlighted the same prophetic texts as those found in Augustine's *City of God* but interpreted them historically. A good example of the difference between Augustine and Jerome can be seen in their treatment of the angel Gabriel's prophecy in Daniel 9 that seventy weeks of years would pass until the destruction of Jerusalem. Jerome carefully calculated the years based on historical evidence of the length of various rulers' reigns. Augustine avoided all of that, complaining that although Daniel had specified the time that Christ would come, "it would be a tedious business to demonstrate this by computation, and it has been done by others before us."[100] He then moved on to discuss what Daniel had to say about the eternal power of Christ and his Church. Jerome's literal explications provided the kind of information these scholars needed for rational proofs. Accordingly, numerous citations of Jerome appear in these questions. Bede was similarly useful. His *De temporum ratione* provided the basis for most of the calculations of the time of the messiah's arrival. Some of this material came directly from the Fathers, but much of it probably came through other medieval exegetes or polemicists, including Peter Alfonse, Andrew of St. Victor, and, in Roger Marston's case, Robert Grosseteste.[101]

Looking for some connection between the authors of these quodlibeta, we find that they were all from England or France, were all Franciscans, and were all part of what might loosely be identified as an Augustinian school. Three of our figures studied in Paris, while the fourth studied with a teacher who had been trained in Paris. Strong intellectual ties bound England and France in the thirteenth century, with lines of influence running in both directions. Bonaventure studied under Alexander of Hales and William of Middleton before becoming himself a mentor to Peter Olivi, who became in turn the teacher of Peter of Trabes. Roger Marston, an Englishman, and Peter Olivi, a Provençal, both studied in Paris under the English theologian John Pecham. Archbishop Pecham was likely a student of Roger Bacon when both men were at the university in Paris. The Oxford-produced summary of Bonaventure's *Sentences* commentary, which Richard Rufus of Cornwall made for students there, shows the movement of ideas back from Paris to England.[102] English Franciscans brought with them to Paris their interest in literal readings of Scripture and Hebrew study and carried back with them theological positions forged in the Parisian university environment.

The paths of these men all crossed in one way or another. A direct connection with Bonaventure exists for Peter Olivi, who, as a student in Paris in 1268, heard him preach, and who had a personal relationship with the minister general in addition to being well acquainted with his works. Roger Marston and Peter of Trabes studied with students of Bonaventure; a teacher-pupil relationship existed between Peter Olivi and Peter of Trabes; Olivi and Marston were fellow students in Paris of John Pecham. Raymond Rigauld is harder to trace, but we do know that he studied at Paris, presumably for some number of years before he became regent there in 1287. We can assume that he lived in the Franciscan convent there, where he would have been a part of the same circle of Franciscan scholars in a Bonaventuran/Augustinian tradition.

In addition to the obvious geographical connection through Paris, it is noteworthy that all of these quodlibetal questions on the advent of Christ were written by Franciscans who identified themselves as part of an Augustinian tradition. Franciscans as a group seem to have been especially interested in developing epistemology and exploring the process by which human beings gained knowledge of the natural world and of God.[103] As we have also seen, Franciscans as a group demonstrated a particular interest in history generally and literal historical exegesis specifically. They served as a driving force in the exploitation of Hebrew and Jewish traditions in literal exegesis. The intersection between these two interests, evident to some degree in the questions explored thus far, comes to the fore when we look ahead to the work of Nicholas of Lyra. Nicholas disputed his quodlibet more than a decade after Peter of Trabes, when the concerns of the day were somewhat different. By 1309, the worst tensions between Franciscan and Dominican theologians over Thomism were dissipating, the nature of epistemological debate—still led by Franciscans—had moved off in new directions, the Jews had been expelled from both England and France, and hundreds of Hebrew manuscripts had been lost to inquisitorial fires. And yet, just as Nicholas's achievements as Hebraist and literal exegete represented the culmination of a thirteenth-century movement, so we see in his quodlibet a continued exploration of ideas and themes that had particular resonance for an earlier time. Here again, as in his commentary, exegesis, polemic, and broader theological debate are linked.

Wrestling with Rashi: Nicholas of Lyra's Quodlibetal Questions and Anti-Jewish Polemic

By the early fourteenth century, when Nicholas of Lyra disputed his questions on "whether the Jews knew Jesus of Nazareth to be the messiah promised to them" and "whether from Scriptures received by the Jews it is possible to prove effectively that our savior was both God and man," the parameters of such questions had already been well established.[1] Nicholas of Lyra may not have been familiar with the range of specific thirteenth-century questions on the topic, but he certainly would have been familiar with the general concerns. Like those thirteenth-century scholars, Nicholas acknowledged the challenge that Jewish unbelief presented to Christian interpretations of Old Testament texts and was intent on guarding those prophecies that had long served as "proof" of Christ's advent. And Nicholas, too, employed an epistemological framework in his exploration of the problem, considering the process of cognition as he addressed unbelief. The particular epistemological ideas in play were different in Nicholas's day, as he was active a generation after figures like Peter Olivi and Peter of Trabes, but the discussion of cognition and noetics was no less vital.

Nicholas arrived in Paris in 1302, around the same time that Duns Scotus, the most important new voice on cognition and natural theology, arrived from Oxford. Though they stood on opposite sides of the controversy between pope and king that sent Scotus into a brief exile in 1303, the two men lived together at the Franciscan convent until Scotus left for Cologne in 1308, and Nicholas could scarcely have avoided being influenced in some way by the "subtle doctor's" thought.[2] Katherine Tachau has emphasized the impact of Scotus's ideas on contemporaries, remarking that "at his death, Scotus left behind at each *studium* students and colleagues who, if they did not agree with all that he taught, recognized clearly and found heuristically fruitful the new framework he had given to many issues."[3] Nicholas was interested enough in epistemological questions to have assembled an abridged edition of Henry of Ghent's quodlibeta, preserved in several manuscripts including one from the Bibliothèque Mazarine with an *explicit* indicating that the collection was "arranged by Brother Nicholas of Lyra, Franciscan master of Paris."[4] Nicholas's interest in epistemology emerged elsewhere in his own work as well, notably in a question placed into his commentary on Daniel 1:17, where he discussed the nature of prophetic cognition.[5] When Nicholas set the problem of prophecy and Jewish unbelief in epistemological terms, he reflected an environment in which theories of knowledge were profoundly important.

Unlike the Franciscan authors of previous questions on proving the Advent through Jewish or prophetic texts, Nicholas did not stake a major claim in the ongoing discussion of epistemology. He was above all a student of the Bible who, by the time he determined these questions, had already developed an approach to literal exegesis that depended upon the Hebrew Bible and rabbinic commentary, especially Rashi's, in the interpretation of Christian Scripture. Although Nicholas was necessarily familiar with and had opinions on the pressing theological issues of his day, the Hebraism and investment in Jewish exegesis that helped establish his reputation were most important in defining the character of his work and set his treatment of these questions apart from earlier models. Nicholas used the quodlibetal disputation as an opportunity to address Jewish error through an interplay of exegesis and polemic—an approach that he continued for decades afterward and that enabled him to make extensive use of Jewish commentaries without, for the most part, being charged with Judaizing. Of course the intersection of exegesis and polemic was ages old in both Christian and Jewish circles, but Nicholas's situation was distinctive in that he made more thoroughgoing use of medieval rabbinic commentary than any Christian contemporary and that he did so at a time when "modern" Jewish opinions were increasingly suspect and Jewish books were being censored and burned.[6] That the only three questions to survive from Nicholas's quodlibetal disputation involved exegesis suggests that contemporaries were also most interested in Nicholas's contributions in this area.[7]

The two questions on knowing Christ and his nature through Jewish Scripture were clearly disputed in the same quodlibet: they appear alongside each other in Bibliotheca Apostolica Vaticana MS Vat. lat. 869 with a direct reference in the first to the second. Discussing the texts by which the Advent could have been known to the Jews, Nicholas cut his argument short, saying simply, "many other similar authorities are introduced in the next question."[8] A survey of sources adduced in the second question shows a clear correspondence with those introduced in the first. While the first question explored whether the Jews indeed recognized that Jesus was the messiah at the time of his advent, the much longer second question explored in detail the specific texts by which such knowledge could have been attained. In both cases Nicholas considered not only whether one could, by means of Jewish Scripture, know that Jesus was the messiah but also whether his full divinity and humanity could be discerned by such means. Both questions ended with an attempt to resolve the problem of Jewish unbelief in some way, concluding with rational explanations for Jewish failure to follow Christ that went beyond an assignment of simple blindness or malice.

The timeline of Nicholas's career at Paris, along with internal evidence from the question on the advent of Christ, dates the quodlibet to 1308–9.[9] Although scholars have readily accepted this composition date, many have followed Nicholas's early twentieth-century biographer, Henri Labrosse, in assuming that the question on the advent of Christ was later revised, sometime between 1331 and 1334.[10] A close examination of the manuscript tradition of the text, however, makes it clear that the question took on its final form very shortly after the disputation itself,[11] since the earliest manuscript copies of the text contain all of the passages that Labrosse associated with the revision. Nicholas returned to the question at various points in his later exegetical work, summarizing pieces in his Ezechiel commentary, for example, but he did not revise the work and distribute it as a new treatise later in his career. The dating of the text to 1309 shows Nicholas's Hebrew- and Rashi-inspired exegesis to have been firmly in place from his earliest years at Paris; it demonstrates the direction of movement for the many parallel passages between the question and the *Postilla litteralis* and enables us to identify the relevant contexts for Nicholas's work, linking his efforts clearly with thirteenth-century Franciscan Hebraism and epistemological discourse and placing the emergence of his distinctive exegetical style in the years immediately following the dramatic expulsion of the Jews from France (1306) in the context of Hebrew book burnings and increasingly hostile responses to Jewish traditions.

Nicholas's questions on recognizing the advent of Christ from Jewish Scripture stand out from earlier approaches to the question in his regular appeal to the Hebrew Bible and its Aramaic translation, his frequent use of rabbinic commentary as Christian prooftexts, and his ongoing dialogue with Jewish tradition, presenting and refuting Jewish objections to Christian interpretations of Old Testament passages. While the question on whether the Jews recognized Christ at his advent is fairly brief, the question on proving the Advent and dual nature of Christ was considerably longer than any thirteenth-century versions of the question. That may have been in part due to the fact that questions as a genre came to be significantly longer in the fourteenth century than they had been in the thirteenth, but it also surely had to do with the fact that, because of his expertise in this area, he had so many sources, both Jewish and Christian, to bring to bear on the question. He addressed many of the same well-worn prophetic passages as his predecessors, but he handled them more expansively because of the insights he gained from his Hebraically oriented Bible study. And unlike the earlier authors who often argued from New Testament passages or with Christian interpretations of Old Testament text, Nicholas strove to demonstrate that it was possible to know Jesus as messiah from a Jewish perspective as well as a Christian one and then to account for the fact that, in spite of this, Jews failed to follow the evidence to its logical conclusions.

In the first of the two questions, "whether the Jews perceived Jesus to be the Christ promised to them, which does not appear to be the case,"[12] Nicholas did begin with New Testament texts both for and against the notion that the Jews rejected Jesus knowingly, as a way of setting up the problem from a Christian perspective. Against the proposition he cited 1 Corinthians 2:7–8, *But we speak the wisdom of God in a mystery, a wisdom which is hidden, which God ordained before the world, to our glory, which none of the princes of this world knew. For if they had known it, they would never have crucified the Lord of Glory*; Acts 3:17, *And now, brothers, I know that you did it through ignorance, as did also your rulers*; and Luke 23:34, *And Jesus said: "Father, forgive them, for they know not what they do,"* each of which suggested that the Jews did not know what they were doing in rejecting Jesus. In favor of the proposition, he cited John 15:24, *now they have both seen and hated both me and my Father*; and Matthew 21:38–9, *But the husbandmen seeing the son, said among themselves, "This is the heir; come, let us kill him, and we shall have his inheritance." And taking him, they cast him out of the vineyard and killed him*, both of which suggested that the Jews knew perfectly well who Jesus was and rejected him out of pure malice. Once the problem was set out, his arguments proceeded on the basis of Jewish texts almost exclusively.

In resolving the question, Nicholas followed the tradition of many before him, including Bonaventure and Thomas Aquinas, by distinguishing between the educated elite and the common people (*maiores* and *minores*).

The common people were familiar with the Ten Commandments and understood what they needed to do to fulfill the Law, but they were essentially ignorant of the writings of the prophets, and so they could not have been expected to read the signs of Jesus' coming.[13] The rest of the question focused on the leadership of the community, those who were knowledgeable in the words of the prophets. Nicholas highlighted their responsibility to the majority, citing Deuteronomy 32:7, *Remember the days of old, think about every generation; ask your father, and he will declare to you, your elders and they will tell you.* Having established the authority of the priests and elders over the community, Nicholas insisted that these leaders must have recognized Christ, as the signs of prophetic fulfillment were clear.[14]

Nicholas distinguished recognition of Jesus as the messiah sent by God from further recognition of the divinity within Jesus, and he argued that St. Paul's comment in Corinthians was meant to indicate their ignorance of Christ's divinity, even while they recognized his human messiahship. Yet in spite of St. Paul's comment, Nicholas argued that just as it was possible to read the signs of the messiah's advent through prophecies, including the seventy weeks of years in Daniel 9, the cessation of Jewish kingship predicted in Genesis 49, and the arrival of Jesus in poverty and humiliation as prophesied in Zachariah 9, so, too, should the messiah's divinity have been evident through prophecies like Jeremiah 33 and Isaiah 9, both of which specifically referred to the messiah as God, through the use of the Tetragrammaton. Nicholas argued that since Jewish authorities read these passages messianically just as Christians did, they should have understood the implications of the messiah's divinity. Although Nicholas was correct in his assertion that these passages were read messianically by Jews, he neglected to clarify that Jewish authorities understood the association of the divine name with the promised messiah in these passages as a praise of God rather than identification of the messiah as God himself, a position he would go on to challenge in the second question. In any case, Nicholas concluded this brief discussion by claiming that at least initially, the Jewish elite did have knowledge (*haberent cognitione*) that Jesus must have been the messiah promised to them, and further, that they had this knowledge in terms of his divinity as well as his humanity.

Nicholas reconciled the apparent contradiction between New Testament assertions of ignorance and knowing by an appeal to Aristotle's *Nichomachean Ethics*. The *Ethics* had been translated with commentary by Robert Grosseteste in the mid-thirteenth century, and the study of moral virtue and weakness of will had become important components of theological study by the late thirteenth century.[15] As the principles of ethics made clear, a certain thing could be known habitually (in the universal), while a full, actual knowledge of that thing (in the particular instance) could be disrupted. Nicholas introduced the notion of incontinence (moral weakness), distinguishing it from the intentional immorality of intemperance. Where the intemperate man adheres to a false moral code, the incontinent man knows right from wrong but, swept away by passion, fails to transform his habitual (universal) knowledge to actual knowledge in a particular situation, and so he pursues a course of action that he would otherwise know is morally wrong. Nicholas was trying to make sense of the Jewish failure to accept Jesus by means of this analysis, but he was not trying to absolve the Jews of responsibility in Jesus' death. Although passion leads the incontinent man to failure in cognition, and so to behavior of which he himself does not approve, he is still responsible for his actions. As Bonnie Kent explains, "the incontinent suffers from a temporary but culpable ignorance."[16] According to Nicholas, at least some of the educated Jewish leadership knew, both habitually and actually, of Jesus' status in the beginning, but when he began to preach against them, he so aroused their ire that passion interfered with their cognitive ability. In that moment, they still possessed a habitual knowledge of him, but they failed to know actually that he was the messiah, both God and man, and so they conspired in his death.[17]

While many learned Jews thus should have known Jesus in his humanity and his divinity, Nicholas allowed that some of the elite may have been ignorant at a deeper level. Since prophetic signs are by nature ambiguous (*prophetie possunt aliquando varie exponi*), even learned Jews could only have attained probability and verisimilitude rather than certainty about the Advent.[18] Nicholas thus devised a fairly elaborate scheme for understanding the failure of the Jews to follow Christ, a scheme in which malice pure and simple played only a limited part. The majority of the Jews had no basis for recognizing the signs, since they were not learned in the writings of the prophets. Since certitude through the available evidence was elusive even for the learned, some of the elite really were ignorant concerning Jesus. Finally, even those who did at first fully know Jesus to be the messiah, both God and man, experienced a failure in cognition when Jesus' criticisms aroused their passion. When biblical texts alluded to the Jews' ignorance, they referred to actual rather than habitual cognition.

Jeremy Cohen used this question (as presented in Nicholas's *Postilla* in Matthew 21) to demonstrate a shift in Christian thought toward increasing Jewish culpability for Christ's death over the course of the thirteenth century. Cohen argued that Nicholas's insistence that the Jewish leadership knew not only of Jesus' messiahship but also of his divinity was a departure from earlier thought, which posited either complete ignorance or knowledge only of his messiahship.[19] For Cohen, Nicholas's conclusions here represented the culmination of a broad move away from Augustinian toleration of the Jews toward a delegitimization of postbiblical Judaism; the traditional position that the Jews rejected Christ out of ignorance gave way here to a new charge of knowing complicity in the killing of God in the Crucifixion.[20]

While Nicholas's position may have further encouraged those who wanted to highlight the Jews' role in the Crucifixion as an intentional rejection of God and the covenant, Nicholas's response does not fit neatly into Cohen's scheme of ignorance versus intentionality. Rather than rejecting the Augustinian notion of Jewish ignorance, Nicholas worked here to preserve it by redefining ignorance in Aristotelian terms. This enabled him to explain how the Jews could have been described by Jesus and St. Paul as being ignorant of their crime while simultaneously insisting on the knowability of the Advent through prophecy. The point of the last paragraph of the question was not so much that the Jews killed Jesus out of malice, the point was that the emotional state of anger and jealousy aroused by Christ's rebukes caused a real lapse in cognition.[21] Since the ignorance of which the Gospels and Epistles spoke took place at the level of actual rather than habitual cognition, it reflected neither on the usefulness of prophecy for determining the Advent nor on Jewish ability to read and understand their own texts. Peter Olivi simply dismissed the Jews' error as one born of blindness or a resistance to the spirit of grace by means of which they might have accurately read their own Scripture.[22] That was not a helpful approach for Nicholas, who so admired Jewish interpretation of Scripture that he often sided with Jewish interpreters over Christian ones in his commentaries.

Nicholas's innovation in the treatment of the Jews' knowledge of Christ, apart from his important insistence on the ability to know Christ in his divinity as well as in his humanity, was to stress a temporary ignorance derived from moral weakness that was distinct from their customary perceptiveness. This was not a moral defense of the Jews at the time of the Crucifixion or for continued Jewish unbelief; describing the Jewish elite as incontinent and captive to passion was hardly flattering. But by providing a rational explanation for Jewish failure to grasp the truths of Christianity, he could separate those failings from what he saw as an invaluable ability to discern the meaning of Scripture.

This tension between a positive valuation of Jewish exegesis and persistent Jewish unbelief was even more apparent in the following question, where Nicholas argued against the proposition that one could prove the dual nature of Christ by means of Jewish Scripture by stating that if one could prove the proposition by means of Jewish texts, then it was unlikely that the Jews, with so many clever, exceptionally learned men among them, would have remained so long in their error.[23] Although Nicholas had yet to publish his *Postilla litteralis* on the whole Bible, it is clear that he was already incorporating Jewish exegetical material into his own lectures on the Bible. Pursuing this path during a time when rabbinic texts were increasingly met with suspicion, censored, and burned as both blasphemous and absurd, required, perhaps, some explanation. In the last question, Nicholas explained the inability or unwillingness of the Jews to respond to Christ's call in the Advent. In the following question, Nicholas provided a similar explanation for the Jews' continued resistance to the demonstrable truths of Christianity. In Nicholas's emphasis on literal readings of Scripture, we see an attempt not only to prove Christianity against Jewish unbelief but also to uphold his rigorously historical reading of Scripture. In this question, Lyra repeatedly maintained that the Christological meaning of various Old Testament passages was perfectly clear in the literal sense without recourse to any particular insight provided by grace.

Nicholas began by asking "whether from Scriptures received by the Jews it is possible effectively to prove our Savior to have been both God and man."[24] He immediately divided the question into two distinct parts, one pertaining to the dual nature of Christ and the other to the time of the Advent. His unique framing of this question—proving the nature of the messiah rather than simply the time of the Advent from Jewish Scripture—links this question firmly with the preceding one. Just as he had indicated, he introduced many more proofs here to show that Jewish Scripture read according to the literal sense gave witness to the joined humanity and divinity of the messiah as well as the time of the Advent.

Nicholas argued first for the proposition that one could prove the dual nature of Christ with Jewish texts by citing Jeremiah 23:5. *Behold the days come, says the Lord, and I will raise up to David a just branch, and a king shall reign, and shall be wise and shall execute judgment and justice in the earth* served as proof of Christ's full humanity, while the next line of the text, *In those days Judah shall be saved, and Israel shall dwell confidently. And this is the name that they shall call him: "The Lord our just one,"* served as proof of his full divinity. To support the second part of the proposition, that the time of the Advent was past, Nicholas cited Haggai 2:8, *And the desired of all nations shall come: and I will fill this house with glory: says the Lord of Hosts*, which indicated that the messiah would come in the days of the Temple. Since Titus and Vespasian had long ago destroyed the Temple, the time of the Advent was clearly past. Against both parts of the proposition Nicholas argued that there had been and continued to be many learned and intelligent men among the Jews. If one could prove these Christian truths through Jewish Scripture, it seems unlikely that they would have held on to their error for so long.[25]

Incipit version 2, "whether through Scriptures received by the Jews it is possible to prove that the mystery of the Christ promised in the law and prophets has already come," framed the question only in terms of time.[26] It argued in favor of the proposition by citing, as Raymond Rigauld and Peter Olivi among others had done before, John 5:39, *Search the Scriptures: for you think in them to have life everlasting. And the same are they that give testimony of me.* The brief argument against the proposition is essentially the same as that introduced in incipit version 1, that the Jews would not have persisted in their error if one could prove the Advent from their own Scriptures. With the response the two texts become identical for the remainder of the question. There can be little doubt that incipit version 1 represents the question as originally offered in the quodlibet. As we have seen, MS Vat. lat. 869 explicitly linked the question on whether the Jews knew Christ at his advent with this one. Framing the question around proving the dual nature of Christ as well as the time of the Advent not only connects this question with the previous one but also is most consistent with the internal structure of the question, which does focus on proving the dual nature of Christ as well as the time of the Advent.

Neither the framing of the question in incipit version 2 nor the citation of John 5:39 in support of the proposition fits the question that follows particularly well. While the Old Testament passages adduced in the opening to incipit version 1 are treated in depth later in the body of the question, there is no return to John 5:39 or even the idea of John 5:39 later in the question; there is a clear disjunction between the opening of incipit version 2 and the question that follows. Sometime within Nicholas's lifetime, this second version of the question began to circulate.[27] It would be difficult, perhaps impossible, to discover whether Nicholas rewrote the incipit and opening argument himself or whether, as I suspect, this may have been done by a copyist somewhere along the line. In any event, the deviations of the second incipit are so small that they require no further attention here.

As Nicholas intended for his evidence to be drawn only from Jewish Scripture and postbiblical texts accepted as authoritative by the Jews, he prefaced the main body of the question with a summary of the writings that should be included. Since most Christians knew only the Vulgate version of Hebrew Scripture, Nicholas outlined the structure of the Hebrew Bible itself, naming each of the twenty four canonical books and dividing them into the three categories defined by Jewish tradition: the Law, the Prophets, and Sacred Writing. Nicholas then introduced the Targum, Aramaic interpretive translations of the Bible. Attributing them all to Jonathan b. Uzziel, he claimed that his writing was

so valid among the Hebrews that no one dared to contradict him, on account of which in the notable books of the Jews, pure Hebrew is placed in one column and Aramaic written by this Jonathan in Hebrew letters in the other, and the Jews use the Aramaic for explanation because some things which are very obscure in pure Hebrew are made clearer and explained, as it were, in that Aramaic, as will be most evident below. Therefore, that translation is necessary to dispute with Jews in many passages.[28]

With this comment, Nicholas made it clear that his intent was not only to demonstrate that one could prove certain Christian truths from Jewish Scripture but also to engage with Jewish interpretations of contested passages. Nicholas's approach here shows the influence of thirteenth-century Dominicans like Paul Christian and Raymond Martini, who used rabbinic traditions to prove the truth of Christianity to Jews in forced sermons and disputations. Nicholas's question differed somewhat in that his concern was not the conversion of the Jews but staking his claim to disputed biblical territory. The disputing that Nicholas cited here was one that took place within the Christian community itself, in the context of Bible study, as he set out to demonstrate against Jewish unbelief that Hebrew Scriptures properly read clearly and unmistakably pointed the way to Christian doctrine and that, furthermore, this proper reading was one which could be done entirely at the literal level without need of any special "light" or "spirit of grace."[29]

Nicholas also included the Septuagint version of the Bible among the Sacred Writings accepted as authoritative by the Jews; since it was written by seventy of the wisest and best Jewish leaders of Ptolemy's day, he argued, it must be accepted as legitimate by present-day Jews. Of course, this would hardly have convinced a contemporary Jewish audience, but again, this seems not to have been Nicholas's concern. Nicholas was speaking to a community of Christian theologians situated in universities on this matter, not to an imagined Jewish audience. Moving from Scripture and its various translations, Nicholas next discussed the Talmud, presenting it dispassionately as canonical text, the oral complement to Moses' written law. He cited the first chapter of *Pirke Avot* on the transmission of the tradition, explaining how Moses handed the oral law down to Joshua and the elders in the Israelite community by word, just as he had received it, and how those men did the same, from generation to generation, until it was finally written down by later authors. After the written and oral law Nicholas introduced rabbinic commentaries on the Bible, which he claimed were even more authoritative than Christian ones, arguing that the authority of the rabbis was legitimized by Deuteronomy 17:11, *Neither shall you lean to the right hand nor to the left hand.* Though the biblical texts intended obedience to the priests, who were the arbiters of the Law, rabbis had come to serve that function, and their opinions had to be followed without discussion.[30] Nicholas defended the range of his material by arguing that even though many falsities were found within rabbinic tradition, it nevertheless could be used to construct effective proofs, just as the Jews used prooftexts from the Gospels and Epistles in their polemic, even though they believed that those books contain falsehoods.[31]

Having established his literary parameters, Nicholas turned to the first part of his response, proving Christ's dual nature. Once more, he divided his effort into two distinct parts, explaining that he needed first to establish the biblical basis for Trinitarian doctrine before he could effectively demonstrate the humanity and divinity of Christ. His argument focused on the use of the plural name for God, *Elohim*, following book 1, distinction 2, of Peter Lombard's *Sentences.* Having set out the Christian argument, Nicholas turned to a series of Jewish objections and responses.

In answer to the Jewish objection that whenever the name *Elohim* appears in relation to God it must be interpreted in the singular, Nicholas introduced a series of examples where the name *Elohim* was used with intentional plurality to speak of God and no other. For each text he used, Nicholas cited first from the Vulgate, then presented a Latinized version of the text as found in the *Hebraica veritas*. One such proof came from Jeremiah 23:36, *for you have perverted the words of the living God, of the Lord of Hosts, our God.* Nicholas explained that where the Latin read, "the words of the living God," the *Hebraica veritas* employed the plural "*verba Heloim viventium*"; and where it read, "the Lord of Hosts," the Hebrew used the Tetragrammaton. Nicholas argued that by pairing the plural name *Elohim* with the Tetragrammaton, the symbol of pure divine essence, within the same passage, Scripture was demonstrating a plurality in the intrinsic essence of the divine. Furthermore, Nicholas argued, plural verbs were often used with the name *Elohim* or other singular references to God, as in the phrase *iverunt Heloim* in 2 Kings 7:23, or *rex eum fecerunt* in Ecclesiastes 2:12.

Nicholas introduced contradictory Hebrew interpretations of some of these passages so as to dismiss them. He was particularly interested in a Hebrew interpretation of Ecclesiastes 2:12 and Asaph's threefold invocation of God's name in Psalm 49 (50). Following the approach outlined in Raymond Martini's *Capistrum Iudaeorum* and *Pugio fidei contra Mauros et Iudaeos*, Nicholas embraced elements of these interpretations as true and effective proofs of Christianity while rejecting their problematic aspects.[32] Nicholas cited the teaching of a "Hebrew gloss" that Asaph's call to God indicated God's creation in three distinct properties as a trinitarian proof of the three properties, "paternity, filiation, and spiration," within divinity. But then he complained that later Jews distorted this truth by claiming that the three properties were divine wisdom, goodness or kindness, and power, and that the use of the plural with respect to God in Genesis 1:1, among other passages, was meant to indicate these three attributes of God. Nicholas argued against the rationality of such a position, explaining that attributes like power, wisdom, and love can only be fully differentiated in God's creation (rather than in God's being), and so these three attributes belonged to the act of creation rather than to God per se.[33] Nicholas's final word on plural references to God in the quodlibetal disputation invoked Moses' purpose in writing down the Law, which was to lead people toward God and away from idolatry. Nicholas argued that, knowing how prone to idolatry the Israelites were, it was unlikely that Moses would have risked confusing them with this language of plurality unless he intended to embed critical, but subtle, hints about the Trinitarian nature of the one God.[34]

At this point Nicholas broke off to introduce new material that he had not included in the original quodibetal disputation, saying, "These are the things that I said about this matter when I determined this question. But after that a little book written in Hebrew came into my hand where the above matter was otherwise dismissed."[35] Living in Paris during the years immediately following the expulsion of the Jews from royal France, Nicholas would have had access to any number of confiscated Hebrew books, many of which had been brought to the Franciscan and Dominican convents for inspection. With the increasing length of quodlibetal questions in the fourteenth century came an increase in the time between the oral determination and the subsequent writing of the text. It would seem that

Nicholas encountered this new book during the months between oral and written phases of the work. The Hebrew book dismissed the Christian attempt to prove Trinitarian doctrine through the existence of plural references to God, arguing that the Bible applied plural nouns to single individuals not only with respect to God but also to others, as in 1 Kings 28:14, which used the plural to describe Samuel's being raised up from the dead, and Ezechiel 46:6, which spoke about the sacrifice of a pure calf, placing "pure" in the plural with "calf" in the singular. Furthermore, the opposite was also true; verbs of plural number were sometimes joined with nouns of singular number, as in Song of Songs 1:3, which read, *Draw me, we will run after thee.*

Nicholas refuted the book on the reading of these three passages and then, calling to mind Peter of Trabes's assertion that if one proof did not convince, perhaps another might, Nicholas introduced further proofs for God's plurality that did not depend upon the plurality implicit in the name *Elohim.*[36] These proofs dealt with passages in which God took on more than one role simultaneously, as, for instance, in Psalm 44:7–8, *God, your God has anointed you with the oil of gladness above your companions*; and Isaiah 48:16–17, *Come near unto me, and hear this: I have not spoken in secret from the beginning, from the time before it was done, I was there, and now the Lord God has sent me, and his spirit.* In these sorts of instances, Nicholas argued, one had to conclude that one person within the divine was speaking to another person. The psalm spoke of God both anointing and being anointed to distinguish between the Father as the God anointing and Christ as the anointed Son. Furthermore, the name of God anointing was doubled to indicate the involvement of both God the Father and the Holy Spirit, and so the passage proved not only a general plurality in divinity but specifically the Trinity. In Isaiah 48:16–17, Nicholas argued, Isaiah was speaking in the person of God himself, evident from the claim that he had been present from before the giving of the Law as well as the explicit identification in the following sentence, *Thus says the Lord your redeemer.* Since it is impossible for one person to be both sender and sent, this must represent two distinct persons within one. God speaking about having been sent was clearly God the Son, while the sender must have been God the Father. As the text also specifically invoked the Spirit, Nicholas triumphantly concluded that the passage provided clear proof of "a Trinity of persons in the divine: of God having been sent and of God sending and of his spirit. God having been sent we call the Son incarnate of the Lord, God sending and his Spirit we call the Father and the Spirit."[37]

Where someone like Peter Olivi was generally satisfied simply to present the Christian interpretation as the only rational one, Nicholas introduced and refuted contradictory Jewish readings. He focused particular attention on what he called a "fable" or "falsehood" (*mendacium*) found in Rashi's commentary. The controversial reading had to do with a rabbinic midrash on the phrase *from the time before it was done, I was there*, which projected Isaiah as having been present at Sinai with Moses and all of the other prophets, at which time they first accepted the prophecies that they would deliver later at the appropriate time.[38] Nicholas declared the tradition "false" (*patet falsum multipliciter*) and at least one element of it "completely absurd" (*valde absurdum*), appealing to Scriptural evidence to demonstrate not only that it was impossible for the souls of the prophets to have come into being before their bodies but also that the dramatic biblical descriptions of the prophets gradually coming to understand and accept their callings would be invalidated if this teaching were true. After a long and labored argument incorporating various "Hebrew glosses" in support of his position, he finally exclaimed that "it is thus evident that the saying of Rabbi Solomon is not only against all of the prophets . . . but even against all of the Scripture of the Old Testament."[39] He railed similarly against the "perversion" of another "ancient gloss" that he said recognized in Ecclesiastes 4:12, *A three-fold cord is not easily broken*, a mystery of three in God, complaining that the Trinity acknowledged in the earlier rabbinic gloss had been twisted here into the three attributes of power, wisdom, and goodness.[40]

Nicholas concluded the first section of his question with a determination that a plurality in divinity, and even more, the Trinity specifically, could be clearly demonstrated from Jewish Scripture.[41] This lengthy section, ranging widely over literal exegesis of key passages of Hebrew Scripture with the support of certain "Hebrew glosses" and the refutation of others, established a framework for the rest of the question. Jewish unbelief notwithstanding, Nicholas insisted that Christian truth could be found through a purely literal reading of the Bible as received by the Jews.

Having demonstrated that a plurality in divinity could be discerned from the Hebrew Bible with the aid of various Jewish interpretations, Nicholas next set out to demonstrate from those same texts the incarnation of one of those persons as God and man simultaneously. This is the part of the question that continued, as promised, the work of the previous one, arguing that the Jews could have recognized the divinity and humanity of Jesus as messiah at his advent. He began and ended with prooftexts that had been introduced briefly in the previous question, developing additional arguments in the middle.

Nicholas chose texts that he knew Jews read messianically and then attempted to demonstrate allusions to divinity embedded within those texts. The first two arguments addressed prophecies introduced in the previous question, Jeremiah 23:5 (and the line's reprise in 33:16) and Isaiah 9:6, focusing on the use of the Tetragrammaton. There were two parts to the argument: first, Nicholas had to establish the Tetragrammaton as a distinctive name for God's pure essence with certain theological implications, then he had to link that essence with the messiah himself. Because the argument could only be made by appealing to the Hebrew text, this was just the sort of place where Nicholas's response stood out from those of his colleagues. Not only could he gather the necessary evidence from the Hebrew Bible, he could also access rabbinic texts, both "ancient" and "modern," that would support his reading. To demonstrate that the Tetragrammaton was used in Hebrew Scripture only to refer to God in his most pure essence, Nicholas turned to the Bible itself, rabbinic commentary, and Maimonides' *Guide of the Perplexed*.

Nicholas confirmed the Christian reading of Jeremiah 23:5, *Behold, the days come, saith the Lord, and I will raise up to David a just branch* as a reference to Christ by asserting that all Hebrew commentators (*expositores Hebrei*) also understood the passage messianically "according to the letter" (*ad litteram*). This agreement established the promised messiah's humanity. He continued the argument by insisting that the use of the Tetragrammaton for "Lord" in the subsequent line of text, *and this is the name that they shall call him: The Lord our just one*, proved Christ's divinity.

Since his argument depended upon the idea that Hebrew Scripture only used the Tetragrammaton with respect to "the True God" (*Deus verus*), he introduced and dismissed the claims of some who denied this on the basis of passages like Genesis 22:14, Judges 6:24, Exodus 17:15, and Ezechiel 48:35, each of which showed the Tetragrammaton being used otherwise. In Ezechiel 48:35, for example, *and the name of the city from that day: the Lord is there*, the Tetragrammaton was used in clear reference to a city. Similarly, in Genesis 22:14, *And Abraham called the name of that place, the Lord seeth*, the Tetragrammaton described a location rather than God.

Nicholas dismissed the argument, insisting that such names were all meant to refer to an effect of the true God. He likened the use of the Tetragrammaton in these passages to the use of the name "God" in the Latin names *Adeodatus* or *Deusdedit*; the name of God was invoked by those names, but clearly the person himself was not being called God.[42] And so in Ezechiel, Nicholas explained, the Tetragrammaton referred not to the city but to the true God for which the city was named. Nicholas introduced the Targum here for support, saying that it understood the use of the Tetragrammaton to mean "the Lord made his divinity descend in that place."[43] Nicholas handled the other three passages in similar fashion, turning to the Targum to confirm his reading of the text and insisting by the end that "it is evident from the above that the Tetragrammaton is never used except with respect to the true God alone."[44] To bolster his claim, already supported by the Targum, he turned to Maimonides' *Guide of the Perplexed*, reporting that "Rabbi Moses" says, "all divine names are derived from divine works, excepting the name of God Tetragrammaton which is appropriated to the highest creator."[45] Since the Tetragrammaton represented "the divine essence, naked and pure" (*divina essentia nuda et pura*), Nicholas argued, it can never refer to anyone or anything else. When Jeremiah said that the people would call the messiah "the Lord, our just one" using the Tetragrammaton, it necessarily indicated the divinity of that messiah.

But there was a problem, Nicholas acknowledged, in this Christian argument because Latin and Hebrew grammar differed in the passage. The Hebrew text contained the verb "to call" in the singular future tense, thus holding out the promised messiah as testimony of God's righteousness, while the Latin Bible contained the future plural form of the verb, shifting the subject in the phrase and identifying the promised messiah (Jesus Christ) as the righteous God himself. Noting that the Aramaic Targum supported the Christian reading, Nicholas defended Jerome's Latin translation and, turning to a longstanding Christian suspicion, alleged that the Jews intentionally corrupted that passage of text in order to deny the messiah.[46] "Against this solution," he wrote, "it is not possible to argue except by showing that the Jews have corrupted the text in order to deny the divinity of Christ. This could best be done by obtaining ancient Bibles that have not been corrupted in this passage and in which the divinity of Christ may still be mentioned . . . Now while I myself have not seen such Hebrew Bibles which are not corrupted in this passage, nevertheless I have heard from men who are worthy by reason of knowledge and life who faithfully declare by oath that they have seen such ancient Bibles which have the passage as in Jerome's translation."[47]

In the absence of such pristine Hebrew Bibles, Nicholas suggested turning to other translations "that the Jews cannot reasonably deny."[48] Although he considered the Septuagint a legitimate source, it was not helpful in this case because Greek did not distinguish all of the different names for God used in Hebrew, substituting only the general term *Kirios* (Lord) for the Tetragrammaton. Unlike Jerome, who omitted such distinctions because of the limitations of Latin, Nicholas claimed that the Septuagint translators intentionally avoided the Tetragrammaton in the Greek for fear that King Ptolemy would misunderstand and presume that they worshipped two separate gods. Although the Septuagint did read "they will call him," just as in Jerome's Latin translation, without the use of the Tetragrammaton the argument unfortunately failed. As he did so often in this question, Nicholas finally called upon the Aramaic Targum on Jeremiah 23:5 and 33:16,[49] which, according to Nicholas, not only explicitly stated that God would establish from David a "just messiah," but also continued *this is the name that they will call him, the Lord, our just one*, using the Tetragrammaton. Nicholas claimed that this proved that the Hebrew Bible must have originally read *vocabunt* instead of *vocabit*. Nicholas dismissed Jewish claims that the passage meant only that the messiah would be called by the name of the God who sent him, not that the messiah would actually be God, by arguing that the messiah could not possibly be the "most holy prophet and holier than Moses" as the Jews expect if he were to allow himself to be called God when that was not the case, for that would have been blasphemy.[50]

Nicholas used another text from the previous question, Isaiah 9:6, *For a child is born to us, and a son is given to us, and the government is upon his shoulder: and his name shall be called, Wonderful Counsellor, God the Mighty, the Father of the world to come, the Prince of Peace*, in the same way. He held that Christ's humanity was illustrated by the phrase, "a child is born to us," while his divinity was shown by the phrase that followed. Nicholas charged the Jews once again with manipulating the text to avoid identifying the Tetragrammaton with the promised child. The Jews read "to call" in the future active rather than the future passive of the Latin and Septuagint versions, and so they associated the divine names, including the Tetragrammaton, with God as the speaker of the sentence. The final name in the series, "Prince of Peace," was then understood to be in the accusative case and to refer to the child. The sense of the passage in the Hebrew was thus, "a child is born to us . . . and the Wonderful Counsellor, God the Mighty, Eternal Father will call his name *Prince of Peace*." Nicholas admitted that he could devise no argument against the claim that "Prince of Peace" was in the accusative, as there was no grammatical distinction between the cases in Hebrew, and so he focused instead on the question of the verb's voice. The Targum supported Christian interpretation, since, like the Latin and the

Septuagint, it used the future passive. Furthermore, it explicitly identified the promised child as the messiah. Nicholas used this fact along with other evidence to dismiss Rashi's identification of the promised child with King Hezekiah, who brought peace to the beleaguered people of Judah following the assault of King Senacherib's army.[51]

Nicholas took the appearance in the Targum of the distinctive phrase *de ante* before the attribute-names to signify that Christ would first be named by God and the angel Gabriel, as described in the Gospels of Luke and Matthew. He further linked the Aramaic addition "and he will accept the Law above himself to preserve [it]" with Matthew 5:17, *I came not to destroy the Law but to fulfil [it]*. The Targum, Nicholas argued, provided irrefutable proof that the text represented a messianic prophecy, and its use of the Tetragrammaton in the verse proved the divinity of that promised messiah.[52] While Nicholas found that only the Targum on this passage provided convincing proof of the full humanity and divinity of Christ, the Hebrew text did contain its own hidden testimony to the mystery of the Incarnation itself. Nicholas described the unusual placement of a final *mem* in the middle of the verb "to multiply," contrary to Hebrew orthography. Instead of the open mem always used at the beginning or middle of a word, the Hebrew word לםרבה (*lemarbeh*) was written with the final, closed form of the letter. "This . . . closed *mem* is placed in the middle of the word against the nature of the letter and the manner of writing to denote that Christ, about which the prophets spoke, was to be born of a closed virgin and against the manner of nature, and that the mystery of the incarnation was closed and secret."[53]

While these efforts to establish messianic references and to link them with the Tetragrammaton took up most of the second section, Nicholas added several other, brief proofs of the dual nature of Christ at the end, each of which made use of the Targum and/or other rabbinic interpretation to support Christian readings of the text. The messianic prophecy of Micah 5:2, affirmed as such by the Targum's translation, served as proof of Christ's dual nature by joining the messiah's birth from among men with his eternality: *And you, Bethlehem Ephrata, are a little one among the thousands of Judah: out of you shall come to me the one that is to be the ruler in Israel, and his going forth is from the beginning, from the days of eternity.*

Nicholas complained that Jewish commentators tried to explain away this eternal existence of the messiah by claiming that the end of the passage referred to God's creation of seven things before the world: the name of the messiah, the Law, repentance, *Gehenna*, the house of the sanctuary, the throne of glory, and the Garden of Eden.[54] After charging that "this saying is so irrational that it does not need refutation," Nicholas went on to refute it anyway. The Law could not have been created before the world because it could only exist in the context of human or angelic intellect, which did not exist until after the creation of the world. Similarly, repentance could not have existed before sin, which could not have existed before the creation of humans in the world. Although he suggested that it would have been a simple matter to continue this rational attack on the midrash, Nicholas said he would refrain because it was so clearly "silly and absurd."[55]

The citation of this passage provides important information about Nicholas's Jewish sources. Noting the many parallel passages in Nicholas's question on the Advent and Raymond Martini's *Pugio fidei contra Mauros et Iudaeos*, Jeremy Cohen once suggested that Nicholas used the Spanish Dominican's text as a primary source of information on rabbinic traditions. Indeed, this midrash is found in Raymond Martini's *Pugio fidei*, but a comparison of the two Latin texts shows that Nicholas invoked the Talmudic version rather than the one from the midrashic collection *Sifre B'midbar* favored by Raymond. While Raymond subsequently offered the alternate version from Pesahim 54a (identical to yet another version in Nedarim 39b), Nicholas presented the seven things in a different arrangment.[56] This may simply mean that he was working from memory, but it is also possible that he found the list—which he attributes only to "the rabbis"—elsewhere. Neither did Raymond elaborate on the creation of the Garden of Eden as Nicholas did in his question; it seems that Raymond was not Nicholas's source in this passage, even though they both discuss the tradition. The encyclopedic *Pugio* discussed most of the rabbinic texts that Nicholas invoked as proof of the Christian faith or erroneous opinions, but that does not mean that Nicholas necessarily drew directly from Raymond. Rather, Rashi (and Theobald de Sézanne's *Extractiones de Talmut* with its companion selection of texts from Rashi's Talmud and Bible commentaries)[57] may have served as a common source for both men.

After a brief argument from the Song of Songs that used the rabbinic reading of the text as an allegorical depiction of the relationship between God and Israel to argue for the simultaneous humanity and divinity of God in the Solomon figure, Nicholas ended with a short reprise of a text introduced in the previous question, Zacharia 9:9, which Nicholas claimed demonstrated the messiah's simultaneous humanity and divinity through his arrival as both pauper and king. In both cases, Nicholas cited the support of "all the Hebrew doctors" (*omnes doctores Hebrei*) to defend his interpretation of the Hebrew text, dismissing the interpretations of "certain other Jews" (*aliqui Iudei*) who denied the Christian interpretation in question. The distinction between "Hebrew" and "Jew" here is somewhat unusual for Nicholas, since he tends to call Jews "Hebrews" in their exegetical role whether he perceives them to be right or wrong in their conclusions. It may be that he was trying to distinguish between Hebrew expositors, on the one hand, and the Jewish community generally on the other.[58] Nicholas concluded the section by stating unequivocally that "it is possible to prove the incarnation of a divine person from Scriptures received by the Jews."[59]

To prove the third part of his question, that the time of the Incarnation was past, Nicholas developed elaborate arguments based upon Genesis 49:10, Haggai 2:7–10, Daniel 9:24, Daniel 2:31–45, and Isaiah 66:7. As this part of the question finally addressed the time of the Advent, it contained the most overlap with the thirteenth-century questions examined in the last chapter, although Nicholas moved beyond them in his regular appeal to the Hebrew version of the Bible and the Targum and by responding regularly to various Jewish interpretations of the texts in question. There are a number of subtle ways in which Nicholas's focus differed from that of earlier authors, who were most interested in whether Christian truth could be demonstrated from Old Testament prophecy. Nicholas, perhaps influenced by Raymond Martini, was interested in demonstrating Christian truth by means of Jewish Scripture much more broadly defined. Preparing to discuss Isaiah 66:7, he noted that "After having proved that the time of Christ's advent is past by canonical Scripture, the same thing may be proved by glosses and sayings of the Hebrew doctors that are considered authentic among them."[60]

Where other authors simply linked the prophecy of Genesis 49:10 with its fulfillment in the reign of Herod, Nicholas first carefully detailed the messianic nature of the prophecy from the Targum and established the conversion of the gentiles at the messiah's advent from the Hebrew reference to "the nations" in the passage before invoking Herod's reign as outsider and the murder of all descendants in the royal line as fulfillment of the prophecy that the scepter would fall away at that time. He also added an argument from "events transpired," suggesting that 1309 years without rulership was surely enough to indicate that the scepter was gone forever. When Nicholas discussed God's promise in Haggai 2:7–10 that in "a little while" the "desired of all the nations" would come, he did more than simply calculate, as Peter Olivi had, the number of years that had passed since that prophecy. Nicholas established that "all the Hebrew commentators" (*omnes expositores Hebreorum*) identified the desired one with the messiah, calculated the years since Haggai's prophecy, dismissed a Jewish argument that "a little while" could be understood in the context of God's eternality rather than in a realistic human time frame, and then presented Scriptural evidence that the house that would be "filled with glory" in the messiah's advent could have been none other than the second Temple, destroyed by Titus and Vespasian. Since he had no proof from the Hebrew Bible or the Targum to demonstrate that God moved "not only earth, but also heaven" at the time of Jesus' birth, he turned to evidence from Josephus's *Antiquities* and *The Jewish War*. Nicholas followed the same approach in a lengthy proof from the Book of Daniel but stopped his discussion short in a number of places, referring the reader back to an earlier commentary on Daniel, where, as detailed earlier in the chapter, he treated the material fully. During a lengthy discussion of Daniel 9 on the seventy weeks of years that would be "shortened" upon Israel, Nicholas invoked the *Hebraica veritas* and Jewish practice and commentary to dismantle a longstanding interpretation of the Venerable Bede. The frequent turn to Hebrew sources to counter the opinions of esteemed Church authorities that was so much a part of Nicholas's *Postilla Litteralis super Bibliam* was already in use during this early part of his career. Bede's opinion, included in the *Glossa ordinaria*, argued that the "shortening" of seventy weeks was meant to indicate that the seventy weeks (of years) ought to be calculated according to the Jewish lunar calendar rather than the solar calendar. Roger Marston, Peter Olivi, and Peter of Trabes had all incorporated this teaching into their own calculations, but Nicholas challenged it outright, stating firmly that with all due respect to Bede, he was simply wrong here. Turning to the Hebrew text, Nicholas explained that the reference to a "shortening" of weeks was not meant to distinguish lunar from solar years but simply to indicate precision, "because in Hebrew *abreviate* means precise and denotes a specific indication of time, neither more nor less."[61] He explained that the Jews themselves recognized the need to harmonize their lunar calendar with the solar one through intercalation, so that holidays would continue to come at their appointed seasons. Nicholas then went on to conduct his own calculations based upon the solar calendar.

In addition to proofs from Hebrew Scripture, the Targum, "Hebrew glosses" (usually Rashi), and other rabbinic texts, Nicholas also suggested turning to proofs from various "traditions" authentic among the Jews. Among these was the widely known midrash on the six-thousand-year duration of the world, which Peter Olivi also used.[62] Nicholas's version, however, was far more detailed than that found in most Christian sources and included an important introduction to the text that legitimized it by claiming a Jewish attribution of the prophecy to the widow of Zarephath's son, "whom Elijah raised from the dead and who afterward had the spirit of prophecy."[63]

In addition to all of these textual forms of evidence, Nicholas also suggested that arguments based upon reasoned assumptions drawn from Scripture constituted legitimate proof, and in this category he turned, as Peter of Trabes had done, to a common Christian argument based upon the prolonged exile of the Jews after the destruction of the Temple. Nicholas pointed out that throughout the Old Testament, the welfare of the Jews rose and fell according to their deeds and their obedience to God. When they were faithful, they were rewarded, and when they fell into idolatry or killed their prophets or sinned in some other way, they were punished. Since the punishment meted out ought to fit the crime and the terrible idolatry of the first Temple period was punished with only seventy years of exile, the incredibly long duration of this exile indicated a crime of such magnitude that it could only have been "to have denied, persecuted and cruelly killed the messiah promised to them in law and the prophets."[64] Nicholas supported his interpretation by citing Maimonides' *Mishneh Torah* on the Jewish response to Jesus' teaching. Nicholas was distorting Maimonides' position here; although Maimonides did, indeed, write that Jesus was "put to death by the court" and that the Jews were "dispersed and humiliated" because of him, he did so to demonstrate the *falseness* of messianic claims, charging Jesus with "changing the Torah and causing the world to err and serve another besides God."[65]

In spite of the weight of textual evidence Nicholas adduced in support of Christian teaching, he found it important to argue for the validity of nontextual evidence as well. After concluding his main arguments and before embarking on a presentation and refutation of twelve Jewish objections to Christian teaching on the Advent, Nicholas addressed himself explicitly to the question of how knowledge of divine things might be attained, explaining that doctrine could be demonstrated in two ways. One of these involved recourse to "first principles" by means of evidence; this method applied to those things connected to the action of natural intellect.[66] But he also insisted on the efficacy of demonstration through divine/prophetic witness; a given doctrine could be confirmed by the relation of miracles such as raising the dead, giving sight to the blind and so on, acts "that could not be achieved except by means of divine virtue."[67] He took it as a given that God cannot provide false testimony, so if a particular divine act seemed to support a matter of doctrine, the prophecy of that act and the description of that act in Scripture could serve as sufficient proof of the doctrine. This second type of proof was necessary when the thing to be understood exceeded natural intellection, and Nicholas stressed that the Jews resorted equally to such proofs, as in those truths spoken by Moses, Joshua, and the elders. Nicholas pointed out that the Jews themselves acknowledged Jesus' performance of miracles, as recorded in the *Book of the Generations of Jesus* and in Josephus' *Antiquities*, among other places. Dismissing the rabbinic contention that he performed them by magically invoking the Tetragrammaton against God's will, Nicholas argued that those miracles proved Jesus to have been the Christ sent by God, truly man and truly God.

With all of his evidence in place, Nicholas finally concluded that "when Scripture declares a certain future event and a specific time, place and manner, if all those things concur in one, it is clearly evident that that which was predicted has been fulfilled." According to Nicholas, Scripture did more than just predict the advent of Christ, it also specifically named the time of his coming (with the transfer of power away from Judah—Genesis 49), the place in which he would be born (Bethlehem—Micah 5), the manner in which he would live (as a pauper—Zechariah 9), and the manner of his death (in humility and submissiveness—Isaiah 53). "All these things clearly were fulfilled in Jesus the Nazarene, from which it is reasonably demonstrated that he himself was truly Christ."[68] While he had been willing to grant in his previous question that there may have been some doubt at the moment of Christ's appearance, like Peter of Trabes he turned around and insisted that by the time Jesus' career on Earth was finished, the weight of the evidence served as conclusive proof that Jesus was the messiah, divine as well as human.

Against this evidence, corroborated by "Hebrew doctors" themselves, Nicholas conceded that there were "Jews" who argued against his conclusions "in many ways." Nicholas briefly presented and then responded to twelve Jewish objections to Christian messianic proofs. This part of the question has a distinctly different character from the rest. Most of the objections were well known among Christians and had been discussed by numerous other Latin authors. In this section, Nicholas frequently turned to arguments based strictly on Christian sources or interpretations of history, something he was careful not to do in the rest of the question, though he did supplement this material with evidence from the Targum or other rabbinic traditions.

Nicholas determined that it was clearly possible to come to Christian truth by means of evidence available to the Jews. But he was left with the problem raised in the opening; if the advent of Christ could be known by a reading of Jewish Scripture as he had just demonstrated, why had those Jews who were wise and learned in their tradition not understood the truth and given up their error? This question may have had a particular urgency for Nicholas because his exegesis was so dependent upon postbiblical Jewish commentary on the tradition. In any case, he avoided the usual simplistic explanations of blindness or stubbornness; his response was unusually careful and constructed in such a way as to maintain the possibility of important Jewish insights into sacred things in spite of their rejection of Christ.

Nicholas first reminded his readers that many among the most learned Jews at the time of Jesus—Nathaniel, Nicodemus, and Gamaliel, for example—did understand that Jesus was the messiah. Paul and Apollos were likewise men learned in Scripture who came to follow Christ.[69] Nicholas also pointed out the charge of John 12:42 that many other learned men also recognized Jesus to be the messiah but refused to follow him because they feared being cast out of the community by the Pharisees. Nicholas passed over the reasons that most Jews in the time of Jesus failed to acknowledge his messiahship, probably because he had covered the problem in the previous question. He focused the rest of his conclusion on the problem of ongoing Jewish unbelief. He offered three reasons why contemporary Jews, learned in Scripture, failed to follow their own sacred texts to their logical Christian conclusion.

The first reason was the cupidity of the Jews and their fear of poverty; since their law gave frequent assurance of material wealth, they had come to abhor the opposite.[70] As a Franciscan, particularly as one active in the early fourteenth century amid great turmoil over the definition of poverty in the order, Nicholas's attention to this issue is not surprising. In spite of the controversy over rigor and definition, there was agreement on all sides of the Franciscan controversy on the spiritual value of poverty.[71] Nicholas obviously noticed that Jews did not seem to share this value. Moving beyond the nature of Franciscan spirituality, this explanation also drew from a general stereotype of Jewish greed in medieval Christian culture, one that undoubtedly had particular resonance in 1309, three short years after the expulsion of the Jews from royal France, allegedly for usury.[72] The explanation that Jews feared poverty if they accepted Christianity ought also to be understood in the context of the requirement that Jews give up their possessions upon conversion to Christianity; the fear of poverty was not an abstract one based upon differences between Jewish and Christian law but reflected a real impoverishment resulting from conversion.

The second explanation Nicholas offered was that Jews were reared from infancy in an environment of hatred toward Christ and Christian law, with Christians cursed "every day" in synagogues. Alluding once again to Aristotle's *Nichomachean Ethics*, he argued that since those things to which one is habituated from childhood become part of one's nature, Jews became unable to exercise proper judgment and turned away from the truth.[73] The final reason Jews failed to embrace Christianity was the sheer difficulty of Christian theology regarding the plurality of persons in divinity, the dual nature of Christ, and the mystery of the Eucharist, which caused Jews to perceive Christians as polytheistic idolators. The Jews thus remained turned toward those things that they had long known.[74] This final point is rather remarkable in its willingness to concede that loyalty to God (misdirected though it may have been) played a part in the Jews' obstinacy. Their unbelief was hardly acceptable, and one could not call Nicholas's attitude philojudaic in any sense. Yet Nicholas's presentation of comprehensible, if unfortunate, reasons for Jewish persistence in error worked to preserve the possibility of learning from the insights of these unbelievers.

For all of the above reasons, Nicholas wrote, Jews "turn away from the Catholic faith, and many who had been baptized revert to Judaism."[75] Just as Nicholas's comment about the Jews' fear of poverty was rooted in recognizable experience, so these final words about rejecting conversion and the relapse of converts would have resonated deeply at the time they were written. Among those few Jews who converted around the time of the expulsion in 1306, there were several cases of relapse in fairly short order. The continuation of the chronicle of Guillaume de Nangis mentioned two separate instances of converts tried for reverting to Judaism in the year 1307, and another relapsed Jew was burned in the Place de Grève in 1310, alongside Marguerite Porete. Since Nicholas participated in Marguerite's trial, he may have been involved in that of the relapsed Jew as well. In any case, he would certainly have been aware of the legal proceedings.[76] Nicholas answered here not only for persistent Jewish rejection of Jesus but also for the failure of conversion to stick.[77]

All of the features that made Nicholas's *Postilla litteralis* so distinctive in its time are already in evidence in these questions: a rigorous commitment to the most basic signification of the literal sense; an appeal to the *Hebraica veritas*, Hebrew grammar, and rabbinic traditions to illuminate the literal sense of Christian Scripture and to challenge traditional Christian authorities and interpretations; the use of alternative ancient Jewish translations, such as the Septuagint or the Aramaic Targum and other ancient authorities (e.g., Josephus or simply "ancient Jewish doctors") to challenge Jewish "errors"; and a preoccupation with matters of Jewish faith and unbelief. In fact, almost every passage discussed in the questions eventually found its way into an appropriate section of the *Postilla litteralis*; the active engagement with Jewish interpretation was clearly a vital part of Nicholas's exegetical process.

Nicholas of Lyra's entire career was influenced by his Hebraism and engagement with rabbinic tradition. His status as one of the preeminent scholars of his day was gained in large part through his remarkable exegetical talent, the inspiration for which came not only from the Victorines and his Franciscan predecessors but also, perhaps above all, from Rashi and his followers in the northern French school. Although we do not know exactly where or from whom he learned Hebrew and Aramaic, we do know that he was an accomplished linguist early in his career, certainly before he came to Paris just after 1300. The redating of Nicholas's question to a single 1309 edition makes it clear that while still a theology student, he already had an impressive knowledge of Hebrew and rabbinics. In addition to the command of Jewish tradition evident in the vast array of sources he brought into the question itself, Nicholas's reference in the 1309 work to his earlier commentary on Daniel and Hebrews proves that by the first few years of the new century, he had already begun to incorporate Jewish texts into his literal exegesis.[78]

In the questions outlined here, we see Nicholas, the Bible scholar, bringing his Hebraic learning to a familiar question, treated in a scholastic context by a number of Franciscan brothers before him. Given his language abilities and interest in literal exegesis, it was only natural that he would bring to the question a fuller accounting than had previously been done, making use of his familiarity with Jewish glosses and relevant Hebrew variants. But while Nicholas's questions reflect some of the same important theological debates that emerged in the writing of thirteenth-century versions of the question, they also reflect the challenges that new attitudes and policies toward Jews must have posed to Christian scholars continuing the Victorine tradition of Hebraism in Bible study. Since the Talmud trials of the 1240s Christians had been censoring and burning Jewish texts. In 1242 James I in Aragon established a policy of forcing Jews to listen to the preaching of Dominican friars. In 1263 the Jewish convert Paul Christian engaged in a critical disputation with Rabbi Moses ben Nahman of Gerona

(Nahmanides) at the Aragonese court. In 1267 Raymond Martini published the *Capistrum Iudaeorum,* and in 1278 Raymond completed his *Pugio fidei* and Pope Nicholas III issued the bull *Vineam soreth* to both the Dominican and Franciscan orders, urging them to redouble efforts to convert the Jews by forcibly gathering them in synagogues to hear Christian sermons.[79]

When Nicholas, following an old charge, suggested that Jews had purposely corrupted the vocalization of certain portions of the Hebrew Bible in order to deny the divinity of Christ, he was actually maintaining the essential validity of Jewish interpretations of Scripture. By showing a pattern to Jewish error, he could salvage the rest of Jewish teaching for Christian use: Jews like Rashi did have a remarkable insight into God's word, from which Christians like Nicholas (and his students in Bible lectures) could learn a great deal, but since the Jews occasionally distorted what they knew to be the truth in order to cling to their false religion, it was necessary to be very careful in borrowing from their books. Written near the beginning of Nicholas's career, the questions offer a defense of his approach to literal exegesis, obviating charges of Judaizing. They demonstrate that however dependent he may have been upon the expertise of the Jews, he was still able to separate the "false" from the "true." Better than any other late medieval Christian exegete, Nicholas managed to navigate around the challenges presented by Jewish interpretation of the Bible, fashioning Jewish teaching into a Christian image.

Both of Nicholas's questions on the Advent were far more widely disseminated than most scholastic questions. Nicholas placed the first in his commentary on Matthew 21, where it enjoyed the exceptionally wide audience achieved by the *Postilla litteralis.* The second was often copied in scholastic miscellanea, in collections of Nicholas's work, along with the *Responsio ad quendam Iudaeum* and the *De differentia nostrae translationis ab Hebraica littera Veteris Testamentis,* in *Adversus Iudaeos* collections, as well as at the end of multivolume copies of Nicholas's *Postilla.* The question on the advent of Christ particularly took on a life of its own, unquestionably because Nicholas's reputation as Hebraist and exegete, solidly established in his own lifetime, made him just the right person to tackle Jewish unbelief for a Christian audience. The question on the advent of Christ was not only read, it was used, torn apart, cut and pasted into other scholars' work. The reception of Nicholas's questions, together with his *Postilla,* tells the remarkable story of the absorption of Jewish traditions into late medieval Christian culture.

Christian Ownership of Jewish Text: Nicholas of Lyra as an Alternative Jewish Authority

As remarkable as Nicholas's literary output was, perhaps even more impressive is the tremendous range of uses to which his writing was put once it left his hands. Few medieval theologians enjoyed such wide diffusion of their work into so many different settings. As Klaus Reinhardt has commented with respect to Nicholas's Bible commentary, the ubiquity of the text alone commands our attention.[1] If one mark of a work's success is its adaptability to different needs and purposes, its ability to speak to a wide audience across space and time, then it is clear that Nicholas's work was enormously successful. And as different as the purposes could be— Nicholas's Bible commentary was employed both as a study aid and, in luxuriously illuminated volumes, as a status symbol; his question on the advent of Christ was put into massive scholastic collections of theological texts alongside the likes of John Duns Scotus and also copied into pocket-sized collections of anti-Jewish polemic designed for use by German Dominican friars sent off to preach Christianity to Jews—the cumulative effect both reflected and enhanced a sense of authority around Nicholas's perceived command of Hebrew. Whether that Hebrew knowledge was understood as a key that could unlock the insight of the Jews into the meaning of Scripture or as a weapon in the fight against Jewish unbelief, Nicholas was widely understood to be the single most important Christian authority on Jewish traditions in the medieval Church.[2] His polemical engagement with rabbinic tradition encouraged confidence that he was not following Jewish positions uncritically, as had appeared to be the case with some earlier literal exegetes who had turned to Jewish exegetical traditions a bit too eagerly, like Andrew of St. Victor. Nicholas, it seemed, was able to separate the wheat from the chaff; since he so clearly addressed "erroneous" Jewish interpretations, those he followed could legitimately be understood as consonant with Christian truth, even if they contradicted dominant Christian positions or the teachings of Church Fathers.

It would be hard to overestimate Nicholas's reputation in late medieval Christendom. His *Postilla litteralis* became the standard work on the Bible in the late Middle Ages, despite the fact that his approach to the literal sense was becoming distinctly out of fashion even as he wrote it. Klaus Reinhardt, Philip Krey, and, most recently, Christopher Ocker have all pointed out the gap between the popularity of Lyra's commentary and the limited influence it had on subsequent exegetes. Reinhardt noted that, within the Iberian Peninsula, Nicholas was widely read but not often imitated, and further that in certain circles there was by the fifteenth century an outright discomfort with Lyra's restrictive approach to the literal sense and ready embrace of rabbinic interpretation over that of the Church Fathers.[3] Krey has stressed that in spite of the wide readership the Apocalypse commentary enjoyed, Nicholas had "few followers in approach."[4] Ocker has similarly argued that "when Lyra was appreciated, it was as a tool and not as a model," citing figures as diverse as John Wyclif and Denys the Carthusian, who turned to Nicholas for the literal sense, historical information, and Hebrew and rabbinic interpretation but whose own commentaries moved in an entirely different direction.[5]

It is all the more interesting, given the fact that the understanding of literal exegesis was moving in a new direction, that Nicholas's effort struck such a powerful chord. While subsequent exegetes may not have been drawn to imitate and further the approach that Nicholas laid out so carefully in his works, they did feel that the information he provided was in some way crucial to their own understanding of sacred text, and they referred to him frequently. In some sense, Nicholas's perceived success at uncovering the contribution of Hebrew scholarship to Christian understanding of the Word may have made further efforts in that direction superfluous. His work, covering the entirety of Scripture, was comprehensive. It is in this sense that Nicholas came to serve as a quasi-authority on Hebrew and Jewish text in the Latin Christian world, and, as we will see, it was this quasi-authority that drew the sharp critical response of individuals like Paul of Burgos and Denys the Carthusian—they responded not just to Nicholas's commentary itself but also to the ready acceptance of that material by their contemporaries.

The history of the dissemination and reception of Nicholas's work could easily fill a book itself, and what follows must be understood as a preliminary sketch only. Nevertheless, my hope is that this survey of the reception of two of Nicholas's works, the 1309 *Quaestio de adventu Christi* and the *Postilla litteralis super Bibliam*, will help to create a sense of how medieval and early modern readers perceived his expertise and read and used his work. As will be seen, the enthusiastic reading, unattributed borrowing, direct invocation of, and hostile reaction to Lyra's work were equally inspired by Nicholas's position as arbiter of Jewish tradition for Latin Christian audiences. Nicholas took Jewish interpretations and converted them into Christian ones. He demonstrated an unusual independence of mind as he wrestled with his sources, both Christian and Jewish, defending both his understanding of the literal sense against that of other Christian exegetes and his Christocentric reading of Scripture against unbelieving Jewish exegetes. In the process, Nicholas brought an extensive body of Jewish learning to a Christian audience that was increasingly unable or unwilling to access such material directly.

The Question on the Advent of Christ

Nicholas's 1309 *Quaestio de adventu Christi* began to circulate almost immediately after its composition and was frequently copied throughout the fourteenth and fifteenth centuries; there are well over one hundred extant manuscripts in libraries across Europe. Within the manuscript tradition, the question circulated in three distinct forms: as a theological/scholastic question or treatise, as a work of anti-Jewish literature, and as an appendix to Nicholas's *Postilla litteralis super Bibliam*.

The most common way that the *Quaestio de adventu Christi* appears in manuscripts is as an independent treatise in collections of works by other authors. This is the case in twelve of the twenty-five fourteenth-century manuscripts I consulted, and seventeen of the thirty-four fifteenth-century manuscripts (see the Appendix). Sometimes the work was placed in collections of theological treatises or questions, sometimes in collections of anti-Jewish and/or antiheretical literature. Even though the text of the treatise remained the same, its presentation affected how it was perceived by the readers of each manuscript, and so its use. Read in a theological context, it continued the work of those scholars presented in Chapter 3, who struggled with the problem of Jewish unbelief and questioned whether Jewish tradition could, on its own terms, be used effectively to prove key articles of Christian faith. As we have seen, Nicholas's Hebrew learning and familiarity with Jewish text made him uniquely qualified, in contemporary minds, to answer such a question. Set within a manual for anti-Jewish disputation, the text provided missionaries with valuable arguments to counter Jewish objections to their proofs for the Catholic faith. Rubrics often set the tone for the work and range from the relatively neutral, scholastic *Treatise proving by Scriptures received by the Jews that Christ was truly the messiah promised in Law*, found in a fourteenth-century Abbey of St. Victor manuscript,[6] to the more overtly polemical *Disputation against the Jews, proving that which they deny, namely the trinity of persons in God, divinity in Christ, and that Christ has already come*, found in a fourteenth-century German monastic manuscript.[7]

The fourteenth-century theological miscellany found in BAV Vat. lat. 869 provides an example of the early circulation of the *Quaestio* as a theological work. This manuscript places the *Quaestio* in its original quodlibetal context, alongside two of the other questions from Nicholas's 1309 quodlibet. This is the only manuscript so far identified containing the question *Whether the Jews recognized Jesus of Nazareth to be the Christ promised to them*, which Nicholas later placed in his *Postilla* on Matthew 21, and one of only a small handful of manuscripts with the question *Whether by Sacred Scripture one can prove effectively the final salvation of Solomon*, later set into his commentary on Kings. The manuscript also contains a second, incomplete version of the question on the Advent, written in another hand toward the end of the collection.

Nicholas's *Quaestio* also circulated as a freestanding theological treatise outside of its quodlibetal context. Sometime around 1320, a Paris scribe framed the question as part of a theological trilogy along with two treatises by John of Paris, O.P., on the advent of Christ in the flesh (proofs from pagan sources) and the advent of Antichrist. The question took on a second life as part of this trilogy when shortly thereafter the German Dominican Nicholas of Strassburg came across the three texts in a St. Germain des Prés manuscript (now Paris BNF lat. 13781) and claimed them as his own.[8] In 1323, Nicholas of Strassburg dedicated the trilogy to Archbishop Baldwin of Trier under the rubric *On the advent of Christ, proofs from the books of the gentiles; On the advent of Christ, from Scripture which evidence all Jews accept*; and *On the advent of Antichrist and the end of the world.*[9] The only changes Nicholas made in the texts were to write a dedication and an introduction to the trilogy as a unit, devise new chapter divisions within each individual treatise, add very brief introductions to the beginnings of each of these chapters, and change all dates to correspond to the year in which he dedicated the work. In the case of Nicholas of Lyra's treatise, Nicholas of

Strassburg also edited out all of Lyra's self-referential statements, including references to Lyra's other works.[10] Nicholas of Strassburg clearly thought that the works he was copying reflected well on his theological learning; his use of Nicholas of Lyra's question on the advent of Christ alongside John of Paris's questions demonstrates its value in a theological (as opposed to explicitly exegetical) context.

The treatise was copied far more frequently when identified as Nicholas of Lyra's own work, however. Conrad of Gelnhausen (d. 1390), a friend of Henry of Langenstein and an important early advocate of conciliarism during the Great Schism, donated a theological miscellany containing *Questio magistri Nycolai de Lyra, qua probat ex scriptura Hebreorum Christum iam venisse in carnem* to the University at Heidelberg.[11]

In the fourteenth century, the question was often incorporated into collections of Nicholas's work, most typically along with the *Responsio ad quendam Iudaeum*, *De visione divinae essentiae*, and *De differentia nostrae translationis ab Hebraica littera Veteris Testamentis*. At least one manuscript of this type appeared in Nicholas's lifetime (1343); a similar fourteenth-century manuscript belonged to the library at the Abbey of St. Victor in Paris.[12] The St. Victor manuscript was evidently copied there, as the scribe wrote in the margin of Nicholas's treatise on the beatific vision, "Note how this doctor de Lyra held Hugh of St. Victor in great respect."[13] Nicholas clearly commanded enough respect himself in the school for his admiration of Hugh to be noteworthy. These collections had their widest appeal within the academic environment of fourteenth-century Paris, although many such manuscripts left Paris sooner or later for use in other parts of Europe; only one collection of this sort is found among the fifteenth-century manuscripts of any provenance listed in the Appendix. By the fifteenth century, many of the concerns that Nicholas had addressed in his other scholastic works had become dated and less relevant; his works dealing with Jewish exegesis remained vitally compelling for centuries.

In general, the application of the question as anti-Jewish literature was stronger in the fifteenth century than in the fourteenth, and more common in German lands than in the west. Twelve of the fifteenth-century manuscripts I consulted included the question with anti-Jewish or antiheretical material or specifically introduced it as an anti-Jewish text, as opposed to only six fourteenth-century manuscripts. Nine of the manuscripts that presented the question as an anti-Jewish treatise can be traced to German lands, only three to France. It bears remembering in this context that, with brief and limited exceptions, there were no Jews living in royal France during this period, and hence no program of preaching to them. Further, the German manuscripts tend to date from fifteenth rather than the fourteenth century, and the critical factor may be temporal rather than geographic.

When copied into portable quarto, or even octavo-sized volumes, the *Quaestio de adventu Christi* lent itself especially well to missionaries' purposes. BAV Vat. lat. 4265, copied (in tiny script) in Lobegestecz in 1381 by Nicholas Gruenenberg, is a good example of such a small manuscript. The question and the *Responsio ad quendam Iudaeum* are present along with numerous anti-Jewish and antiheretical works, including the *Pharetra fidei contra Iudaeos* and the *Disputatio Iudaeorum contra Sanctum Anastasium* translated from the Greek in the twelfth century by Pascalis de Roma. Two fourteenth-century octavo volumes, one of the *Quaestio* alone, the other with the *Responsio*, are found in Munich Clm 23656 and 23615. Munich Clm 24840 is a fifteenth-century quarto volume presenting the *Quaestio* by itself, also intended for active use.

The tradition of including the *Quaestio* as an appendix to the *Postilla litteralis super Bibliam* began in the first half of the fourteenth century, becoming more prevalent in the fifteenth and eventually entering into the print tradition.[14] This demonstrates the question's usefulness as a corrective to the *Postilla*'s dependence on Jewish tradition. The fact that the *Postilla* enjoyed tremendous success in times and places that were intensely anti-Jewish demonstrates how well Nicholas tamed the rabbinic tradition from which he borrowed. Nevertheless, as I discuss in the section on the *Postilla* below, there were some who were uncomfortable with the extent to which Nicholas relied on Jewish works, and appending the question to the *Postilla* seems to have provided an extra measure of safety lest any reader be confused about the relative truth of Christianity and Judaism. While the same anti-Jewish arguments were present throughout the *Postilla*, the *Quaestio de adventu Christi* provided a concise treatment of the issues and gave the Christian faith the last word.

The Dominican friar George Naddi of Siena (d. 1398) devised just such a corrective to the sympathetic reception of Jewish interpretation in literal exegesis by incorporating Nicholas's entire question into a treatise detailing 116 Old Testament prophecies of Christ's advent.[15] George insisted that these prophecies from Hebrew Scripture could be understood Christologically according to the literal sense. He leveled the familiar charge that the Jews failed to understand the meaning of their own prophetic texts, but where earlier Christian writers had attacked the Jews for their failure to move beyond the literal sense to the spiritual, George accused them of failing to understand the literal sense itself. Whereas for Nicholas, Rashi's *peshat* interpretation could be, and often was, equated with the literal sense, for George the true literal sense could be found only in a Christian theological context. Jewish interpretation of the letter remained by definition carnal because the literal sense could ónly be properly understood within the fullness of the Christian faith. By implication, those Christians (like Nicholas) who followed Jewish exegetes in the letter were likewise in danger of falling into error. By setting proper Christian interpretations alongside erroneous Jewish readings of the same texts (as found in Nicholas's question), George encouraged his readers to distinguish between the truly literal and what he deemed the merely carnal.[16]

George placed almost every word of Nicholas's question somewhere in his text. Except for the arrangement of the material, which followed the order of the books of the Christian Bible rather than Nicholas's scholastic format, the text followed Nicholas of Lyra verbatim, as can be seen in the following example, which concluded a refutation of Rashi's explanation that Isaiah first accepted his prophecies on Mt. Sinai with Moses and all of the other prophets:

Nicholas of Lyra: Et sic patet quod dictum Rabi Salomonis non solum est contra totam prophetiam que dicit animam non procedere corpus, sed etiam contra totam scripturam veteris testamenti, ut patet ex predictis.

George of Siena: Et sic patet quod Rabi Salomonis non solum est contra totam prophetiam que dicit animam non procedere corpus, sed contra totam sacram scripturam veteris testamenti, ut patet ex predictis.[17]

George tampered with the text of the question just enough to eliminate Nicholas's references to earlier exegetical works and to revise the dating passages, substituting the year 1388 for Nicholas's 1309. Only once did George mention Nicholas by name. In the midst of quoting Nicholas's discussion of Daniel 9:24, *Seventy weeks are shortened upon your people*, he stopped at the charge that the Venerable Bede misread the seventy weeks of years as lunar rather than solar. Stepping out of his unattributed quotation of Nicholas's text, George invoked Nicholas by name before offering the critique, writing, "There is another explanation, such as that of Nicholas of Lyra who says that Bede has not explained the passage properly" and "according to that which Nicholas of Lyra says, this [interpretation of the years as lunar] is not valid." After allowing Nicholas to bear responsibility for the challenge to Bede's authority, George returned to a word-for-word quotation of Nicholas's text as if it were his own.[18]

Named master in theology by papal fiat in 1380, George served his order in a variety of important positions in the large Dominican province of Rome, at the *studium generale* in Florence and in the Siena convent, including turns as master of students at the Florence *studium*, *diffinitor* in charge of monitoring the orthodoxy of fellow friars, and master of the Sisters of Penitence associated with the Dominican order in Siena.[19] He had a reputation as an especially accomplished preacher and enjoyed a rare appointment as Dominican preacher general, which gave him a lifetime privilege to preach where and when he saw fit.[20] Throughout his career, he lectured extensively to fellow friars on the Bible, and it is in this context that we ought to read and understand the treatise on Old Testament prophecies. In George's concern to show his students how the rabbinic (and Judaizing Christian) reading of the letter *carnaliter* differed from proper Christian reading *litteraliter*, the work reflects the changes taking place in late medieval Christian Bible hermeneutics.[21] George's students would unquestionably have encountered and used Nicholas's *Postilla* in their study of Scripture; the treatise on Old Testament prophecies warned against the danger of Judaizing inherent in too enthusiastic a reception of the Jewish interpretation presented there.[22]

The *Quaestio de adventu Christi* was read and used often, and to collect citations of it even just for one century following its composition would be an enormous undertaking. As we have already seen in Nicholas of Strassburg's and George of Siena's examples, scholars might take the text and repackage the entirety to serve their own needs. More commonly, though, the text was a source of information on either useful or troubling Jewish teachings (depending on the context). One passage was picked up by a German monk for use in a text having nothing otherwise to do with Jews. A scribe from the Carthusian monastery in either Basel or Mainz inserted Nicholas's description of the Jewish tradition that the world would endure for six thousand years into the middle of a series of eschatological predictions taken from the Franciscan Hugh of Novocastro's 1315 work, *De victoria Christi contra Antichristum*. The scribe cited Nicholas by name and gave a faithful report of the passage as it appears in the *Quaestio*.[23] This Jewish teaching was of obvious interest to apocalyptic thinkers, and, like Peter Olivi, who referred to this same tradition as a "Hebrew truth," the Carthusian scribe was happy to incorporate it into a Christian consideration of the end of days. Although the tradition was well known in the Christian world and had been incorporated into a range of Christian commentaries over the years, it was Nicholas's version that was most accessible and most authoritative for this Carthusian and his audience.

In addition to the extensive manuscript tradition, at least twenty-five printed editions of the *Quaestio de adventu Christi* were published between the work's first printing as an independent treatise in 1470 and its inclusion with Nicholas's *Postilla litteralis super Bibliam* in the 1634 Antwerp edition of the Bible.[24] In seventeen printed editions, the *Quaestio* appeared as an appendix to the *Postilla litteralis*; in nine it was printed as an independent treatise. While the *Postilla* was the most frequently published of Nicholas's works, almost half of the thirty-six *Postilla litteralis* editions contain the *Quaestio de adventu Christi* as well.

Nicholas of Lyra's quodlibetal question on the advent of Christ was readily adapted, as we have seen, to many purposes. Nicholas did not write the text with missionary fervor, but it suited the purposes of those who possessed such zeal. More important for Nicholas and his readers, however, was the role the question played in making Jewish insight into the literal meaning of Scripture available to Christians by filtering the teachings of the rabbis and separating Jewish wisdom from Jewish error. Motivated by an interest in the use of Jewish tradition for the literal exegesis of the Old Testament, Nicholas wrote a treatise designed to show Christian scholars how Jewish texts could be incorporated into a Christian understanding of divine truth in Scripture. It was not unusual for late medieval Christian thinkers to allude to the dichotomous nature of Jewish literature, but Nicholas was the only one to attempt to provide a comprehensive guide through the thicket.

The *Postilla litteralis*

Nicholas's *Postilla litteralis super Bibliam* quickly became, along with the *Glossa ordinaria*, the most widely used Christian reference work on the Bible. The Paris book trade churned out copy after copy of each commentary as soon as it came into print.[25] The commentaries on individual books began circulating all across Europe as soon as they were completed, as the manuscript tradition attests. In the 1330s, when the literal commentary on the Bible was finally complete, large multivolume collections of the entire *Postilla litteralis* with Bible text and illustrations of key passages began to make their appearance. Describing the sorts of works produced by the *pecia* system, a relative mass production of particularly desirable works at the university in Paris, Louis Jacques Bataillon named Nicholas's *postillae* "above all." The same *pecia* evidence confirms the overwhelming preference for Nicholas's literal commentary over the moral. While Bataillon identified over twenty-three *pecia* manuscripts of the literal commentary, he could find only one of the moral commentary.[26] Klaus Reinhardt, surveying the manuscript tradition of Nicholas's corpus in medieval Iberia, found seventy-six copies of the *Postilla litteralis* (in whole or in part) and only one copy of the moral commentary.[27] While more copies of the latter work circulated in northern Europe than in Spain, the balance of interest was similarly skewed toward the literal over the moral commentary. Nicholas's *Postilla litteralis* continued to be one of the most frequently copied and eagerly sought-after works of any kind in the Latin West well into the early modern period. Its popularity withstood the test of time, finding an equally eager audience in the fourteenth, fifteenth, and sixteenth centuries. Nicholas's *Postilla litteralis* was the very first Bible commentary to be set into print in 1471; the final print edition of the text appeared in 1634.

Nicholas's presence in Paris for more than four decades may have contributed to the early success of his commentary. While most mendicant scholars were sent to a university for training, stayed to teach for a few years, and then were sent on to provincial schools, Nicholas remained at the Franciscan convent his entire life. His remarkable ability to lead the Franciscan order (as provincial minister of France and Burgundy) while staying above the political fray over poverty, his strong connections with the French and Burgundian rulers, and his special talents as Hebraist and teacher of the Bible combined to keep him in Paris, the undisputed center for the study of theology in his day. The steady stream of scholars moving in and out of the university there meant that over the years, hundreds of students came to sit at Nicholas's feet in study, and his reputation quickly spread across Latin Christendom. The young Franciscan Poncio Carbonell (1260–1350), for example, studied with Nicholas in Paris in 1308 and shortly thereafter returned home to Barcelona a great admirer. He seems to have obtained a number of Nicholas's commentaries on individual books of the Bible as soon as they were available from the Paris scriptoria, immediately incorporating their contents into his own Bible commentaries. Poncio referred to Nicholas with a deference bordering on awe and cited his work extensively, trying to bring a sense of his own excitement to his students.[28] Poncio was hardly alone in his appreciation of Nicholas's work; Klaus Reinhardt has identified over forty extant manuscript copies of the *Postilla litter-*

alis in Iberian libraries, including a few in Castilian translation. Only the *Glossa ordinaria* was more widespread, and fifteenth-century criticisms of Nicholas's approach by some Iberian figures, most notably the Jewish convert and archbishop Paul of Burgos, must be understood in the context of this tremendous popularity.[29]

The Englishman John Baconthorpe, O. Carm. (d. ca. 1348) made extensive use of Nicholas's commentary during his own lifetime. John, a student of Robert Walsingham in Oxford and Guido Terrena in Paris, incepted as regent master in Paris 1324–25 and later taught at both Cambridge and Oxford. He served as the English provincial master for the Carmelites between 1327 and 1333.[30] Based on internal evidence, Beryl Smalley dated John's *Postilla* to around 1336, when he was teaching in England. John's prologue makes clear that he intended the work for student lectures; Smalley saw in the work an opportunity to explore "the close connexion between Oxford and Avignon in the early fourteenth century," as well as the character of Oxford university culture during what she termed a "little-known period."[31] With those interests in mind, Smalley focused her attention on John's exegetical method and his political theory, particularly with regard to questions of papal authority. In terms of the former, she emphasized above all his rejection of the then-popular use of moralized fable in favor of a more rigorous theological interpretation of the text. Smalley noted that John's attention to the literal/historical sense of the gospel was confined for the most part to expansive borrowing of verbatim material from Nicholas's *Postilla*, going so far as to say that "whenever one finds an arresting example of literal exegesis, it proves to be borrowed from the *Postilla litteralis* on St. Matthew."[32] But Smalley's understanding of what literal exegesis ought to look like was formed in large part through her study of an earlier period. John's notion of the literal sense reflected the late medieval shift toward an increasingly full literal interpretation; John approached the letter with the assumption that theological speculation was a necessary element of the literal sense. Christopher Ocker turned to Baconthorpe's Matthew commentary as an important example of how fluid the movement between letter and spirit had become for fourteenth-century exegetes, noting how thoroughly "the letter and its spiritual meaning collapse into one another."[33] As Ocker pointed out, John "colored biblical interpretation with theological arguments as much as he used the Bible in theology."[34]

The fact that Nicholas's commentary was so extensively worked into lectures on the Bible by a non-Franciscan whose primary exegetical interests were quite different from his serves as an important indicator of how the *Postilla litteralis* came to serve as a fundamental tool in the interpretation of Scripture. John was especially interested in the spiritual meaning that he thought resided within the letter, but he also accepted that Nicholas's straightforward interpretations were necessary to understand the text fully. John borrowed vast passages of Nicholas's commentary on Matthew, generally without attribution. That being the case, it is particularly instructive to see where he cited Nicholas by name. Almost invariably, John did so in situations where Nicholas's authority on Hebrew text or Jewish tradition seemed to be called for. John did not have firsthand knowledge of Hebrew himself, and he gladly made use of Nicholas's expertise. In his commentary on the first chapter of Matthew, for example, John cited Nicholas's critique of Jerome, quoting Nicholas's *Postilla* verbatim: "Note that there are no holy women named in the genealogy of the savior but only those whom Scripture reproves as sinners, to show that Jesus was born of sinners on account of sinners in order to eliminate sin, wherefore in consequence Rahab the harlot, Ruth the Moabite and Bathsheba, the wife of Uriah are mentioned here, as says Jerome." At that point, where Nicholas had written "but this does not seem likely," John introduced Nicholas into the text, writing, "But Nicholas of Lyra says that this does not seem likely."[35] John then presented Nicholas's arguments against Jerome verbatim, stressing the obvious virtue of Mary, mother of God, in the genealogy and then highlighting the evident virtue of each of the named women in turn, utilizing Hebrew text and rabbinic interpretation to do so. At the conclusion of Nicholas's arguments, he included Nicholas's assurance that this challenge to Jerome should not cause undue concern but then moved in his own direction, with the acknowledgment that that "it is not easy to cast off Jerome's teachings and so one can argue against Nicholas in this manner."[36] John then returned to a faithful rendering of Nicholas for the rest of the genealogy with no further need to cite Nicholas by name or to distance himself from Nicholas's opinions.

When John arrived at the figures of Aminadab and Nashon in the genealogy, he included Nicholas's appeal to rabbinic interpretation of the Song of Songs as a way of linking these figures to the Exodus and highlighting the nobility of Jesus' line.[37] Later, at Matthew 1:18–25, in a spirited defense of the doctrine of the Incarnation and especially of Mary's virginity, John turned to Nicholas for help with evidence from Hebrew text, introducing his Franciscan contemporary as someone "highly trained in Hebrew."[38] John found Nicholas helpful and invoked him by name in a discussion of how "at the end of the sabbath" ought to be understood in Matthew

28:1, particularly in light of the difference in language between this passage and Mark 16. After laying out the argument that Matthew intended here Sunday dawn rather than the middle of the night, John used Nicholas to corroborate the opinion, saying "Nicholas of Lyra concurs" and then incorporating a verbatim section from Nicholas's *Postilla litteralis super Matthaeum,* "Among the Jews, each day in the week is named in relation to the sabbath, and so the day immediately after the sabbath is called the first from the sabbath, and the second day is the second from the sabbath and so on."[39] In addition to his outright borrowing from Nicholas's commentary, John's inclusion of a concise listing of proofs "that Christ was the messiah promised in the Law, which the Jews deny" at the opening of Matthew, immediately before a brief introduction to his mode of proceeding (according to the instruction of book 2 of Augustine's *On Christian Doctrine,* with extensive consideration of theological matters) and a lengthy treatment of the conception of the Virgin Mary, likewise shows the influence of Nicholas's writing.[40] John fully incorporated Nicholas's question on whether the Jews recognized Christ to be the messiah into his commentary on Matthew 21:46 without naming his source and without further comment or reaction to Nicholas's position on the impediment of passion to the Jews' ability to recognize Jesus as the messiah.[41]

During the same period, another Englishman, Henry Cossey, O.F.M. (d. ca. 1336), turned likewise to Nicholas in composing his Psalm commentary.[42] Henry began his studies at Oxford and entered the Franciscan order there. He went on to teach at Cambridge, incepting as regent master in 1325–26. Henry shared Nicholas's interest in constructing literal interpretations of Scripture based on the *Hebraica veritas* and Jewish interpretation. He apparently had access to Robert Grosseteste's Hebrew-Latin Psalter, known as the *Superscriptio Lincolniensis,* and had enough facility in Hebrew to utilize that material effectively in his commentary.[43] Henry also names "Rabbi Y, a recent convert" as a guide to the Hebrew. Nevertheless, Henry seems to have drawn his citations of rabbinic sources—Rashi, the Targum, the Talmud, and Moses ha-Darshan—from Nicholas directly.[44] Henry occasionally turned to Nicholas for support for his own reading of the literal sense against Jewish interpretation. For example, in the important messianic prooftext from Psalm 49, *Congregate illi sanctos eius,* Henry writes, "The Jews say that this is to be fulfilled in the advent of the messiah when all of the Jews dispersed across the globe will be gathered together in Jerusalem. From which it seems to me and to Lyra that this psalm speaks prophetically according to the letter regarding Christ."[45] Indeed Lyra does introduce the psalm as a prophecy of Christ, adding a refutation of those Christian exegetes who argue that the literal sense refers to the giving of the Law on Mt. Sinai and those Jewish exegetes who argue that the literal sense refers to the future ingathering of the exiles in Jerusalem. In his discussion of Psalm 109, Henry reproduces much of Lyra's *Postilla* on the text, especially the marshaling of arguments in favor of a messianic reading of the text. When he introduces Jewish authority into the text, whether it be the Targum or a modern rabbi, Henry invokes Lyra as the source of such information, as when he explains that "Rabbi Moses ha-Darshan on Genesis 18 says that the literal sense of *dixit Dominus* here is to be understood about the messiah . . . so says Lyra."[46]

Scholars continued to turn to Nicholas's commentary throughout the fourteenth century. As his reputation grew, legends about the source of his Hebrew training circulated throughout the university and monastic world—some said he must have been a convert from Judaism, others that his impoverished family must have sent him as a child to study at the presumably less expensive Jewish schools in Normandy.[47] Even those few late medieval scholars who had the ability to read Hebrew themselves seem to have turned to Nicholas as a reader and interpreter of Hebrew and Jewish text. Jacques Legrand (ca. 1360–1415) is a case in point. An Augustinian friar and master of theology, he lived and worked his entire life in the area around Paris. Among his works are a *Sentences* commentary, psalm commentary, *Sophilogium*, and several works in French aimed at a royal audience. He studied Hebrew, as he explained in the French version of his *Sophilogium, L'Archiloge Sophie*. In the text, he described the language, compared its grammatical structure with Latin, presented the letters individually, and provided other relevant information necessary for a beginning student. Yet, as Gilbert Dahan and Evencio Beltran have shown, despite the fact that Jacques clearly had at least a basic command of the language, when he cited Jewish commentators in his Latin writing he turned to Nicholas's summary of Rashi in the *Postilla*, not to Rashi himself as a source.[48] It may be that in a Paris without Jews, Jacques had no obvious place to turn for Jewish texts. Many of the books that had been seized during the 1306 expulsion and that lay readily at hand in Nicholas's day had been returned to the Jewish community during their brief readmission in 1315. In a world without Jews or their books, Nicholas had come to serve in satisfactory fashion as the voice of Rashi and rabbinic tradition on the meaning of the biblical letter.

Clearly, Nicholas was not the first Christian to be used as a source for

Jewish interpretations. Peter Alfonse's *Dialogi contra Iudaeos* was enthusiastically plundered not only for polemical material but also for interesting Jewish exegetical traditions.[49] Andrew of St. Victor served as a source of information on Jewish traditions for twelfth- and thirteenth-century Bible scholars. But it is safe to say that no Christian author since Jerome was used as extensively and consistently as Nicholas as a source for "what the Jews say" about biblical text and, therefore, as the most reliable source for the foundational meaning of the letter. Describing the way in which Nicholas's *Postilla* on Psalms came to supplant Peter Lombard's gloss on the text by the middle of the fourteenth century, Martin Morard invokes as evidence for Nicholas's ascendance a remarkable manuscript copy of the Dominican master John of Aversa's psalm commentary, written in Naples around 1339. In the Biblioteca Ambrosiana manuscript (second half of the fourteenth century) containing the most complete version of the commentary, passages where John had quoted Thomas Aquinas on the literal sense of the text have been corrected, with numerous elements crossed out and replaced with Nicholas of Lyra's parallel text.[50]

So widely and enthusiastically was Nicholas's commentary with its careful integration of rabbinic commentary into a Christian reading of the Bible received that by the fifteenth century, it began to draw some critical responses. As we have already seen, George of Siena's treatise on Old Testament prophecies was meant at least in part as a correction to the sort of literal hermeneutics employed by Nicholas, perceived as too restrictive and as valuing non-Christian interpretation too highly. Denys the Carthusian (1402/3–1471) criticized Nicholas's *Postilla* openly (rather than implicitly) on the same grounds. Denys Turner has gone so far as to describe the Carthusian mystic's spiritual and moral commentaries as "reverting to an older monastic style of commentary in reaction to the new scholarship of Nicholas of Lyra."[51] Denys the Carthusian opened his Song of Songs commentary with a brief prologue explaining the general allegory of the text and stating his intention to get right to the exposition without further delay. But he had a few important preliminary comments without which he said his reader would not be able to understand the commentary that followed. Those brief comments began with a fairly extensive quotation and critique of Nicholas of Lyra's introduction to the Song. Denys complained that Nicholas got it wrong, both in his acceptance of Jewish interpretation of the text and in his critique of Christian authors. Denys invoked Origen, Jerome, Anselm of Canterbury, Saint Bernard, and Saint Gregory the Great (in that order) to defend "traditional" interpretations of the text against Nicholas's innovation.[52] Denys's words are biting, as after presenting his defense of Christian interpretation of *ecclesia* as inclusive of the ancient synagogue, he writes, "It is thus clear from the witness of so many and such great Catholic Fathers that this book treats of Christ and the Church, not of the Church in its separation from the Synagogue, but as including it; and as including not the Synagogue only, but all the Saints from the beginning of the world, who, before the Law was written, lived under the law of nature. So the Catholic doctors are not to be placed at one extreme of interpretation and set against the Jewish scholars at the other extreme, so that some scholar of modern times can represent himself as occupying the middle ground, as the first to publish a true interpretation of this text."[53] Clearly writing with Nicholas's *Postilla* at his side, Denys went on to challenge Nicholas on specific readings throughout the commentary, generally rejecting Nicholas's definition of the literal sense and insisting on a theologically rich letter.

Denys's resistance to Nicholas's *Postilla* was necessarily limited to a critique of hermeneutics, since he could not address the validity of Nicholas's reading of Hebrew text. Another critic who could make such judgments, Bishop Paul of Burgos (a convert formerly known as Rabbi Solomon ha-Levi), had a far more powerful impact on the way Nicholas was read. Klaus Reinhardt has described Paul's *Additiones* to Nicholas commentary (composed 1429–31) as a response to the widespread embrace of Nicholas's commentary.[54] In 1429, thirty-eight years after his conversion, Paul wrote extensive marginal notes in a copy of the *Postilla* for his son's use. Paul was clearly concerned about the popular perception that Jewish exegesis as presented in Nicholas's commentary was as authoritative as the Church Fathers and the Christian *Glossa ordinaria*—often, as we have seen, as even more authoritative. He defended the traditional interpretations of Jerome and the *Glossa ordinaria* over Nicholas and Rashi, often by arguing that Nicholas did not properly understand the sense of the Hebrew.[55] But even after his *Additiones ad Postillam magistri Nicolai de Lyra* began to circulate fairly extensively, they did not change the perception of Nicholas as an authority on all things Jewish and, by extension, on the literal meaning of the Christian Bible. The German Franciscan Matthew Döring quickly wrote a response to Paul's critique defending Nicholas, and there is no manuscript or printed volume of Nicholas's commentary containing the *Additiones* that does not also contain Matthew's *Replicationes*. While Paul's caution did not curtail the popularity of Nicholas's *Postilla*, his corrective made a significant impact on the print tradition, with twenty-two of thirty-six print editions of the complete *Postilla litteralis* published between 1471 and 1643 carrying the work.[56] Luther's dependence on Nicholas of Lyra is well known and attested, but Luther acknowledged indebtedness to Paul's *Additiones* for information on the Hebrew text and Jewish interpretation as well.[57] Paul may not have cast doubt on Nicholas's reliability in the way he might have liked, but he did serve as a source for arguments against rabbinic interpretation, in favor of alternate readings from the Church Fathers and Thomas Aquinas.

The manuscript tradition of the *Postilla litteralis* is enormously complex and still awaits systematic study. For our purposes in tracing the reception of Nicholas's text in the fourteenth and fifteenth centuries, it will suffice to examine briefly the range of the tradition, which shows the commentary circulating in scholastic, monastic, and lay contexts. Numerous copies of the *Postilla* were made on fine vellum, beautifully illuminated with rich colors and gold leaf of varying quality. Some of these elaborately illuminated texts belonged to ecclesiastical figures such as bishops and cardinals. Oxford MS Bodl. 251, for example, a manuscript illuminated so luxuriously that it was at a later time plundered, some of its gold-leafed images cut away for sale on the art market, belonged at one time to William Courtenay (1342–96), Archbishop of Canterbury, head of the English Church.[58] Another fourteenth-century manuscript, Vat. Archivio di S. Pietro D200, bears the insignia of Cardinal Orsini on the opening folio. The manuscript contains Nicholas's postilla on the Evangelists and two Jewish treatises (written in a different hand) and was undoubtedly once part of a multivolume copy of the complete commentary.

The *Postilla* was quickly embraced by monks as well as friars and other university scholars, and numerous copies found their way into monasteries during the fourteenth century. The elaborately illuminated Bibl. Mun. Reims MS 178—made for the Royal Abbey of Reims sometime in the second half of the fourteenth century—opens with a scene of Nicholas teaching a group of clearly tonsured religious figures. The multivolume fourteenth-century Paris, Bibl. Mazarine MS 166–168 was made for the Abbey of St. Victor, Paris; in addition to the *Postilla litteralis*, the volume contains Nicholas's two Jewish treatises, the *De visione divinae essentiae*, and *De differentia nostrae translationis ab Hebraica littera Veteris Testamentis*.

Many manuscripts, as already noted, were made in the context of the university book trade. Some, like BAV Vat. lat. 162, bear the *pecia* marks associated with mass production. An explicit tells us that the manuscript, containing Nicholas's 1326 commentary on Psalms, was copied in Paris by Gervais Wallence in 1329.[59] The lavishly illuminated Princeton Art Museum

MS y1937–266, dating to the second quarter of the fourteenth century, was similarly made by a Paris university scribe.[60] The manuscript was copied by the hand of Johannes Brito, most probably the same scribe who was registered as *librarius* in the university book trade from 1314 to 1326.[61] The author portrait at the opening to the prologue on the Gospels presents an intriguing classroom scene, with tantalizingly elusive hints as to patronage (Figure 3). In the illumination, Nicholas is teaching a diverse group of students, including a young woman of indeterminate, apparently nonreligious dress as the central figure. A man on her right holds her arms, presenting her, as it were, to Nicholas for instruction. This man appears not to be tonsured, another layperson in the image. The manuscript is unquestionably a product of the university trade, but its destination remains a puzzle.

The unusual composition of the manuscript is worth noting, as it suggests a special interest in Nicholas's engagement with Hebrew text and Jewish tradition. This is the only copy of the *Postilla* of which I am aware that contains only the Pentateuch, the Gospels, and the two treatises on Jews. Extensive marginal notation, the majority of which highlights those places where Nicholas either embraced or refuted a position of Rashi or "the rabbis," confirms the interest implicit in the decision to include the two Jewish treatises in this collection of the first sets of books in the Old and New Testaments. On fol. 3r, for example, we find the marginal notes *nota opinio Rabi Salomonis*; *opinio Rabi Iosue*; *opinio Rabi Eliezer*. On fol. 9v we find the following set: *opinio Iudeorum*; *opinio Rabi Salomon*; *contra*; *opinio catholicorum*. Alongside Nicholas's commentary on the Ten Plagues, marginal notes read *opinio Iudeorum*; *prima plaga*; *Iudeorum opinio*; *contra*; *Iohannes*; *opinio propheta*; *secunda plaga*; *opinio Iudeorum*; *contra*; *solutio*. Although Nicholas almost always uses the term *Hebraei* to refer to the Jews in their collective exegetical role, the annotator consistently uses the term *Iudaei* instead.[62]

In addition to monastic and scholastic copies of the *Postilla*, a number of elaborately illuminated copies may have been destined for use at court, as seems to have been the case with British Library MS Royal 3.D.VII, a fourteenth-century vellum manuscript of Nicholas's commentary on Genesis through Chronicles, in which the crowned patrons of the text stand directly in front of Nicholas without intermediary, eagerly absorbing the wisdom his text has to offer (Figure 4). The identity of the royal couple, he wearing a blue robe decorated with fleurs-de-lis, holding a pair of gloves, she with a small animal in her arms, is unknown, although the British Library catalog suggests that the coat of arms appearing on three corners of a

Figure 3. Nicholas of Lyra Teaching. Author initial, *Postilla litteralis super Bibliam*. Princeton University Art Museum. Museum Purchase, Carl Otto von Kienbusch, Jr. Memorial Fund. MS y1937-266, fol. 119r. Photograph by John Blazejewski.

Figure 4. Nicholas of Lyra Instructs a royal couple with Moses' Aid. Author initial, *Postilla litteralis super Bibliam*. British Library MS Royal 3.D.VII, fol. 1r.

border on folio 1 is most probably English.[63] The manuscript follows the continuous *Postilla* format employed in scholarly copies; the biblical text is not present except as reference points for the commentary.

While these deluxe volumes are striking, there are far more workhorse volumes with rough drawings at the relevant points in Nicholas's illustration cycle rather than the elaborate illuminations of some of the finer copies. Rome Casanatense MS 10, for example, is an octavo volume in both paper and parchment with the Pentateuch through Ezra, clearly designed for scholarly use, with heavily abbreviated text and extensive marginal notation. The spaces for Nicholas's illustration cycle have mostly been left blank, with the exception of some fairly simple diagrams in the Book of Numbers.

Bibl. Mun. Tours MS 52 (Figure 5) is a fascinating example of a late (c. 1500) deluxe copy made for a presumably lay owner, lavishly historiated with illustrations on the opening pages of the prologue and each of the books of the Pentateuch. Although images within the text are restricted to Nicholas's own cycle, these illustration pages focus on subjects of more general narrative interest, with depictions in Genesis, for example, of Cain killing Abel, Noah's Ark, the Tower of Babel, the birth of Jacob and Esau, Jacob's dream, and so on. Each illumination is accompanied by a short rubric explaining the subject matter.

With the advent of print in the late fifteenth century, Nicholas's commentary began to reach an even wider audience as relatively inexpensive editions of the work became available to eager readers.[64] In addition to the Latin *Postilla litteralis* itself, translations of the commentary were also marketed, especially in High and Low German. These Bibles began to appear in print almost as early as Bible commentary itself. The first Bible commentary to appear in print was Nicholas's *Postilla litteralis et moralis super Bibliam*, Rome 1471–72, and by 1478, Heinrich Quentell of Cologne had published a Low German translation of the Bible with Nicholas's commentary.

The Quentell commentary differs from the far more numerous Latin editions of the *Postilla* in many ways: written in the vernacular, it is clearly directed toward a lay audience (in fact, a prologue by the printer explains the value of Bible study to the lay reader); instead of taking the form of other printed versions of the text, in which biblical text was surrounded by marginal gloss, carefully edited portions of the *Postilla* were woven into the biblical text itself (presented in story form); all superfluous scholarly material, such as William Brito's *Expositiones*, Paul of Burgos' *Additiones*, and Matthew Döring's *Replicationes*, are absent. Even the woodcuts accompanying this German text deviate from the standard set of thirty illustrations put in place by Nicholas. Here one hundred fifty woodcuts supplement the written text in order to hold the attention of the reader—this is essentially a picture book. As stated in the prologue, the pictures were inserted to help make the Bible come alive to the reader. There are pictures of the Ten Plagues, of the Israelites crossing the Red Sea, Moses receiving the Commandments, Joshua battling the Canaanites, and so on. In fact, the only element of the tabernacle (so important in Nicholas's own illustration cycle) to be illustrated in the German volume is the ark of the covenant, and that appears only incidentally in a picture of Moses and the priests.

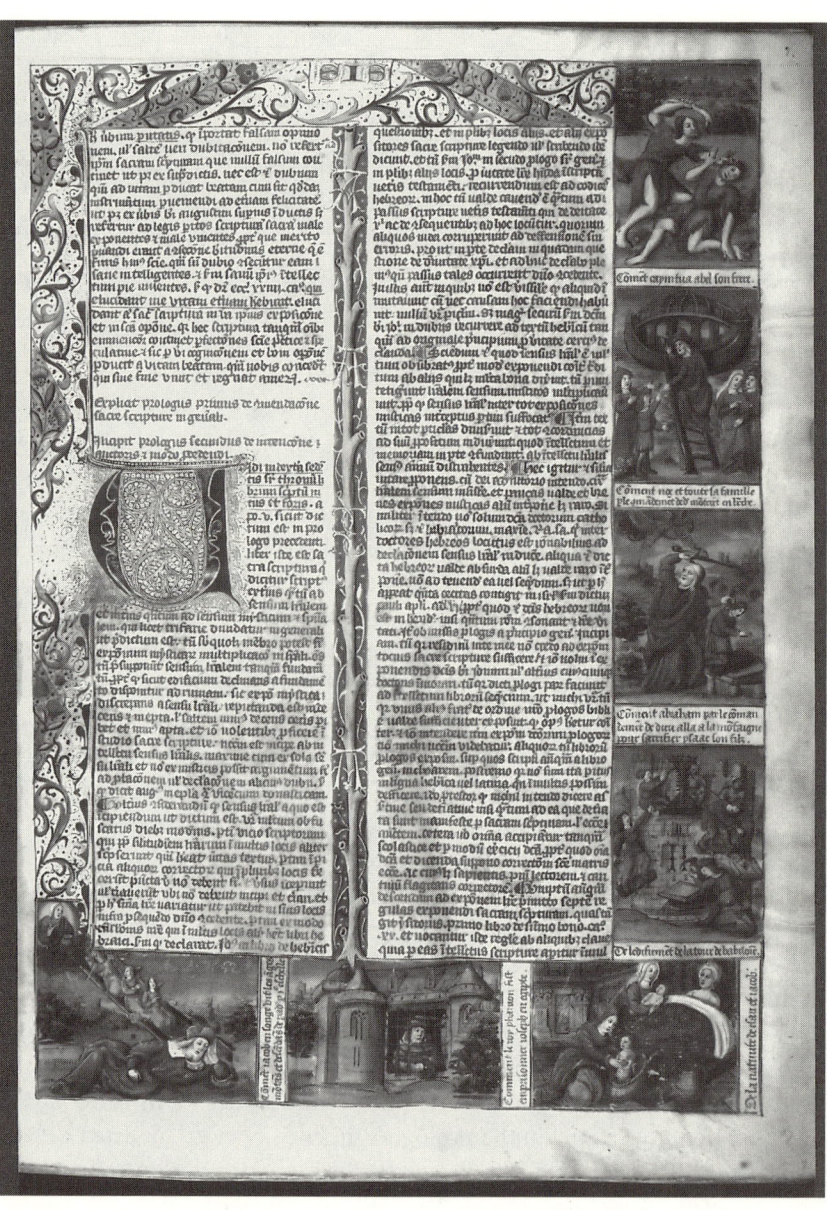

Figure 5. First Page of Genesis, with Narrative Scenes. *Postilla litteralis super Bibliam*. Bibl. Mun. Tours MS 52, fol. 2r.

This edition also has woodcuts in the New Testament, illustrating the life of Jesus and the Acts of the Apostles. Given the clearly different purpose for which this book was designed, it is not surprising to find that it differs completely in composition from Latin editions of the *Postilla*. But it is fascinating to see how important Nicholas of Lyra remained and that the *Postilla* was perceived, at least in this case, as the single most valuable commentary on the Bible to present in a vernacular work.

The overwhelming preference for Nicholas's literal over his moral commentary continued into the print tradition. Edward Gosselin's survey of print editions of the *Postilla super Bibliam* shows that editions of the literal commentary outnumbered the moral by a three-to-one margin, with thirty-six known editions of the *Postilla litteralis* to only thirteen editions of the *Postilla moralis*. This calculation includes the nine known editions of the literal and moral commentaries presented together. If we compare those editions that contain only the literal or the moral commentary, the numbers are considerably more skewed, with only four editions of the moral commentary to twenty-seven editions of the literal commentary, all four printed between 1475 and 1481. Looking at editions of individual books or groups of books, we find only two editions of the *Postilla moralis* (on the Gospels and Epistles) on its own, in contrast with twenty-five editions of the *Postilla litteralis* on its own and fourteen editions of the *Postilla litteralis* and *moralis* together, all on the Gospels and Epistles.[65]

Widely read as Nicholas was, he became a common reference point for a range of authors outside of the schools and formal Bible lectures. A number of scholars have argued that Nicholas's Bible commentary played an important role in the development of vernacular literary traditions as well as in the study of the Bible. In England, the Lollards relied upon on Nicholas's commentary for the translation and study of Scripture in English. Mary Dove, among others, suggests an influence on Chaucer and other vernacular literature via those translation efforts.[66] Mark Hazard, meanwhile, links Nicholas's commentary on the Gospel According to John with a range of English vernacular texts.[67]

Nicholas of Lyra as an Authority on Jewish Tradition

The juxtaposition of two very different images of Nicholas in two elaborately illuminated fourteenth-century manuscripts, one from MS Paris BNF lat. 14247 (Figure 6) and the other from Brit. Lib. MS Royal 3.D.VII (Figure

Figure 6. Nicholas of Lyra at the Feet of Jerome. Author initial, *Postilla litteralis super Bibliam*. MS Paris BNF lat. 14247, fol. 1r.

4), communicates better than any words the role that Nicholas played for later medieval Christians. In the first manuscript, Jerome is the teacher, Nicholas the student sitting at his feet. The more than eight centuries separating the two men dissolve away, as Nicholas takes up the Father's mantle as authoritative commentator on the true meaning of God's word as preserved by the Jews. Like Jerome, Nicholas read the Old Testament in its original Hebrew. Like Jerome, he focused on the literal, historical sense of the Bible rather than on the spiritual, allegorical, or theological implications that might derive from that historical reading. Like Jerome, Nicholas utilized the teachings of the Jews to gain a fuller understanding than would be otherwise available to a Christian reader. Both men showed a love of the letter and a passion for unraveling a level of detail that most Christian readers of the text simply ignored. The link with Jerome is, of course, inescapable, but the image belies the relative power of the two men that emerges from the *Postilla* itself. While, according to the medieval understanding of authority, it was appropriate to depict Nicholas sitting as a small man at Jerome's giant feet, by the time Nicholas had completed his magisterial Bible commentary one might argue that a more accurate image would have Nicholas towering over Jerome, or at the least standing on his shoulders, taking up his mission and his method but reaching, with the help of Rashi, heights Jerome had not been able to attain.

The image in Brit. Lib. Royal 3.D.VII tells a somewhat different story. No longer a student eagerly writing down the words of Jerome, Nicholas hears the Word of God directly from Moses himself and communicates it to the Christian world—to noble patrons, to male and female, to clergy and laity alike. Nicholas is no longer the second Jerome, working at his master's feet. Here Nicholas drinks directly from the font of Moses, copying into his codex the true meaning of the Hebrew letter as it appeared on Moses' original scroll. With his Christian faith and Jewish insight equally at hand, the image suggests that Nicholas has the most accurate text possible of God's word and that, plain and useful doctor that he was, he could make that truth available to the entire Christian world, to the laity as well as to the university theologians. At the precise moment when Jews were being pushed farther and farther to the margins of Latin Christian society, then, we see the most important figure in Christian Bible scholarship attaining his stature on the basis of his perceived knowledge of Hebrew text. Carefully interweaving exegesis and polemic, Nicholas successfully Christianized medieval rabbinic text for his readers, bringing the fruits of Jewish learning to a phenomenally broad Christian audience.

Appendix: Manuscripts Consulted Containing Nicholas of Lyra's Quaestio de adventu Christi

In the following descriptions, Incipit 1 = *Utrum ex scripturis receptis a Iudaeis possit eficaciter probari salvatorem nostrum fuisse hominem et Deum* and Incipit 2 = *Utrum per scripturas a Iudaeis receptas possit probari misterium Christi in lege et prophetis promissi esse iam completum.* The manuscripts have been arranged in chronological order insofar as was possible; many of the manuscripts are only very roughly datable. This appendix does not aim to provide complete descriptive information on the manuscripts listed, but to give a sense of the variety of contexts in which the *Quaestio de adventu Christi* circulated.

Paris BNF lat. 13781 fols. 55v–71v. Probably prior to 1323. St. Germain des Prés. Incipit 1. With fragment of Nicholas's question, *Utrum per sacram scripturam possit efficaciter probari salus Salamonis* (fols. 71v–71bisv), John of Paris, *De adventu Christi secundem carnem* and *De Antichristo; Vita Beatae Annae, Prophetia Beatae Hildegardis.*

Princeton Art Museum MS y1937–266 fols. 214r–219v. Second quarter fourteenth century. Paris, Iohannes Brito, scribe. Incipit 2. With the *Postilla litteralis* on the Pentateuch and Gospels and the *Responsio ad quendam Iudaeum.* This appears to be the earliest of a group of fourteenth-century manuscripts that misdate the text to 1809: *nunc fluxerunt mille octigenti ix anni ad anno incarnationis scriptum est opud istus.*

BAV Archivio S. Pietro D202 fols. 62v–74r. 1343. Provenance uncertain, Iohannes de Morreyo, scribe. Incipit 2. With collected works of Nicholas: *Responsio ad quendam Iudaeum, De differentia nostrae translationis ab Hebraica littera Veteris Testamentis, De visione divinae essentiae.* One of several related

MSS bearing *mille octingenti ix* as the date of composition, in place of 1309. Bears ownership mark of Petrus Sonatis, O.P.

BAV Vat. Lat. 869 fols. 130r–138r and fols. 222r–225v. First half fourteenth century. Provenance uncertain. Incipit 1. Collection of miscellaneous theological and philosophical questions, including some by John Duns Scotus, O.F.M., and Richard of Middleton, O.F.M. The first version of the *Quaestio de adventu Christi* in the collection is presented with two other questions by Nicholas from the same quodlibet, *Utrum Iudei cognoverunt Jesum Nazarenum esset Christum sibi promissum* and *Utrum per sacram scripturam possit efficaciter probari finalis salvus Salomonis.* The second version of the question on the Advent is incomplete.

BAV Archivio S. Pietro D200 fols. 251–276v. Fourteenth century. Rome. Incipit 2. With the *Postilla litteralis* in the Gospels and the *Responsio ad quendam Iudaeum*. Insignia of Cardinal Orsini on fol. 1. The *Postilla litteralis* is in a different hand than *Quaestio de adventu Christi* and the *Responsio ad quendam Iudaeum.*

Assisi Bibl. Comm. MS 172 fols. 189r–192r. Fourteenth century. Provenance uncertain. Incipit 1. With various theological treatises and questions, including Nicholas's question on the salvation of Solomon found in BAV Vat. lat. 869 and Paris BNF lat. 13781, *Utrum per sacram scripturam possit efficaciter probari salus Salomonis.*

Assisi Bibl. Comm. MS 571 fols. 24v–49r. Fourteenth century. Provenance uncertain. Incipit 2. With *Responsio ad quendam Iudaeum* and other anti-Jewish texts, including Isidor of Seville, *Contra Iudaeos.*

Paris BNF lat. 8860 fols. 200v–208v. Fourteenth century. Provenance uncertain. Incipit 2. With *Responsio ad quendam Iudaeum* and *Postilla litteralis* on New Testament.

Paris BNF lat. 13643 fols. 1–35r. Fourteenth century. Provenance uncertain. Incipit 2. Small octavo volume with *Responsio ad quendam Iudaeum*; Question disputed by Durand of Saint-Pourçain, O.P.

Paris BNF lat. 14503 fols. 144r–154r. Fourteenth century. Abbey of St. Victor, Paris. Incipit 1. Miscellaneous collection, including Bernard of Clairvaux's *Liber de contemptu mundi*, Marsilius de Padua, *Defensor pacis*; *Liber Alchorani* (translations by both Marcos of Toledo and Peter of Toledo).

Paris Bibl. Mazarine MS 168 fols. 184r–192r. Fourteenth century. Abbey of St. Victor, Paris. Incipit 2. At end of second volume of *Postilla litteralis super Bibliam* with *Responsio ad quendam Iudaeum, De visione divinae essentiae, De differentia nostrae translationis ab Hebraica littera Veteris Testamentis*.

Munich Clm 5526 fols. 74r–82r. Fourteenth century. From monastery at Diessen an Ammersee in Bavaria. With other theological questions. Related to Paris BNF Lat. 2384, possibly its model, which contains the same rubric: *Ad disputandum contra Iudeos et probandum que ipsi negant, scilicet trinitatem personarum in Deo, in Christo divinitatem, et Christum iam venisse de preterito*.

Munich Clm 8872 fols.139r–148r. Fourteenth century. From the library of the Franciscan convent in Munich. Incipit 1. In a theological miscellany.

Munich Clm 23615 fols.1–24r. Fourteenth century. Provenance uncertain. Partial text—begins with *[redemp]tor tuus sanctis Israel. Item quod dicit Isayam fuisse in Monte Synay*. Octavo volume with *Responsio ad quendam Iudaeum*.

Munich Clm 23656 fols. 2r–11r. Fourteenth century. Provenance uncertain, Johannis de Beyer, scribe. Incipit 1. *Quaestio de adventu Christi* in a twelve-folio octavo volume by itself.

Paris BNF lat. 16523 fols. 63r–76r. Fourteenth century. Provenance uncertain. Incipit 2. With anti-Jewish works, including Peter Alfonse, *Dialogi contra Iudaeos*; *Contra Iudaeos* (attributed to John Baconthorpe, O. Carm.); Guido Terrena, O. Carm., *De Antichristo*; *Testamenta XII patriarcharum*. *Liber contra hereses Katarorum* added to end of manuscript later.

Paris BNF lat. 3262 fols. 338r–342r. Fourteenth century. Provenance uncertain. Incipit 1. With John of Freiburg, O.P., *Summa confessorum* and a letter from Pope John XXII to Paris University faculty, November 21, 1324.

BAV Vat. Chigi A.IV.95 fols. 44r–58v. Late Fourteenth century. Provenance uncertain. Incipit 2. With *Postilla litteralis super Ecclesiastem*.

Paris BNF lat. 17260 fols. 17v ff. Late Fourteenth century. Paris? Incipit 2. With collected works of Nicholas: *De Susanne, De visione divinae essentiae, Responsio ad quendam Iudaeum, De differentia nostrae translationis ab Hebraica littera Veteris Testamentis.*

BAV Vat. lat. 4265 fols. 1–26v. 1381. Lobegestecz, Nicolaus de Gruenenberg, scribe. Incipit 1. With the *Responsio ad quendam Iudaeum,* the *Pharetra fidei contra Iudaeos,* and other anti-Jewish and antiheretical works. The manuscript has been described in Alexander Patschovsky, ed., *Quellen zur böhmischen Inquisition im 14. Jahrhundert,* Monumenta Germaniae Historica. Quellen zur Geistesgeschichte des Mittelalters 11 (Weimar: Böhlau, 1979), 152–57.

Rome Bibl. Angelica 76 fols. 1–17r. 1390. Pisa, Nicolai de Lanfreducciis, doctor of law, scribe. Incipit 2. Miscellaneous collection, including works by Aristotle, patristic texts, St. Gregory on Ezechiel, and Nicholas of Lyra's Apocalypse commentary. The text provides the opening arguments of incipit 1 along with the question and opening arguments of incipit 2.

Paris Bibl. Arsenal MS 537 fols. 115r–129r. 1397. From the library of the Grand-Augustins in Paris. Incipit 2. With the *Responsio ad quendam Iudaeum* and a number of other texts, including Bindo de Senis, O.S.A., *Distinctiones sive concordantie hystoriales Veteris ac Novi Testamenti,* Iohannes Cochinger, O.P., *Postilla super Epistolas Pauli.*

Paris Bibl. Arsenal MS 580 fols. 367r–374v. 1407. From the library of the Grand-Augustins in Paris, Guillelmus Cronier, scribe. Incipit 2. One of several related MSS that erroneously date the text to the year 1809 (*mille octigenti ix anni,* fol. 371v).With the *Postilla super Novum Testamentum* and *Responsio ad quendam Iudaeum.* The scribe's colophon on fol. 366v indicates that this was once part of a complete multi-volume copy of the *Postilla litteralis.*

Paris BNF lat. 3655 fols. 120v–135v. 1424. Montpellier, Amédée Bovier, scribe. Incipit 2. With Nicholas's *Responsio ad quendam Iudaeum*; Alan of Lille, *De fide catholica contra hereticos*; Francis de Meyronnes, O.F.M., *Tractatus de principatu temporali, Quaestio de haereticis,* and *De conceptione Virginis Mariae*; *Quaestio de papae auctoritate*; *Contra Machometum*; *Contra errores Graecorum*; Peter Olivi, *Tractatus de venditionibus et emptionibus.*

Munich Clm 12715 fols. 8r–23v. 1429. Ranshofen, Christianus Perger de Ekkenfelden, scribe. Incipit 2. With anonymous *De symbolo, De fuga mulierum, De gratia infusa,* Nicholas's *Postilla litteralis super Psalmos* and other miscellaneous texts.

Munich Clm 3243 fols. 376v–389v. 1447. Provenance uncertain. Incipit 2. With *Postilla litteralis super Epistolas Pauli, Responsio ad quendam Iudaeum,* and other anti-Jewish works, *Letter of Rabbi Samuel, Pharetra fidei contra Iudaeos, Extractiones de Talmut.*

Paris Bibl. Arsenal MS 19 fols. 1–9r. 1449. Incipit 2. Third volume of Nicholas's *Postilla litteralis super Bibliam,* containing *Postilla litteralis in Novum Testamentum, Responsio ad quendam Iudaeum* and *De differentia nostrae translationis ab Hebraica littera Veteris Testamentis.*

Paris BNF lat. 3359 fols. 1–9r. 1462. Paris? Incipit 2. With *Responsio ad quendam Iudaeum, De visione divinae essentiae, De differentia nostrae translationis ab Hebraica littera Veteris Testamentis,* and Augustine *Super Psalmos.*

BAV Pal. Lat. 1794 fols. 131r–145v. 1465. Italy. Incipit 1. With varied works, religious and secular, including *Modus conficiendi,* Petrarch's *Griselda, Laudes Italie.* Brief excerpt from Nicholas's *Postilla litteralis* on fol. 127, excerpt from *Postilla litteralis super Matthaeum* on poverty on fol. 129.

Munich Clm 3042 fols. 87r–100r. 1468. Provenance uncertain. Incipit 2. With *De miseria conditionis humane (De contemptu mundi),* Thomas Aquinas, *De sacramente,* and other theological works.

Munich Clm 19610 fols. 106r–132v. 1468. From Tegernsee. With anti-Jewish treatises. Incipit 2.

Paris Bibl. Arsenal MS 78 fols. 28v–65r. 1477. Padua. Incipit 2. With a Jewish legend on the Birth of Christ told by Theodore the Jew to Philip l'Argentier, the *Testamenta duodecim patriarcharum,* John of Paris's *De adventu Christi secundem carnem* under the title, *De probatione fidei christiane,* Prophecies of the Ten Sibyls, and *Sibylla Erithrea Babilonica.*

BAV Vat. Chigi B.V.71 fols. 3r–21v. Fifteenth century. Provenance uncertain. Incipit 2. With *Responsio ad quendam Iudaeum* and *Letter of Rabbi Samuel.*

BAV Vat. lat. 1990 fols. 73r–130r. Fifteenth century. Provenance uncertain. Incipit 1. Mistakenly attributed to John Baconthorpe in the Vatican Library's catalog. Text appears to have been copied from Nicholas of Strassburg's version of the text rather than Nicholas directly. With Josephus, *Antiquities*.

BAV Vat. Lat. 4272 fols. 167r–181v. Fifteenth century. Provenance uncertain. Incipit 1. With the *Responsio ad quendam Iudaeum* and a work of Andreas de Novocastro.

BAV Vat. Lat. 6209 fols. 371r–389v. Fifteenth century. Provenance uncertain. Incipit 1. With collection of sixteenth-century records of Church councils.

BAV Vat. Lat. 8724 fols. 125r–167r. Fifteenth century. Provenance uncertain. Incipit 2. With *Responsio ad quendam Iudaeum* and other anti-Jewish treatises, including *Letter of Rabbi Samuel* and Peter Alphonse, *Dialogi contra Iudaeos*.

Assisi Bibl. Comm. MS 561 fols. 151r–185r. Fifteenth century. Provenance uncertain. Incipit 2. With anonymous Latin sermons.

Paris BNF lat. 3644 fols. 1–30r. Fifteenth century. Provenance uncertain. Incipit 1. *Quaestio de adventu Christi* in a volume by itself.

Paris BNF lat. 2384 fols. 191v–235v. Fifteenth century. Paris. Incipit 1. With Letter of Rabbi Samuel; bound together with earlier manuscript sections (ninth– through twelfth–century) containing a variety of texts on the Bible by Jerome, Bede, Gregory the Great and Alcuin (fols. 1–153). *Quaestio de adventu Christi* begins on fol. 191v, ends abruptly after two pages, then begins again. MS is related to, and was probably the model for, Munich Clm 5526. They both have the following rubric (here on fol. 193v): *Ad disputandum contra Iudeos et probandum que ipsi negant, scilicet trinitatem personarum in Deo, in Christo divinitatem, et Christum iam venisse de preterito.*

Paris Bibl. Arsenal MS 532 fols. 184r–194v. Fifteenth century. Provenance uncertain. Incipit 2. With *Responsio ad quendam Iudaeum* in a large miscellany, including works by Hugh of St. Victor, Richard of St. Victor, Thomas

Aquinas, O.P., Giles of Rome, O.S.A., Francis de Meyronnes, O.F.M., Jean Gerson, and others.

Munich Clm 4207 fols. 205r–217v. Fifteenth century. Provenance uncertain. Incipit 1. With *Postilla litteralis super Isaiam, Ieremiam, Baruch* and *Responsio ad quendam Iudaeum*. A later hand added on fol 217v, *Supradicta questio convenit formam in aliis terminis, videlicet sic: utrum per scripturas* . . .

Munich Clm 8392 fols. 205r–215v. Fifteenth century. Provenance uncertain. Incipit 2. With *Responsio ad quendam Iudaeum*; various works of Hugh of St. Victor, including *De Archa Noe*; and Ludolph of Saxony, O. Cart., *Libellus de vita Jesu Christi*. One of several MSS that erroneously present 1809 as the year in which the work was written.

Munich Clm 8960 fols. 282v–289r. Fifteenth century. From the Franciscan convent in Munich. Incipit 1. With a collection of quadragesimal and other sermons in a quarto volume.

Munich Clm 14232 fols. 196v–209r. Fifteenth century. Regensburg, from the Benedictine monastery of S. Emmeramum. Incipit 2. Collection of theological texts, including Robert Holcot, O.P., *Questiones theologice in Librum Sapientie*, and anti-Hussite works.

Munich Clm 14891 fols. 152r–166r. Fifteenth century. Regensburg, from the Benedictine monastery of S. Emmeramum. Incipit 2. Theological miscellany, with *Responsio ad quendam Iudaeum, Letter of Rabbi Samuel*.

Munich Clm 15567 fols. 138v–142r. 1469. Provenance uncertain, from the Benedictine monastery in Rot ad Oenum. Incipit 1. Incomplete text. Theological miscellany, including works by Hugh of St. Victor, St. Bernard, Jean Gerson, Johannes Nider, and others.

Munich Clm 16431 fols. 96v–113v. Fifteenth century. Provenance uncertain, from the monastery of S. Zenonis at Reichenhall. Incipit 2. With *Postilla litteralis super Duodecim Prophetis et Epistolas Pauli*.

Munich Clm 17833 fols. 379r–390r. Fifteenth century. Provenance uncertain. Incipit 2. With papal documents, account of Huss's death at Constance, condemnation of John Wyclif.

Munich Clm 18630 fols. 233r–244v. Fifteenth century. From Tegernsee. Incipit 2. Incomplete text. With miscellaneous texts.

Munich Clm 24840 fols. 1–52r. Fifteenth century. Provenance uncertain. Incipit 1. *Quaestio de adventu Christi* in a volume by itself.

BAV Vat. lat. 5992 fols. 124r–132r. Fourteenth or Fifteenth century. From the Conventu SS Apostolorum Urbis. Incipit 1. In theological miscellany.

Paris BNF lat. 3968 fols. 187r–190v. Fifteenth century. Provenance uncertain. Incipit 1. With miscellaneous texts.

Rome Bibl. Casanatense 159 fols. 36r–68r. 1511. Spain, Gondissalvus Garcias de Sancta Maria (iuris civilis doctor). Incipit 2. With the *Responsio ad quendam Iudaeum* and *Pharetra Fidei contra Iudaeos*. The *Quaestio* appears at the beginning of the *Responsio* under the rubric, *Incipit responsio fratris Nicolai de Lira ad quendam Iudeum ex verbis Evangelii secundum Mattheum contra Christum nequiter arguentem, quod opusculum completum fuit per eundem Nicolaum maxima cum diligentia et suptilitate.* The text of the *Quaestio* then begins, followed immediately by the *Responsio* with no distinction between the two texts.

Notes

Introduction

1. "In contrarium arguebatur quod inter Iudeos sunt et fuerunt multi ingeniosi in scripturis legis et prophetarum valde studiosi. Ergo, si predicta possent haberi efficaciter per scripturas ab eis receptas, non est verisimile quod stetissent tamdiu in errore, ergo, etc." Biblioteca Apostolica Vaticana (hereafter BAV) MS Vat. lat. 869, fol. 130r. On the manuscript tradition for the text, see Chapter 4. In the manuscript citations that follow I have modernized capitalization and punctuation, but I have followed the orthography of the manuscript, except for providing v for consonantal u, and I have refrained from standardizing variant spellings in the text.

2. I use the term "unbelief" rather than "disbelief" here because the question of whether Jewish lack of (Christian) faith represented an intentional act of "disbelieving" or an inability to believe (divinely ordained or the result of moral weakness) was subject to debate. Although Nicholas occasionally accused modern Jews of disbelief, he tended much more to a position of unbelief. See Chapters 3 and 4.

3. Jeremy Cohen, *The Friars and the Jews: The Evolution of Medieval Anti-Judaism* (Ithaca, N.Y.: Cornell University Press, 1982), and *Living Letters of the Law: Ideas of the Jew in Medieval Christianity* (Berkeley: University of California Press, 1999).

4. Three helpful historiographical surveys on changes in Jewish-Christian encounters during the later Middle Ages can be found in Jeremy Cohen, "Recent Historiography on the Medieval Church and the Decline of European Jewry," in *Popes, Teachers, and Canon Law in the Middle Ages: Essays in Honor of Brian Tierney*, ed. Stanley Chodorow and James Ross Sweeney, 251–62 (Ithaca, N.Y.: Cornell University Press, 1989); Anna Sapir Abulafia, "From Northern Europe to Southern Europe and from the General to the Particular: Recent Research on Jewish-Christian Coexistence in Medieval Europe," *Journal of Medieval History* 23 (1997): 179–90; and David Berger, *From Crusades to Blood Libels to Expulsions: Some New Approaches to Medieval Antisemitism*, Annual Lecture of the Victor J. Selmanowitz Chair of Jewish History 2 (New York: Touro College Graduate School of Jewish Studies, 1997).

5. For an overview of the Jewish experience in Europe during this period, see Kenneth Stowe, *Alienated Minority: The Jews of Medieval Latin Europe* (Cambridge, Mass.: Harvard University Press, 1992).

6. See Lester Little, *Religious Poverty and the Profit Economy* (Ithaca, N.Y.: Cornell University Press, 1983).

7. On policies concerning Jews in France, see William C. Jordan, *The French Monarchy and the Jews: From Philip Augustus to the Last Capetians* (Philadelphia:

University of Pennsylvania Press, 1989). On the English situation, see Robin R. Mundill, *England's Jewish Solution: Experiment and Expulsion, 1262–1290* (Cambridge: Cambridge University Press, 1998).

8. Peter Alfonse, a twelfth-century Jewish convert to Christianity, made a small body of Talmudic literature available in Latin translation with his *Dialogi contra Iudaeos* (an imaginary discussion between his new Christian self and his former Jewish self, demonstrating that the Christian faith was far more rational and reasonable than Judaism), but this did not result in a new concern to control Jewish error or blasphemy as would be the case with later Christian encounter with Talmudic literature. See John Tolan, *Petrus Alfonsi and his Medieval Readers* (Gainesville: University Press of Florida, 1993).

9. For concise summaries of the Talmud trials and relevant documents, see Solomon Grayzel, *The Church and the Jews in the Thirteenth Century*, 2nd ed. rev. (New York: Hermon Press, 1966); and Gilbert Dahan, *Le brûlement du Talmud à Paris: 1242–1244* (Paris: Cerf, 1999).

10. Grayzel, *Church and the Jews*, 31–32, 250–53.

11. Grayzel, *Church and the Jews*, 274–81.

12. Robert Chazan, *Medieval Jewry in Northern France: A Political and Social History* (Baltimore: Johns Hopkins University Press, 1973), 131, 156.

13. On the fourteenth-century expulsions of the Jews from France, see Isidore Loeb, "Les expulsions des Juifs de France au xive siècle," in *Jubelschrift zum siebzigsten Geburtstag des Prof. Dr. H. Graetz* (Breslau: Schottlaender, 1887), 39–56. Following the expulsion of the Jews in 1306, small numbers were readmitted, with numerous restrictions, to French lands in 1315 by Philip the Fair's son, Louix X. They were expelled once again seven years later by Charles IV and were not readmitted to France during Nicholas of Lyra's lifetime. Elizabeth A. R. Brown reexamines the evidence for the 1322 expulsion in "Philip V, Charles IV and the Jews of France: The Alleged Expulsion of 1322," *Speculum* 66 (1991), 294–329.

14. Eusèbe de Laurière et al., eds., *Ordonnances des roys de France de la troisième race, recueillies par ordre chronologique*, vol. 1 (Paris, 1723–1849), 595–97.

15. See Cohen, *Friars and the Jews*; Robert Chazan, *Daggers of Faith: Thirteenth Century Christian Missionizing and Jewish Response* (Berkeley: University of California Press, 1989); and Hyam Maccoby, ed. and trans., *Judaism on Trial: Jewish-Christian Disputations in the Middle Ages* (Rutherford, N.J.: Fairleigh Dickinson University Press, 1982).

16. Alexander Patschovsky, "Der 'Talmudjude': Vom mittelalterlichen Ursprung eines neuzeitlichen Themas," in *Juden in der christlichen Umwelt während des späten Mittelalters*, ed. Alfred Haverkamp and Franz-Josef Ziwes (Berlin: Duncker & Humblot, 1992), 18–19.

17. Robert Chazan, *Barcelona and Beyond: The Disputation of 1263 and Its Aftermath* (Berkeley: University of California Press, 1992).

18. I consider Nicholas of Lyra's more ambiguous division of Jewish authorities into "ancient" and "modern" categories in Chapter 2.

19. See Cohen, *Friars and the Jews*, 129–69 and *Living Letters of the Law*, 313–63; and Chazan, *Daggers of Faith*. Cohen highlights what he sees as an essentially new theological understanding of Jewish error, while Chazan emphasizes changing

Christian purpose in the development of what he calls the first serious effort to convert the Jews as a body in Latin Christendom. John Hood, like Chazan, sees change in the behavior of the clergy rather than in the realm of theology. John Y. B. Hood, *Aquinas and the Jews* (Philadelphia: University of Pennsylvania Press, 1995). The *Capistrum Iudaeorum* exists in a modern edition with Spanish translation: Raimundi Martini, *Capistrum Iudaeorum*, 2 vols., ed. and trans., Adolfo Robles Sierra (Würzburg: Echter Verlag, 1990). Robles Sierra provides an analysis of distinctions between the two works in his introduction, differentiating the *Capistrum* from the *Pugio* in scope and presentation of Hebrew text: where the *Pugio* addressed a wide range of theological issues, the earlier *Capistrum* attempted only to prove that the advent of Christ had already happened; where the *Pugio* presented extensive passages of Hebrew text, the *Capistrum Iudaeorum* included translations of Hebrew text without providing the Hebrew itself. *Capistrum Iudaeorum*, 25–31. See also Jeremy Cohen, "Raimundus Martini's *Capistrum Iudaeorum*" (Hebrew), *Me'ah She'arim: Studies in Medieval Jewish Spiritual Life in Memory of Isadore Twersky*, ed. Ezra Flaisher, Ya'akov Blidshtain, Karmi Horovits, and Dov Septimus (Jerusalem: Hebrew University of Jerusalem, 2001), 279–96. On the evolution of Christian anti-Jewish polemic, see Gilbert Dahan, *La polémique chrétienne contre le judaïsme au Moyen Age* (Paris: Cerf, 1991).

   20. Jeremy Cohen, in *Friars and the Jews*, "Scholarship and Intolerance in the Medieval Academy," *American Historical Review* 91 (1986), 592–613, and *Living Letters of the Law*, has articulated the position that increasing intolerance towards Jews in medieval Christendom was the result of changing theology (a shift from the Augustinian notion of Jew-as-witness to Christian truth toward a notion of Jew as dangerous heretic), although he stops short of explicitly locating policies of expulsion in theological concerns. The work of scholars like William Jordan and Robin Mundill suggests that theological intolerance was less relevant to expulsion than the particular political and economic circumstances of the day: see William Jordan, "Princely Identity and the Jews in Medieval France," in *From Witness to Witchcraft: Jews and Judaism in Medieval Christian Thought*. Wolfenbütteler Mittelalter-Studien, 11, ed. Jeremy Cohen, 257–73 (Wiesbaden: Harrassowitz, 1996); Mundill, *England's Jewish Solution*.

   21. Jordan, *French Monarchy and the Jews*, 179–86.

   22. Joseph Shatzmiller, *Shylock Reconsidered: Jews, Moneylending, and Medieval Society* (Berkeley: University of California Press, 1990), 62–67.

   23. A brief discussion of the various reports is found in L. Lazard, "Note sur la légend du juif de la rue des Billettes," *Annuaire des archives israelites* 4 (1887–88): 56–60. Lazard examines in particular the entries found in *Recueil des Historiens des Gaules et de la France*, vol. 20, 658; vol. 21, 127; vol. 22, 32–33; vol. 23, 145–46. He seems to have been unaware of the existence of a unique report contained in a thirteenth- or fourteenth-century manuscript, Paris Mazarine MS 1030, fols. 165^v–166^v, which describes the arrest of a man charged with the Rue de Billettes host desecration. See also the article by Gilbert Dahan, "Il y a sept cents ans à Paris (1290): L'affaire des billettes," *Communauté nouvelle* (Paris) 58 (Paris, December 1991): 72–84; and Miri Rubin, *Gentile Tales: The Narrative Assault on Late Medieval Jews* (Reprint Philadelphia: University of Pennsylvania Press, 2004).

24. Jordan, *The French Monarchy*, 194–95.

25. Guillaume de Nangis. *Chronique latine de Guillaume de Nangis de 1113 à 1300 avec les continuations de cette chronique de 1300 à 1368*, ed. Hercule Geraud (Paris, 1843), 1:363–64, 380.

26. Beryl Smalley, *The Study of the Bible in the Middle Ages* (Notre Dame, Ind.: University of Notre Dame Press, 1964), 364–65.

27. See Aryeh Graboïs, "The Hebraica Veritas and Jewish-Christian Intellectual Relations in the Twelfth Century," *Speculum* 50 (1975): 613–34 and Gilbert Dahan, *Les intellectuels chrétiens et les juifs au Moyen Age. Polémique et relations culturelles entre chrétiens et juifs en occident du XIIe au XIVe siècles* (Paris: Cerf, 1990).

28. On the relationship between exegesis and polemic in Christian context, see Dahan, *Intellectuels chrétiens.*

29. See Chapter 5.

30. Nicholas was known by the sobriquet *doctor planus et utilis*, the plain and useful doctor.

31. Quite literally, since the later scholars knew of his work and saw in him a predecessor.

32. Philip Krey, "Many Readers but Few Followers: The Fate of Nicholas of Lyra's 'Apocalypse Commentary' in the Hands of His Late-Medieval Admirers," *Church History* 64 (1995): 185–201.

33. The basic source for biographical information on Nicholas of Lyra remains Henri Labrosse, "Sources de la biographie de Nicolas de Lyre," *Études franciscaines* 16 (1906): 383–404, and "Biographie de Nicolas de Lyre," *Études franciscaines* 17 (1907): 488–505, 593–608. A more readily accessible biography, which draws heavily from Labrosse's work, may be found in Charles V. Langlois, "Nicolas de Lyre, Frère Mineur," in *Histoire Littéraire de la France* (Paris, 1937), 36: 355–401.

34. Labrosse, "Biographie de Nicolas de Lyre," 593–94.

35. We know from the fact that Nicholas became regent master for the year 1308–9, that he must have completed his studies in 1308. Based on the timetable for the course of theological studies outlined in John Marenbon, *Later Medieval Philosophy (1150–1350): An Introduction* (London: Routledge & Kegan Paul, 1987), 20–24, Nicholas must have begun his studies at Paris no later than 1301.

36. Franz Pelster, "*Quodlibeta* und *Quaestiones* des Nikolaus von Lyra O.F.M. (d. 1349)," in *Mélanges Joseph de Ghellinck, S.J.*, vol. 2, *Moyen Age, époques moderne et contemporaire* (Gembloux: Duculot, 1951), 960–61; Palémon Glorieux, *Répertoire des maitres en théologie de Paris au XIIIe siècle* (Paris: Vrin, 1934), 2:215. On the trial of the Templars, see Heinrich Finke, *Papsttum und Untergang des Templeordens* (Münster: Aschendorff, 1907), 2: 310–12; Malcolm Barber, *The Trial of the Templars* (Cambridge: Cambridge University Press, 1978), and Barber, *The New Knighthood: A History of the Order of the Temple* (Cambridge: Cambridge University Press, 1994).

37. Following Nicholas's name in the document is that of another Franciscan, James of Ascoli. James probably succeeded Nicholas as the Franciscan regent in Paris, although Glorieux thought that James was not regent until 1310–11, immediately prior to Bertrand of Tour. According to Prosper de Reggio Emilia, James of Ascoli, Bertrand of Tour and Martin of Abbeville were the Franciscan regent masters from 1311 to 1315. Palémon Glorieux, "Discussiones: D'Alexandre de Hales à

Pierre Auriol, La suite des maîtres franciscains de Paris au XIIIᵉ siècle," *Archivum Franciscanum Historicum (hereafter AFH)* 26 (1933): 264. See also the chronological table of regent masters in Glorieux, *Répertoire des maîtres en théologie*, vol. 1.

38. The document reads April 11, 1309, but the year was actually 1310 (new style), according to Robert E. Lerner, *The Heresy of the Free Spirit in the Later Middle Ages* (Berkeley: University of California Press, 1972), 71, and "An 'Angel of Philadelphia' in the Reign of Philip the Fair: The Case of Guiard of Cressonessart," in *Order and Innovation in the Middle Ages*, ed. W. C. Jordan et al. (Princeton, N.J.: Princeton University Press, 1976), 345. As mentioned above, the new year began at Easter in early fourteenth-century Paris. The year 1309 (old style) extended from March 30, 1309, to April 19, 1310 (new style); thus, there were two April 11ths in 1309. Paul Verdeyen questioned Lerner's date of 1310 in "Le Procès d'inquisition contre Marguerite Porete et Guiard de Cressonesart (1309–1310)," *Revue d'histoire ecclésiastique* 81 (1986): 47–94, noting that after dating the document April 11, 1309, the notary proceeded to offer two contradictory markers, placing the document in the eighth indiction (1310) but the fourth year of the reign of Clement V (1309). Verdeyen favored the earlier date because he believed that notaries often miscalculated the indictions and so the year of the pope's reign was more trustworthy. However, Verdeyen was the one who erred in this case, for the relevant document (Paris, Archives nationales, layette J 428, no. 15) clearly reads *anno quinto* of Clement's reign (1310), not *anno quarto*.

39. Nicholas continued to be involved in university affairs for several decades after incepting as master; there was certainly a place for established masters to participate in university life after their tenure as regent was over. See Labrosse, "Sources de la Biographie," 388; "Biographie de Nicolas de Lyre," 595.

40. The execution of the Jew is recorded in Guillaume de Nangis, *Chronique Latine*, 1:363–64, 380.

41. Labrosse, "Biographie de Nicolas de Lyre," 596–97, 600–601.

42. On the Perugia general chapter meeting, see David Burr, *The Spiritual Franciscans: From Protest to Persecution in the Century After Saint Francis* (University Park: Pennsylvania State University Press, 2001), 268–75.

43. Labrosse, "Sources de la Biographie," 597–600. Kevin Madigan and Philip Krey have both demonstrated that, whatever Nicholas's assumptions about the poverty of Christ and the apostles, he did not politicize his biblical commentary around the poverty issue as did some other Franciscan exegetes. Madigan, "Lyra on the Gospel of Matthew"; Krey, "The Apocalypse Commentary of 1329: Problems in Church History," in *Nicholas of Lyra: The Senses of Scripture*, ed. Philip Krey and Lesley Smith (Leiden, 2000), 195–221; 267–88.

44. Heinrich Denifle and Emile Chatelaine, eds., *Chartularium Universitatis Parisiensis*, (Paris, 1891), 2: 315–16.

45. Denifle and Chatelaine, *Chartularium*, 429–32. A critical edition has recently been published: Michael Scott Woodward, ed., *"De visione divinae essentiae* by Nicholas of Lyra," *Franciscan Studies* 63 (2005): 325–407.

46. Philippe Buc argues for a close relationship between Nicholas and the French crown on the basis of the text of Nicholas's *Postilla litteralis*, which seems to indicate an intimate knowledge of the royal court: "Pouvoir royal et commentaires

de la bible," *Annales: Economies, sociétés, civilisations* 44, no. 3 (1989): 691–709, and "The Book of Kings: Nicholas of Lyra's Mirror of Princes," in Krey and Smith, *Nicholas of Lyra*, 83–109.

47. Labrosse, "Biographie de Nicolas de Lyre," 600–603.

48. Jules Viard, "Date de la mort de Nicolas de Lire," *Bibliothèque de l'école des Chartes* 56 (1895): 141–43.

49. Judith Olszowy-Schlanger, *Les manuscrits hébreux dans l'Angleterre médiévale: étude historique et paléographique*, Collection de la revue des études juives, vol. 29 (Paris: Peeters, 2003). See also Raphael Loewe, "The Medieval Christian Hebraists of England. The *Superscriptio Lincolniensis*," *Hebrew Union College Annual* 28 (1957): 209.

50. These rumors, designed to account for Nicholas's knowledge of Hebrew and Jewish literary traditions, serve to remind us that such knowledge had become a rarity by the fifteenth century. Paul of Burgos's comments on Nicholas's Hebrew skill may be found in his *Additiones* to the *Postilla litteralis*'s prologue: ". . . in littera hebraica ad quam pluries recurrit non videtur fuisse sufficienter eruditus quasi illam in pueritia didicisset, sed de illa videtur habuisse notitiam quasi ab aliis in aetate adulta mendicato suffragio acquisitam." PL 113: 46.

51. Labrosse, "Sources de la biographie de Nicolas de Lyre," 394–96. The author of the biography was identified by Heinrich Rüthing, "Kritische Bemerkungen zu einer mittelalterlichen Biographie des Nikolaus von Lyra," *AFH* 60 (1967): 42–54.

52. On Jewish communities in northern France and Normandy see Robert Chazan, *Medieval Jewry in Northern France*; and Norman Golb, *The Jews in Medieval Normandy: A Social and Intellectual History* (Cambridge: Cambridge University Press, 1998).

53. Olszowy-Schlanger, *Manuscrits hébreux*.

54. See Deeana C. Klepper, "The Dating of Nicholas of Lyra's *Quaestio de adventu Christi*." *AFH* 86 (1993): 297–312.

55. For a thorough treatment of Nicholas's works see Henri Labrosse's serial publication, "Oeuvres de Nicolas de Lyre," *Études franciscaines* 19 (1908): 41–52, 153–75, 368–79; 35 (1923): 171–87, 400–432. Although there are some problems with Labrosse—he mistakenly believed in the existence of a revision of Nicholas's *Quaestio de adventu Christi* and he did not see enough manuscript copies of Nicholas's texts to make definitive judgments on issues of dating and connections between texts—nothing has supplanted his extensive study.

56. Judah Rosenthal was the first to argue this explicitly, in his edition of the twelfth-century work by Jacob ben Ruben, *Milhamot ha-Shem* (Jerusalem: Mosad ha-Rav Kuk, 1963), 141–46, although the possible connection had been raised by Martin Steinschneider early in the twentieth century. A comparison of the arguments presented in book 11 of Jacob's work with Nicholas's responses in his treatise supports Rosenthal's conclusion. Cohen, *Friars and the Jews*, 186–87, lays to rest objections raised by Bernard Blumenkranz in "Nicolas de Lyre et Jacob ben Ruben," *Journal of Jewish Studies* 16 (1965): 47–51. See also Joshua Levy, "*Sefer Milhamot ha-Shem*, Chapter Eleven: The Earliest Jewish Critique of the New Testament" (Jacob ben Ruben, Nicholas of Lyra) (Ph.D. diss., New York University, 2004).

57. Each psalm is preceded by a few lines of verse describing an episode in the life of St. Francis. At the end of this devotional segment of the work follows a literal commentary on the poems and the psalms with an attempt to draw connections between the episodes in the life of St. Francis and the psalms. In addition to the emphasis on the literal sense as defined and pursued in the *Postilla litteralis super Bibliam*, another indication that this is genuinely Nicholas's work is the following phrase found in the preface: "Postquam auxiliante Domino scripsi quedam opera super utrumque testamentum," which is very similar to statements made in the prefaces in Nicholas's *De differentia nostrae translationis ab Hebraica littera Veteris Testamentis* and *Responsio ad quendam Iudaeum*. Further, a passage in the commentary on Psalm 86 refers the reader to something else the author has written on the subject at hand, "sicut dixi diffusius super Librum Psalmorum." This type of self-reference is very common in Nicholas's work, and a comparison of his commentary on Psalm 86 in the *Postilla litteralis* with that in the *Oratio* confirms their connection. See Labrosse, "Oeuvres de Nicolas de Lyre," 35:185–86.

58. The *Postilla moralis* did not evoke nearly the same level of interest as Nicholas's literal commentary. See Chapter 2 and Chapter 5.

59. Nicholas also apparently wrote a commentary on the *Sentences* of Peter Lombard, of which only brief excerpts remain in two manuscripts, University of Cracow MS BB.IV.43 and Brussels, MS Bibliothèque Royal 12.171. Labrosse, "Oeuvres de Nicolas de Lyre," 35:400–401. Following the progression of theological studies outlined in Marenbon, *Later Medieval Philosophy*, 21–22, Nicholas's *Sentences* commentary was most likely written around 1303 when he would have lectured as a *baccalaureus sententiarius* at Paris.

60. Both of these questions appear with the *Quaestio de adventu Christi* in BAV MS Vat. lat. 869, the first on fol. 130r and the second on fols. 138r–140v. The question on whether or not the Jews recognized Christ appears in its entirety in Nicholas's *Postilla litteralis* on Matthew 21:38. The question on the salvation of Solomon appears in part attached to the end of the *Quaestio de adventu Christi* in MS Paris BNF lat. 13781, precedes the *Quaestio de adventu Christi* in Assisi Bibl. Communale MS 172, fols. 189r–192r, and is discussed in the *Postilla litteralis* on 2 Kings 7:15 and 22:51. There must have been a larger number of questions discussed during the disputation, but no one has discovered them to date.

61. Pelster, "*Quodlibeta* und *Quaestiones* des Nikolaus von Lyra," 951–73 and "Nikolaus von Lyra und seine quaestio de usu paupere," *AFH* 46 (1953): 211–50. The texts of the three quodlibeta are preserved anonymously in BAV MS Vat. lat. 982. The first quodlibet, again anonymous, is also found in MS Florence Laurentiana Cod. 3 Plut. 31 dextra (Sancta Croce). The question on the coming of Antichrist has been partially edited in Josep Perarnau, "Guiu Terrena Critica Arnau de Vilanova," *Arxiu de Textos Catalans Antics* 7/8 (1988–89): 221–22. The attribution is problematic; Pelster writes that since the author of the quodlibeta debated the questions in Florence, we must assume that Nicholas spent some time teaching there. However, there is absolutely no evidence to indicate that Nicholas ever went to Florence, and he never mentions the region in his *Postilla litteralis*, whereas he frequently refers to places and events that took place in his native Normandy and his later city of residence, Paris. Rega Wood and Philip Krey have shown that the question on *usus*

pauper is very much at odds with Nicholas's position in his *Postilla litteralis*, so much so that they question whether the same person could have written the two works, even allowing for an evolution of thought over the years. Krey comes to the conclusion (with which I would agree) that, for the present, the quodlibeta should still be considered anonymous. For a discussion of Pelster's thesis and the problems inherent in it, see Rega Wood, "Church and Scripture in Franciscan Gospel Commentaries" (Ph.D. diss., Cornell University, 1975); and Philip Krey, "Nicholas of Lyra: Apocalypse Commentary as Historiography" (Ph.D. diss., University of Chicago, 1990), 14–16, 37–47.

62. See Chapter 2 for a probable chronology of Nicholas's early exegetical work.

63. Wolfgang Bunte, in *Rabbinische Traditionen bei Nikolaus von Lyra: Ein Beitrag zur Schriftauslegung des Spätmittelalters,* Judentum und Umwelt 58 (Berlin: Lang, 1994), provides a valuable listing of rabbinic texts cited in Lyra's *Postilla litteralis*. It should be noted, however, that Bunte lists only those texts mentioned specifically by name or author and that he does not distinguish between Nicholas's own references and those of Paul of Burgos in the *Additiones* to Nicholas's *Postilla*.

64. Herman Hailperin, *Rashi and the Christian Scholars* (Pittsburgh: University of Pittsburgh Press, 1963). On the illustration of Rashi's commentary and possible links with Nicholas's own illustrations, see Mayer I. Gruber, "What Happened to Rashi's Pictures?" *Bodleian Library Record* 14 (1992), 111–24; Bernice Kaczynski, "Illustrations of Tabernacle and Temple Implements in the *Postilla in Testamentum Vetus* of Nicolaus de Lyra," *Yale University Library Gazette* 48, no. 1 (1973):1–11; and Helen Rosenau, "The Architecture of Nicolaus de Lyra's Temple Illustrations and the Jewish Tradition," *Journal of Jewish Studies* 25 (1974): 294–304. Nicholas generally illustrated the same places in the text as Rashi seems to have done.

65. *Peshat* is the plain or literal sense, while *derash* might best be described as an applied, homiletic, or interpretative sense.

66. Gilbert Dahan places the work in the context of medieval Bible criticism (*critique du texte biblique*) and the work of Bible correction in *L'exégèse chrétienne de la Bible en Occident médiéval, XIIe-XIVe siècle* (Paris: Cerf, 1999), 187. Certainly Nicholas shares many of the correctors' concerns and methods, but it is important to distinguish between the scope of the correctors in fixing the Latin text and Nicholas's incorporation of this work as part of his broader exegetical efforts.

Chapter 1. Medieval Christian Use of Hebrew and Postbiblical Jewish Texts

1. An earlier version of portions of this chapter appeared as "Nicholas of Lyra and Franciscan Interest in Hebrew Scholarship," in *Nicholas of Lyra: The Senses of Scripture,* ed. Philip Krey and Lesley Smith (Leiden: Brill, 2000), 289–311; reprinted by permission.

2. *The Cambridge History of the Bible,* vol. 2; Adam Kamesar, *Jerome, Greek Scholarship, and the Hebrew Bible* (Oxford: Clarendon Press, 1993); Dennis Brown, *Vir Trilinguis: A Study in the Biblical Exegesis of Saint Jerome* (Kampen: Kok, 1992).

3. Beryl Smalley, *Study of the Bible in the Middle Ages*, 3rd ed. (Oxford: Blackwell, 1983), 1–36.

4. On the relationship between the emergence of prose narrative and a new interest in the literal sense in both Christian and Jewish circles in northern France, see Michael Signer, "Peshat, Sensus Literalis, and Sequential Narrative: Jewish Exegesis and the School of St. Victor in the Twelfth-Century," in *The Frank Talmage Memorial Volume*, ed. Barry Walfish (Haifa: Haifa University Press; Hanover, N.H.: University Press of New England, 1993), 203–16. The relationship between the new learning in the emerging schools and a new emphasis on literal exegesis is made plain in Hugh of St. Victor's *Didascalicon*, available in both a critical Latin edition and an English translation: Charles Henry Buttimer, ed., *Hugonis de Sancto Victore Didascalicon de studio legendi: A Critical Text*, Studies in Medieval and Renaissance Latin, 10 (Washington, D.C.: Catholic University Press, 1939); Jerome Taylor, ed. and trans., *Didascalicon: A Medieval Guide to the Arts* (New York: Columbia University Press, 1961).

5. Beryl Smalley has probably done more than anyone else to bring about an awareness of medieval Christian Hebraism and the use of Jewish tradition in medieval Christian scholarship. Relevant articles are too numerous to mention here, but references to several are included in *Study of the Bible in the Middle Ages*. The third edition contains a helpful bibliographical essay on modern scholarship up to 1983. Some of the earlier scholars who laid the groundwork for the study of Christian Hebraism include Samuel Berger, *Quam notitiam linguae Hebraicae habuerint Christiani Medii Aevi temporibus in Gallia* (Nancy: Typis Berger-Levrault et sociorum, 1893); and Berthold Altaner, "Zur Kenntnis des Hebräischen im Mittelalter," *Biblische Zeitschrift* 21 (1938): 288–308. On the influence of Rabbi Solomon ben Isaac of Troyes (Rashi, d. 1105) particularly, see Herman Hailperin, *Rashi and the Christian Scholars* (Pittsburgh: University of Pittsburgh Press, 1963).

6. Smalley, *Study of the Bible*, 83–106. For a thorough discussion of Hugh's understanding of Judaism and rabbinic tradition, see Rebecca Moore, *Jews and Christians in the Life and Thought of Hugh of St. Victor* (Atlanta: Scholars Press, 1998).

7. Smalley, *Study of the Bible*, 112–85. Also see the introduction by Michael Signer to his edited volume of Andreas de Sancto Victore, *Expositionem in Ezechielem: Andreas de Sancto Victore Opera* 6, CCCM 53E (Turnhout: Brepols, 1991).

8. Raphael Loewe, "Herbert of Bosham's Commentary on Jerome's Hebrew Psalter: A Preliminary Investigation into Its Sources," *Biblica* 34 (1953): 44–77, 159–92, 275–98.

9. See the brief discussions of Herbert in Smalley, *Study of the Bible*, 186–95 and Aryeh Graboïs, "The Hebraica Veritas and Jewish-Christian Intellectual Relations in the Twelfth Century," *Speculum* 50 (1975): 630–31. Two recent studies focus on Herbert of Bosham's Psalms commentary: Deborah Goodwin, *"Take Hold of the Robe of a Jew": Herbert of Bosham's Christian Hebraism* (Leiden: Brill, 2006); and Eva de Visscher, "The Jewish-Christian Dialogue in Twelfth-Century Western Europe: The Hebrew and Latin Sources of Bosham's Commentary on the Psalms" (Ph.D. diss., University of Leeds, 2003).

10. Smalley, *Study of the Bible*, 196–263.

11. Gilbert Dahan, *L'exégèse chrétienne de la Bible en Occident médiéval: XIIe-XIVe siècle* (Paris, 1999), 91–108; *Les intellectuels chrétiens et les juifs au Moyen Age: Polémique et relations culturelles entre chrétiens et juifs en occident du XIIe au XIVe siècles* (Paris: Cerf, 1990), 298–99; Dahan, "Les interprétations juives dans les commentaires du Pentateuque de Pierre la Chantre," in *The Bible in the Medieval World: Essays in Memory of Beryl Smalley*, ed. Katherine Walsh and Diana Wood. *Studies in Church History, Subsidia 4* (Oxford: Blackwell, 1985), 131–55; Dahan, "Exégèse et polémique dans les commentaires de la Genèse d'Étienne Langton," in *Les juifs au regard de l'histoire: Mélanges en l'honneur de Bernhard Blumenkranz* (Paris: Picard, 1985), 129–48. Smalley, citing a *reportatio* of Langton's commentary on Kings and one of the minor prophets, concluded that Langton did consult with learned Jews. Smalley, *Study of the Bible*, 235–36. Dahan, on the basis of his study of Langton's commentary on Genesis, concluded on the contrary that Langton not only knew no Hebrew but also did not engage such help. According to Dahan, the citations of Jewish opinion in the Genesis commentary came mainly from Peter the Chanter and Peter Comestor. Dahan, "Exégèse et polémique," 140–41. On the "biblical moral school," see John W. Baldwin, *Masters, Princes, and Merchants: The Social Views of Peter the Chanter and His Circle* (Princeton, N.J.: Princeton University Press, 1970).

12. Smalley, *Study of the Bible*, 235; Raphael Loewe, "Alexander Neckam's Knowledge of Hebrew," *Medieval and Renaissance Studies* 4 (1958), 17–34.

13. Smalley, *Study of the Bible*, 264ff., *English Friars and Antiquity in the Early Fourteenth Century* (Oxford: Blackwell, 1960). On language study as part of textual criticism of the Bible, see Dahan, *L'exégèse chrétienne*, 206–17. On Nicholas of Lyra's role as Hebrew "authority," see Chapter 5.

14. See Anna Sapir Abulafia, *Christians and Jews in Dispute: Disputational Literature and the Rise of Anti-Judaism in the West (c. 1000–1150)*, Variorum Collected Studies Series, 621 (Aldershot, Hampshire: Variorum, 1998); and Gilbert Dahan, *La Polémique chrétienne contre le judaïsme au Moyen Age* (Paris: Albin Michel, 1991).

15. See John Tolan, *Petrus Alfonsi and His Medieval Readers* (Gainesville: University Press of Florida, 1993).

16. See the foundational work by Amos Funkenstein in "Changes in the Patterns of Christian Anti-Jewish Polemic in the Twelfth Century" (Hebrew), *Zion* 33 (1968), and in "Basic Types of Christian Anti-Jewish Polemics in the Later Middle Ages," *Viator* 2 (1971): 373–82. Also David Berger, ed., *The Jewish-Christian Debate in the High Middle Ages: A Critical Edition of the Nizzahon Vetus with an Introduction, Translation, and Commentary*, Judaica, Texts and Translations 4 (Philadelphia: Jewish Publication Society of America, 1979); Berger, "Mission to the Jews and Jewish-Christian Contacts in the Polemical Literature of the High Middle Ages," *American Historical Review* 91 (June 1986): 576–91; Graboïs, "Hebraica Veritas," 613–34; and Gilbert Dahan, *Intellectuels chrétiens et les juifs*.

17. See especially Jeremy Cohen, "Scholarship and Intolerance in the Medieval Academy," *American Historical Review* 91 (1986): 592–613; Alexander Patschovsky, "Der 'Talmudjude': Vom mittelalterlichen Ursprung eines neuzeitlichen Themas," in *Juden in der christlichen Umwelt während des späten Mittelalters*, ed. Alfred Haverkamp and Franz-Josef Ziwes (Berlin: Duncker & Humblot, 1992), 13–27; and

Gilbert Dahan, "Un dossier latin de textes de Rashi autour de la controverse de 1240," *Revue des études juives* 151 (1992): 321–336. On the Talmud trial itself, see Judah M. Rosenthal, "The Talmud on Trial: The Disputation at Paris in the Year 1240," *Jewish Quarterly Review* 47 (1956–57): 58–76, 145–69; Joel Rembaum, "The Talmud and the Popes: Reflections on the Talmud Trials of the 1240s," *Viator* 13 (1982): 203–23; and Cohen, *Friars and the Jews*, 60ff.

18. Patschovsky, "Der 'Talmudjude,'" 18–19.

19. Cohen, *Friars and the Jews*, 103–8; Robert Chazan, *Daggers of Faith: Thirteenth-Century Christian Missionizing and Jewish Response* (Berkeley: University of California Press, 1989).

20. See n. 19 of the Introduction above and Robert Chazan, *Barcelona and Beyond: The Disputation of 1263 and Its Aftermath* (Berkeley: University of California Press, 1992).

21. On the differences between the two works, see Robles Sierra's introduction to *Capistrum Iudaeorum*; and Cohen, *Friars and the Jews*, 131–56.

22. Raphael Loewe and Judith Olszowy-Schlanger have both addressed the lack of interest in grammar among the Christian Hebraists of England. Although significant numbers of Christians knew enough Hebrew to utilize it independently in Bible study, they seem not to have dedicated themselves to a rigorous study of the language itself. Loewe, "The Medieval Christian Hebraists of England: The *Superscriptio Lincolniensis*," *Hebrew Union College Annual* 28 (1957): 205–52; Olszowy-Schlanger, *Les manuscrits hébreux dans l'Angleterre médiévale: étude historique et paléographique*, Collection de la revue des études juives 29 (Paris: Peeters, 2003).

23. On Dominican language *studia*, see André Berthier, "Les écoles de langues orientales fondées au XIIIe siècle par les Dominicains en Espagne et en Afrique," *Revue africaine* 73 (1932): 84–102, and "Un maître orientaliste du XIIIe siècle: Raymond Martin O.P.," *Archivum Fratrum Praedicatorum* 6 (1936): 267–311; Berthold Altaner, "Die Fremdsprachliche Ausbildung der Dominikanermissionare während des 13. und 14. Jahrhunderts," *Zeitschrift für Missionswissenschaft* 23 (1933): 233–41; and Chazan, *Daggers of Faith*.

24. Charles Singer, "Hebrew Scholarship in the Middle Ages Among Latin Christians," in *The Legacy of Israel*, ed. Edwyn R. Bevan and Charles Singer (Oxford: Clarendon Press, 1927), 283–314.

25. For an extensive consideration of Franciscan relationship to historical perspective, see Bert Roest, "Reading the Book of History: Intellectual Contexts and Educational Functions of Franciscan Historiography 1226–1350" (Ph.D. diss., Rijksuniversiteit Groningen, 1996).

26. *Monumenta ordinis fratrum praedicatorum historica* (Rome, 1899), 4:34, 38. The relevant passages are discussed in Herbert Stadler, "Textual and Literary Criticism and Hebrew Learning in English Old Testament Scholarship, as Exhibited by Nicholas Trevet's *Expositio litteralis Psalterii* and by MS Corpus Christi College (Oxford) 11" (master's thesis, Corpus Christi College, Oxford, 1989), 10.

27. The English Dominican Nicholas Trevet stands out as a notable exception. See Stadler, cited in n. 26. Theobald de Sézanne, O.P. was also unusual in that he lent his considerable skill in Hebrew not only to anti-Jewish polemic (he translated into Latin allegedly offensive passages from the Talmud and portions of Rashi's

commentaries following the Paris Talmud trial of 1240) but also to biblical scholarship, serving as an adviser on the *Hebraica veritas* for Hugh of St. Cher's *correctorium*. Theobald was not, however, an exegete himself, nor did Hugh make much use of Theobald's Hebraic knowledge in the composition of his school's *Postilla super totam Bibliam*.

28. For a chronology of Grosseteste's career, see Richard W. Southern, *Robert Grosseteste: The Growth of an English Mind in Medieval Europe* (Oxford: Clarendon Press, 1986); and James McEvoy, *Robert Grosseteste* (Oxford: Oxford University Press, 2000).

29. Shortly after Grosseteste became bishop, he asked the Franciscan Adam Marsh to arrange for some Franciscans to be attached to his household. See *Roberti Grosseteste Episcopi quondam Lincolniensis Epistolae*, Rolls Series 25, ed. Henry Richards Luard (London: Longman, 1861), 69–71. On the legacy of Grosseteste's library to the Oxford Franciscans, see Southern, *Robert Grosseteste*, 27.

30. See Southern, *Robert Grosseteste*, 74–75, 112, 170–71. This interpretation of Grosseteste's actions is based on a number of different letters from Grosseteste's own hand, published by Henry Luard in the work cited in n. 29. It is ironic that Jordan's preaching effectively pushed Grosseteste into the arms of the Franciscans; the message of setting spiritual priorities evidently came through more clearly than any specifically Dominican ideal. In any case, Grosseteste maintained strong ties of friendship with a number of Dominicans, including Jordan, even while working with the English Franciscans. On Grosseteste's relationship with both mendicant orders, see McEvoy, *Robert Grosseteste*, 51–61.

31. Recent and ongoing work by Judith Olszowy-Schlanger and a team of researchers at the Institut de Recherches et d'Histoires des Textes in Paris promises to substantially extend our knowledge of these thirteenth-century translation projects. See Olszowy-Schlanger, *Les manuscrits hébreux*.

32. According to Southern, it was Grosseteste's natural science background that led him to his approach to theology. Just as the careful observation of nature leads to scientific understanding, a careful observation of the Bible leads to theological understanding. Southern, *Robert Grosseteste*, 173. Beryl Smalley also discusses Grosseteste's principles of instruction in *Study of the Bible*, 276–77.

33. In this translation, the Latin equivalents appear directly above each line of the Hebrew psalm.

34. Grosseteste's experience with the nature of scientific evidence may also have led to his belief that Latin translations were inferior to the original Greek and Hebrew versions of the Bible, as translations were one step removed from the original word of God. See Southern, *Robert Grosseteste*, 182; and Beryl Smalley, "Hebrew Scholarship Among Christians in Thirteenth-Century England, as Illustrated by Some Hebrew-Latin Psalters," in *Lectiones in Vetere Testamento et in Rebus Judaicis* 6 (London: Shapiro, Valentine, 1939), 1–18. This same group of psalters was also studied by Raphael Loewe in "The Medieval Christian Hebraists of England," 205–52 and in "Latin *Superscriptio* Manuscripts on Portions of the Hebrew Bible Other Than the Psalter," *Journal of Jewish Studies* 9 (1958): 63–71; and, most recently, Olszowy-Schlanger, *Les manuscrits hébreux*.

35. Beryl Smalley, "The Biblical Scholar," in *Robert Grosseteste, Scholar and Bishop*, ed. Daniel A. P. Callus (Oxford: Clarendon Press, 1955), 84–86.

36. Southern, *Robert Grosseteste*, 296.

37. Compare, for example, Roger Marston's question on the advent of Christ, published in G. F. Etzkorn and I. C. Brady, eds., *Fr. Rogeri Marston: Quodlibeta Quatuor*, Bibliotheca Franciscana Scholastica Medii Aevi 26 (1968), 104–45, with Robert Grosseteste's *De cessatione legalium*, ed. Richard C. Dales and Edward B. King (London: Oxford University Press, 1986). Etzkorn and Brady identify numerous additional references to Grosseteste as "Commentator Lincolniensis" or "Domini Lincolniensis" in his other quodlibeta in the same volume.

38. Andrew G. Little, "The Franciscan School at Oxford in the Thirteenth Century," *AFH* 19 (1926), 808.

39. Daniel A. P. Callus, "Robert Grosseteste as Scholar," in Callus, ed., *Robert Grosseteste, Scholar and Bishop* (Oxford: Clarendon Press, 1955), 68. Concerning the first of these three things, "a preference for Augustinian-Platonism," one might argue that this sets off the Franciscans in contrast to the Dominicans and seculars more than it does Oxford and Paris.

40. Adam joined the Franciscan order at Worcester in 1232 or 1233 and was sent almost immediately back to Oxford, where he studied theology under Grosseteste, who was lector to the Franciscans until 1235. See Little, "Franciscan School at Oxford," 833–34.

41. Adam Marsh's correspondence was edited by J. S. Brewer in *Monumenta Franciscana* 1 (London, 1858–82), 77–489.

42. Little, "Franciscan School at Oxford," 809.

43. "Brother Hugh [of Digne]'s fourth friend was Brother Adam March, a Friar Minor and another great scholar, and, like Grosseteste, he was also famous in England and wrote many books." Joseph L. Baird, Giuseppe Baglivi, and John Robert Kane, ed., *The Chronicle of Salimbene de Adam* (Binghamton, N.Y.: Medieval and Renaissance Texts and Studies, 1986), 225. "[Brother Stephen] carried with him a fine little treatise written by Adam Marsh, whose lecture on Genesis I heard him deliver." Baird, Baglivi, and Kane, *Chronicle of Salimbene*, 296.

44. Southern, *Robert Grosseteste*, 283.

45. Although Bacon never incepted as a master in theology, he did study theology in Paris and had very definite views concerning how theology ought to be taught. See Roger Bacon, *Opus maius*, ed. John Henry Bridges, 3 vols. (Oxford: Clarendon Press, 1897–1900. Reprint Frankfurt, 1964); *Opus minus, Opus tertium,* and *Compendium studii philosophici*, in *Opera quaedam hactenus inedita*, ed. John Sherren Brewer, Rolls Series, vol. 15 (London: Longman, 1859).

46. Katherine Tachau raised this possibility during discussion at a session of the International Medieval Congress at Kalamazoo, Michigan in May 1996. On Bacon's apocalypticism, see Mark Abate, "Roger Bacon and the Rage of Antichrist: The Apocalypse of a Thirteenth-Century Natural Philosopher" (Ph.D. diss., Boston University, 2000).

47. Bacon thought that the Crusades were misguided and that the Church should instead have been putting its energy into converting infidels through preach-

ing. On Bacon's philosophy of mission, see E. Randolph Daniel, *The Franciscan Concept of Mission* (Lexington: University Press of Kentucky, 1975), 59–66.

48. *The Greek Grammar of Roger Bacon and a Fragment of His Hebrew Grammar*, ed. Edmond Nolan and Samuel A. Hirsch (Cambridge: Cambridge University Press, 1902), 199–201.

49. Heinrich Denifle, "Die Handschriften der Bibel-Correctorien des 13. Jahrhunderts," in *Archiv für Literatur- und Kirchengeschichte des Mittelalters*, 7 vols. (Berlin: Weidmannsche Buchhandlung, 1885–1900), 4:277–78.

50. Earlier attempts to correct the text of the Bible by monks such as Stephen Harding and Nicholas Maniacoria in the twelfth century were isolated and rare, in contrast to the systematic efforts of the thirteenth century. A summary of twelfth-century corrections can be found in Denifle, "Handschriften der Bibel-Correctorien," 266–76.

51. A summary of Bacon's thought on the Paris Bible and the *correctoria* (which is spread throughout his *Opus maius*, *Opus minus*, *Opus tertium*, and *Compendium studii philosophiae*) can be found in Smalley, *Study of the Bible*, 331–36.

52. Denifle, "Handschriften der Bibel-Correctorien," 545. Berger, *Quam notitiam*, 32–36.

53. Hailperin, *Rashi and the Christian Scholars*, 131–33.

54. Andrew G. Little, *The Grey Friars in Oxford* (Oxford: Clarendon Press, 1892), 215–16.

55. A. B. Emden, *A Biographical Register of the University of Oxford to A.D. 1500* (Oxford: Clarendon Press, 1959), 3:562.

56. Ephrem Longpré, "Guillaume de la Mare," in *Dictionnaire de théologie catholique* (Paris: Letouzey et Ané, 1925), 8: 2467–70.

57. Denifle, "Handschriften der Bibel-Correctorien," 477; Berger, *Quam notitiam*, 46–48.

58. Berger, *Quam notitiam*, 46.

59. Roger Bacon, *Opus tertium*, 88, 94. Bacon, after complaining that irresponsible corrections of the Bible have left the Paris version even more corrupt than before the efforts, goes on to mention one wise man who has applied linguistic tools to achieve a more legitimate correction of the text.

60. Arduin Kleinhans, "De Studio sacrae scripturae in ordine fratrum minorum saeculo XIII," *Antonianum* 7 (1932): 435. Denifle thought that Bacon was referring to William de la Mare: see "Handschriften der Bibel-Correctorien," 298, 545. But William did not incept at Paris until around 1268 and was too young to have spent the kind of time in study that Bacon describes.

61. Southern, *Robert Grosseteste*, 49–53.

62. Arthur Allgeier, "Eine unbekannte mittelalterliche Psalmenübersetzung," *Römische Quartalschrift* 37 (1939): 437–39. The manuscript, now British Library Cod. Egerton 2908, is a small, hand-sized Bible and differs from other Latin Bibles only in the Book of Psalms, which Allgeier demonstrates to be a new translation from the Hebrew text. A list of saints at the back of the manuscript points to an Italian Franciscan origin.

63. Even that which was clearly midrashic was commonly understood to per-

tain to the literal sense of Scripture because it did not address the Christian truth embedded in the spiritual/allegorical sense.

64. Sarah Kamin and Avrom Saltman, ed., *Secundum Salomonem: A Thirteenth-Century Latin Commentary on the Song of Solomon* (Ramat Gan: Bar-Ilan University Press, 1989). Michael Signer sees the anonymous commentary as a clear continuation of the Victorine approach to literal exegesis in which the letter of the Bible serves as "both the lexical meaning of the word and the *historia* . . . both the *res* and the *res gestae*." "Thirteenth-Century Christian Hebraism: The *Expositio* on Canticles in MS Vat. lat. 1053," in *Approaches to Judaism in Medieval Times*, vol. 3, ed. David R. Blumenthal (Atlanta: Scholars Press,1988), 92–93. The commentary is also discussed by Signer in the introduction to *Expositionem in Ezechielem*, xlviii–li; Smalley, *Study of the Bible*, 352–55; and Mark Zier, introduction to *Expositio super Danielem: Andreae de Sancto Victore Opera 7*, CCCM 53F (Turnhout: Brepols, 1990), ix–xii. Smalley and Zier have a slight disagreement as to the dating of the commentary; Zier dates it to the middle of the thirteenth century, while Smalley places it much closer to Nicholas of Lyra's time, around 1300.

65. This information comes to us from James of Fabriano, O.F.M., who composed a table of contents for the volume and indicated the manuscript's origins. See Zier, introduction to *Expositio super Danielem*, ix–x; Signer, introduction to *Expositionem in Ezechielem*, xlviii; Smalley, *Study of the Bible*, 176; and Kamin and Saltman, *Secundum Salomonem*, 47–48. Kamin and Saltman note that there are two Song of Songs commentaries in the manuscript, both in a different hand from that in the Andrew of St. Victor material. They suggest that the anonymous commentary was added to round out the historical treatment of other biblical books. The manuscript also contains an excerpt from Bernard of Clairvaux's much less problematic Sermons on the Song of Songs. *Secundum Salomonem*, 47–48.

66. See Franz Ehrle, "Petrus Johannis Olivi, sein Leben und seine Schriften," in *Archiv für Literatur- und Kirchengeschichte des Mittelalters* (Berlin: Weidmannsche Buchhandlung, 1885–1900), 3: 416.

67. Glorieux, *Répertoire des maîtres en théologie de Paris au XIIIᵉ siècle* (Paris: Vrin, 1933–34), 2:326.

68. William Brito, *Summa Britonis sive Guillelmi Britonis Expositiones vocabulorum Biblie*, 2 vols., ed. Lloyd W. Daley and Bernardine A. Daley (Padua: Antenoreis, 1975). For a summary of the work and William's Latin sources, see Dahan, *Intellectuels chrétiens et les juifs*, 243–44.

69. Decima Douie, *Archbishop Pecham* (Oxford: Clarendon Press, 1952), 276.

70. In addition to the extracts from the Talmud, Theobald assembled extracts from Rashi's Bible commentary under the title *De glossis Salomonis Trecensis*. Dahan, "Un dossier Latin de textes de Rashi."

71. In spite of its polemical tone, Peter Alfonse's *Dialogi contra Iudaeos* provided Christian scholars with a wealth of information on Jewish texts. On the Christian use of the *Dialogi* as a source of information on Jewish exegesis, see Tolan, *Petrus Alfonsi*.

72. In addition to the psalters mentioned above, Samuel Berger describes thirteenth-century English manuscripts containing new Hebrew-Latin versions of

the Pentateuch, Joshua, Judges, Song of Songs, Ecclesiastes, Samuel, and Esther. Berger, *Quam notitiam*, 49–53.

73. See Richard W. Southern, "The Place of England in the Twelfth-Century Renaissance," in *Medieval Humanism and Other Studies* (Oxford: Blackwell, 1970), 158–80.

74. Southern, "Place of England," 160–62.

75. Southern, "Place of England," 164–71.

76. William J. Courtenay, *Schools and Scholars in Fourteenth-Century England* (Princeton, N.J.: Princeton University Press, 1987), 147, 152–53.

77. "These two [Robert Grosseteste and Adam Marsh] were also close friends of the Englishman, Master Alexander, a Friar Minor, who was professor at the University of Paris." *Chronicle of Salimbene*, 225.

78. It should be noted that in Paris the Franciscans readily adapted to the new method of teaching theology. In fact, Alexander of Hales (c. 1186–1245), who joined the Franciscan order in 1236, was the first scholar to pursue this approach to the teaching of theology.

79. A discussion of the conflict can be found in Peter Raedts, *Richard Rufus of Cornwall and the Tradition of Oxford Theology* (Oxford: Clarendon Press, 1987); Stephen F. Brown, "Richard Fishacre on the Need for 'Philosophy,'" in *A Straight Path: Studies in Medieval Philosophy and Culture: Essays in Honor of Arthur Hyman*, ed. Ruth Link-Salinger (Washington, D.C.: Catholic University of America Press, 1988), 23–36; and, in brief, McEvoy, *Robert Grosseteste*, 160–71.

80. Brown, "Richard Fishacre," 23.

81. Brown, "Richard Fishacre," 26–28.

82. Brown, "Richard Fishacre," 33.

83. Raedts, *Richard Rufus of Cornwall*, 25–26.

84. "Et optime novi pessimum et stultissimum istorum errorum [auctorem], qui vocatus est Ricardus Cornubiensis . . . reprobatus Parisius propter errores, quos invenerat [et] promulgaverat . . ." Roger Bacon, *Compendium studii theologiae*, ed. Hastings Rashdall, British Society of Franciscan Studies, 3 (Aberdeen: Typis Academicis, 1911), 52–53.

85. Grosseteste wrote a letter to the Oxford regent masters in theology in the mid-1240s criticizing their teaching methods and warning them to use only the books of the Bible in their lectures. See Raedts, *Richard Rufus of Cornwall*, 123, 139.

86. Raedts, *Richard Rufus of Cornwall*, 141.

87. On the abbreviation of Bonaventure's *Sentences*, see Raedts, 40–63. On the question of Richard's true thoughts concerning the place of the *Sentences* in theology, see 143, 150–51.

88. On the condemnations of 1270 and 1277 and Franciscan-Augustinianism vs. Dominican-Aristotelianism, see John Wippel, "The Condemnations of 1270 and 1277 at Paris," *Journal of Medieval and Renaissance Studies* 7 (Fall 1977), 169–201. On the controversy surrounding Aquinas's work specifically, see Franz Ehrle, "Der Kampf um die Lehre des hl. Thomas von Aquin," *Zeitschrift für katholische Theologie* 37 (1913): 266–318; and Pierre F. Mandonnet, "Premiers travaux de polémique thomiste," *Revue des sciences philosophiques et théologique* 7 (1913): 46–70, 245–62. William de la Mare wrote his *Correctorium fratris Thomae* around 1278 or 1279, ex-

amining 118 articles from Thomas Aquinas's work and countering them primarily with the opinions of Bonaventure. The work was officially adopted by the Franciscan general chapter meeting at Strasbourg in 1282, which ordered that the *Summa* of Aquinas not be taught without the addition of William's *correctorium*. Longpré, "Guillaume de la Mare," 2467–70. Roger Marston attacked Aquinas in a series of questions disputed during his Oxford regency, sometime between 1280 and 1284. See Douie, *Archbishop Pecham*, 284–85. While some scholars in recent years have questioned the very notion of an "Augustinian School," others insist that there are enough lines of connection between associated thinkers to justify the construct. For an account of the scholarly debate, see Bonnie Kent, *Virtues of the Will: The Transformation of Ethics in the Late Thirteenth Century* (Washington, D.C.: Catholic University of America Press, 1995), 10–19, 246–54; and Steven P. Marrone, *The Light of Thy Countenance: Science and Knowledge of God in the Thirteenth Century* (Leiden: Brill, 2001), 1–24, 569–73.

89. For a summary of John Pecham's place in the controversy over Thomistic Aristotelianism in the latter half of the thirteenth century, see Douie, *Archbishop Pecham*, 4–24.

90. Kent, *Virtues of the Will*, 246.

91. Roest, "Reading the Book of History," 164.

92. Southern, *Robert Grosseteste*, 283.

93. "Brother Hugh's third friend was Robert Grosseteste, bishop of Lincoln, one of the greatest scholars in the world." *Chronicle of Salimbene de Adam*, 225.

94. Bernard McGinn, "Bonaventure's Apocalyptic Theology of History," in *Visions of the End: Apocalyptic Traditions in the Middle Ages* (New York: Columbia University Press, 1979), 196–202, 196–97. See also Daniel, *Franciscan Concept of Mission*, 31–32. Bonnie Kent examines Bonaventure's attitude toward Aristotle as expressed in the *Hexaemeron* in *Virtues of the Will*, 46–59.

95. Daniel, *Franciscan Concept of Mission*, 33–35.

96. Roest, "Reading the Book of History," 164.

97. David Burr, *Olivi's Peaceable Kingdom: A Reading of the Apocalypse Commentary* (Philadelphia: University of Pennsylvania Press, 1993), 255.

98. By the time Nicholas reached Paris in 1301 or so, the resistance to the Thomistic Aristotelian synthesis in theology had been largely resolved. While continuing the orientation toward Augustinian theology dominant in Franciscan circles a generation earlier, Nicholas, like the rest of the so-called Augustinian school, also utilized the work of Aristotle and Aquinas extensively.

99. By the early fourteenth century, advanced theology students at Paris were spending two years teaching the Bible as a *baccalaureus cursus* or *biblicus*, one year as a *baccalaureus sententiarius* lecturing on the *Sentences*, and four years as a *baccalaureus formatus*, taking part in disputations and other university functions. After this the bachelor received his license to teach and could incept as a master. See William Courtenay, "The Bible in the Fourteenth Century: Some Observations," *Church History* 54 (1985) 176–87, and John Marenbon, *Later Medieval Philosophy (1150–1350): An Introduction* (London: Routledge & K. Paul, 1987), 20–24.

100. See Chapter 4.

101. See Mark Zier, "Nicholas of Lyra on the Book of Daniel," in *Nicholas of*

Lyra: The Senses of Scripture, ed. Philip Krey and Leslie Smith (Leiden: Brill, 2000), 173–93. A further connection between the two men is suggested by Nicholas's Song of Songs commentary, which was clearly influenced by the Latin Song of Songs translation owned by the cardinal. See Mary Dove, "Nicholas of Lyra and the Literal Senses of the Song of Songs," in Krey and Smith, *Nicholas of Lyra*, 129–46.

102. Little attention has been paid to the influence of Roger Bacon on Nicholas of Lyra, but evidence suggests that a close comparison of their writings would be fruitful in this regard. In the *Postilla litteralis* on Hebrews 1:5, Nicholas borrows Roger Bacon's language on signs when he employs the example of the sign of a circle on a tavern to explain the double literal sense of Scripture. The circle sign on a tavern as a signifier (or false signifier) of wine is used by Roger Bacon in his *De signis* as well as in the *Compendium studii theologiae*. See K. M. Fredborg, Lauge Nielsen, and Jan Pinborg, "An Unedited Part of Roger Bacon's *Opus maius*: *De signis*," *Traditio* 34 (1978): 128 and Roger Bacon, *Compendium of the Study of Theology*, ed. and trans., Thomas Maloney (Leiden: Brill, 1988) 101–5. In his *Quaestio de adventu Christi* and at various points in the *Postilla litteralis*, including the prologue, Nicholas, perhaps prompted by Bacon, repeats a concern voiced by early Christian scholars that the Jews intentionally provided Christians with corrupt texts in order to mislead them. See Chapter 4.

103. Though Jews were officially readmitted to royal lands in France for brief periods after the expulsion of 1306, they were specifically prohibited from bringing books of the Talmud (and any other Jewish books deemed "blasphemous" by Christian authorities) back with them. William Chester Jordan suggests that the terms of readmission assured that few would take advantage of it. "Home Again: The Jews in the Kingdom of France, 1315–1322," in *The Stranger in Medieval Society*, ed. F. R. P. Akehurst and Stephanie Cain Van D'Elden (Minneapolis: University of Minnesota Press, 1997), 27–45.

104. Scholars have long noted the tendency of later medieval exegetes to incorporate spiritual interpretations within literal exegesis. Beryl Smalley located the phenomenon in Thomas Aquinas's application of Aristotelian notions of causality to biblical authorship in *Study of the Bible*, 292–308. Christopher Ocker, in a convincing reassessment of literal exegesis during this period, argues that the blurring of literal and spiritual senses resulted from a shift in emphasis from natural signification in Victorine exegesis to a new emphasis on verbal signification in the later thirteenth century. *Biblical Poetics Before Humanism and Reformation* (Cambridge: Cambridge University Press, 2002), 31–48.

105. See Philip Krey, "Many Readers But Few Followers: The Fate of Nicholas of Lyra's 'Apocalypse Commentary' in the Hands of His Late-Medieval Admirers," *Church History* 64 (1995): 185–201.

Chapter 2. Nicholas of Lyra, O.F.M.: Mediating Hebrew Traditions for a Christian Audience

1. An image in MS Paris BNF lat. 14247, reproduced in Chapter 5, shows Nicholas literally working at the feet of Jerome. The centrality of Nicholas's commentary

for Reformation thinkers has been memorialized in Latin sayings like, "Si Lyra non lyrasset, Luther non saltasset" (If Lyra had not played, Luther would not have danced). Félix Vernet, *Dictionnaire de théologie catholique*, s.v. "Nicholas de Lyre."

2. So widely disseminated was Nicholas's *Postilla litteralis* that hundreds of manuscript copies are still extant in libraries all across Europe, east and west. Philip Krey and Lesley Smith estimate the number of extant manuscripts at eight hundred in Krey and Smith, ed., *Nicholas of Lyra: The Senses of Scripture* (Leiden: Brill, 2000), 16.

3. In addition to the Postilla itself, much exegetical material circulated in his *Quaestio de adventu Christi, Responsio ad quendam Iudaeum, and De differentia nostrae translationis ab Hebraica littera Veteris Testamentis*. On the use of Nicholas as a source for Jewish interpretation, see Chapter 5.

4. "Littera gesta docet; quid credas allegoria; quid agas tropologia; quo tendas anagogia." Nicholas placed this instructive poem, usually credited to John Cassian (360–435), in the prologue to the *Postilla litteralis*. He repeated its instruction at key points in his commentary, as, for example, in his discussion of Paul's allegorical interpretation of Sarah and Hagar in Galatians 4.

5. A. J. Minnis, *Medieval Theory of Authorship* (Philadelphia: University of Pennsylvania Press, 1984).

6. Christopher Ocker, *Biblical Poetics Before Humanism and Reformation* (Cambridge: Cambridge University Press, 2002), 141.

7. Ocker, *Biblical Poetics*, 22.

8. Ocker, *Biblical Poetics*, 216.

9. On Thomas Aquinas's and Bonaventure's understanding of verbal signification and the parabolic literal sense, see Ocker, *Biblical Poetics*, 21–22, 38–43.

10. "Si ego qui generationem ceteris tribuo, etc. Replicatio est cuiusdem sententie ad maiorem affirmationem. Aliqui autem doctores catholici exponunt hoc de eterna generatione filii a patre secundum naturam divinam. Sed hec expositio videtur magis mystica quam litteralis." *Postilla super Isaiam* 66:9.

11. Theresa Gross-Diaz, "What's a Good Soldier to Do? Nicholas of Lyra on the Psalms" in Krey and Smith, *Nicholas of Lyra*, 111–28.

12. Ocker, *Biblical Poetics*, 21–22, 142–44. On Nicholas's use of the parabolic and double literal sense, see the essays by Gross-Diaz, "What's a Good Soldier to Do?"; Mary Dove, "Nicholas of Lyra and the Literal Senses in the Song of Songs"; and Philip Krey, "The Apocalypse Commentary of 1329: Problems in Church History," all in Krey and Smith, eds., *Nicholas of Lyra*.

13. Cf. Thomas Aquinas, *Summa theologia*.

14. On Nicholas's Song of Songs Commentary see Dove, "Literal Senses in the Song of Songs." For a brief comparison of Nicholas of Lyra and Rashi on the Song, see Sarah Kamin, "The Relation of Nicolas de Lyre to Rashi in his Commentary on Song of Songs," in *Jews and Christians Interpret the Bible* (Hebrew) (Jerusalem: Magnes Press, The Hebrew University, 1991), 62–72.

15. Sarah Kamin and Avrom Saltman, ed., *Secundum Salomonem: A Thirteenth-Century Latin Commentary on the Song of Solomon* (Ramat Gan: Bar-Ilan University Press, 1989); Michael Signer "Thirteenth-Century Christian Hebraism: The *Expositio* on Canticles in MS Vat. lat. 1053," in *Approaches to Judaism in Medie-*

val Times, vol. 3, ed. David R. Blumenthal (Atlanta: Scholars Press, 1988), 92–93. See also Chapter 1.

16. "Et hec expositio magis concordat littere quam precedens, utraque tamen potest dici litteralis. Ad cuius evidentiam sciendum quod illud quod est alterius figure necessario est in se res aliquam. Quia quod nihil est non potest aliquid figurare vel significare. Propter quod figura tripliciter potest accipi. Uno modo ut res in se tantum. Alio modo ut figura alterius tantum. Tertio modo ut res in se et figura alterius. Et hic triplex modus invenitur frequenter in sacra scriptura, verbi gratia quod de Salomone dicitur 3 Regum 11, *Depravatum est cor eius per mulieres* etc. Dicitur de eo sensum se tantum et nullo modo ut fuit figura Christi, et sic sensus litteralis est tantum de Salomone. Et illud quod de eo dicitur Psalmus 71 *Ante sole permanet nomen eius*. Non potest intelligi de Salomone sensum se, sed tantum ut fuit figura Christi, propter quod sensus litteralis tantum est de Christo, sicut ibidem fuit plenius declaratum. Istud autem quod dominus dixit de eo 2 Regum 7, *Ego ero illi in patrem, et ipse erit mihi in filium* intelligitur de Salomone sensum se et sensum quod fuit figura Christi, quia fuit filius Dei per adoptionis gloriam saltem in principio regni sui ut patet 2 Regum, et fuit figura Christi que est Dei filius per naturam, quia filiatio perfectior est quam alia. Et sic est ibi duplex sensus litteralis unius, de Salomone ratione filiationis adoptive, alius de Christo ratione filiationis naturalis per illam figurate, et hoc secundo modo inducit apostolus dictam auctoritatem Hebrei 1 ad probandum divinitatem Christi, que probatio non sit per scripturam efficaciter nisi accipiatur in sensu litterali, sicut dicit Augustinus contra Donatistas. Sic autem est in proposto duplex sensus litteralis, et unius est impletus in Silverio Papa et Menna Dei servo, qui fuerunt figura Enoch et Helye, et alius implebitur in Enoch et Helya, cui magis concordat littera ut visum est, et perfectius in eis implebitur propter quod de ipsis est sensus principaliter intentus." *Postilla litteralis super Apocalypsim* 11:11. Philip Krey discusses this passage and the double literal sense extensively in "The Apocalypse Commentary of 1329," and "Nicholas of Lyra: Apocalypse Commentary as Historiography" (Ph.D. diss., University of Chicago, 1990).

17. In *Defining Acts: Drama and the Politics of Interpretation in Medieval England* (Notre Dame, Ind.: University of Notre Dame Press, 2005), Ruth Nisse argues that Nicholas's literal commentary moves so far in the direction of Jewish exegesis as to stand almost outside normative Christian hermeneutics. Ocker notes Nicholas's distinctive understanding of biblical hermeneutics but includes him within the circle of later medieval exegetes influenced by new notions of biblical poetics. Ocker, *Biblical Poetics*, 142–44. By comparing his commentary on Samuel and Kings specifically with the clearly historical twelfth-century commentary of Andrew of St. Victor, Frans van Liere has demonstrated Nicholas's accommodation to later medieval assumptions. "The Literal Sense of the Books of Samuel and Kings: From Andrew of St. Victor to Nicholas of Lyra," in Krey and Smith, *Nicholas of Lyra*, 59–81.

18. On the uses of Nicholas of Lyra in the later Middle Ages, see Chapter 5 and Ocker, *Biblical Poetics*, 179–83.

19. See Nicholas's prologue. I use here an early copy of the text found in BAV Archivio S. Pietro D202 along with Nicholas's *Quaestio de adventu Christi* and *Res-*

ponsio ad quendam Iudaeum. Most copies of the text appear in collections of this sort. See Chapter 5.

20. Eccl. 12:10: "Ac veritate plenos: quia cum veritate litterali continent plures veritates mysticas."

21. "Non tamen intendo omnes sensus mysticos scribere, nec per singula verba discurrere; sed aliqua breviter ordinare, ad que lectores Bibliorum, ac predicatores verbi Dei recurrere poterunt." Prologue to the *Postilla moralis super Bibliam.*

22. Krey and Smith, *Nicholas of Lyra.*

23. Lesley Smith, "The Rewards of Faith: Nicholas of Lyra on Ruth," in Krey and Smith, *Nicholas of Lyra,* 51.

24. Smith, "Rewards of Faith," 54. The most thorough treatment of Nicholas's dependence on Rashi's commentary is still Herman Hailperin, *Rashi and the Christian Scholars* (Pittsburgh: Pittsburgh University Press, 1963), 137–246.

25. Paul of Burgos in his *Additiones* pointed out numerous places where Nicholas drew from Aquinas in his commentary. See also Corinne Patton, "Creation, Fall, and Salvation: Lyra's Commentary on Genesis 1–3"; and Philip Krey, "'The Old Law Prohibits the Hand and Not the Spirit': The Law and the Jews in Nicholas of Lyra's Romans Commentary of 1329," both in Krey and Smith, *Nicholas of Lyra,* 19–43; 251–66; and Yves Delègue, *Les machines du sens: Fragments d'une sémiologie médiévale* (Paris: Editions des Cendres, 1987).

26. Gross-Diaz, "What's A Good Soldier to Do?" 111–28.

27. Rega Wood, "Nicholas of Lyra and Lutheran Views of Ecclesiastical Office," *Journal of Ecclesiastical History* 29, no. 4 (1978): 451–62.

28. Kevin Madigan, "Lyra on the Gospel of Matthew," in Krey and Smith, *Nicholas of Lyra,* 219–21. Michael Signer noted the same tendency in Nicholas's Ezechiel commentary, demonstrating the friar's frequent use of Rashi to challenge patristic interpretations. Signer, "Nicholas of Lyra on the Prophet Ezechiel," 156–157.

29. On Nicholas's understanding of "the Hebrew gloss," see discussion farther on in this chapter.

30. On Rashi's usage of *peshat* and *derash,* see Sarah Kamin, *Rashi's Exegetical Categorization in Respect to the Distinction Between Peshat and Derash* (Hebrew) (Jerusalem: Hebrew University, 1986); and Benjamin Gelles, *Peshat and Derash in the Exegesis of Rashi* (Leiden: Brill, 1981).

31. J. Neumann, "Influence de Rashi et d'autres commentateurs Juifs sur les *Postillae Perpetuae* de Nicolas de Lyre, *Revue des études juives* 26, 27 (1893): 172–82; 250–62; A. Michalski, "Raschis Einfluss auf Nicolaus von Lyra in der Auslegung der Bücher Leviticus, Numeri, und Deuteronimum," *Zeitschrift für alttestamentliche Wissenschaft* 35 (1915): 218–43; 36 (1916): 29–63; Hailperin, *Rashi and the Christian Scholars.* Jeremy Cohen's treatment of Lyra's exegesis is an exception, as he focuses on the infusion of antirabbinic argument in the text. *The Friars and the Jews: The Evolution of Medieval Anti-Judaism* (Ithaca, N.Y.: Cornell University Press, 1982), 170–95. Several scholars have turned their attention to Rashi's influence on the illustration cycle that accompanied the *Postilla,* including Helen Rosenau, "The Architecture of Nicolaus de Lyra's Temple Illustrations and the Jewish Tradition," *Journal of Jewish Studies* 25 (1974): 294–304; Bernice Kaczynski, "Illustrations of

Tabernacle and Temple Implements in the *Postilla in Testamentum Vetus* of Nicolaus de Lyra." *Yale University Library Gazette* 48, no. 1 (1973): 1–11. Based on Mayer I. Gruber's discussion of illustrations in Rashi's commentary, "What Happened to Rashi's Pictures?" *Bodleian Library Record* 14 (1992): 111–24, it appears that Nicholas illustrated his text in the same places as had Rashi.

32. A partial listing of rabbinic texts used by Nicholas in the *Postilla* may be found in Wolfgang Bunte, *Rabbinische Traditionen bei Nikolaus von Lyra: Ein Beitrag zur Schriftauslegung des Spätmittelalters*, Judentum und Umwelt 58 (Berlin: Lang, 1994). Anyone who has delved seriously into Nicholas's *Postilla* on the whole Bible can sympathize with the difficulties inherent in providing a systematic identification of his sources, and Wolfgang Bunte has provided a great service in his attempt to identify all of Nicholas's named references to rabbinic texts. That said, his book must be used with caution, as a preliminary guide to sources rather than a definitive list. In addition to the questionable practice of indexing named references without respect to their appearance in Nicholas's own commentary or in Paul of Burgos' or Matthew Döring's responses, errors abound. For example, two citations of Moses ha-Darshan's *Bereshit Rabbati* as "Rabbi Moses" are erroneously identified by Bunte as Maimonides' *Epistle to Yemen*. Bunte, *Rabbinische Traditionen*, 170, nn. 10, 14.

33. Hailperin, *Rashi and the Christian Scholars*, 142.

34. Minnis, *Medieval Theory of Authorship*, 86. Lesley Smith provides a good sense of how this plays out in Nicholas's commentary in her essay "Rewards of Faith, 45–58. See especially 52–53.

35. Even as we acknowledge that Nicholas reflected new attitudes toward the literal sense, there is no denying that the weight of his commentary rests on the same sort of historical explication employed by the Victorines and other twelfth-century literal exegetes.

36. Madigan, "Lyra on the Gospel of Matthew."

37. Madigan, "Lyra on the Gospel of Matthew," 213.

38. Madigan, "Lyra on the Gospel of Matthew," 219–20.

39. Chapter 4.

40. John Baconthorpe, O. Carm., *Postilla super Matthaeum*, Trinity College Library MS B.15.12, fol. 102v.

41. Gross-Diaz, "What's a Good Soldier to Do?" An exception to this rule seems to be Nicholas's commentary on creation (and cosmology) in the first three chapters of Genesis, where Corinne Patton notes that Nicholas not only turned less frequently to Jewish interpretation than in the rest of his Old Testament commentary, Genesis included, but also rejected eight of the nineteen Jewish interpretations introduced into these chapters, including many from *Bereshit Rabbah*. Patton, "Creation, Fall and Salvation," 20–21.

42. As I show in more detail farther on, he was most likely following Rashi's lead in his selection of passages to illustrate.

43. See Deeana C. Klepper, "Literal Versus Carnal: George of Siena's Christian Reading of Jewish Exegesis," in *Jewish Biblical Interpretation in Comparative Context*, ed. David Stern and Natalie Dohrmann (Philadelphia: University of Pennsylvania Press, forthcoming).

44. Nicholas was not alone in viewing Rashi in this way. Herman Hailperin noted the tendency of thirteenth-century Hebraists like William de la Mare to see Rashi as a Jewish version of the Christian gloss. Hailperin, *Rashi and the Christian Scholars*, 132, 139.

45. "Item Hieremie xxiii, *Ecce dies veniunt dicit Dominus et suscitabo David germen iustum*. Ubi translatio Chaldaica apud Hebreos autentica habet *Statuam David messiam iustum et regnabit rex et sapiens erit, et faciet iudicium et iusticiam in terra*, sequitur, *Et hoc est nomen quod vocabunt eum, "Dominus iustus noster."* Per hoc autem quod dicitur *suscitabo David germen iustum* apparet eius humanitas. Per hoc autem quod sequitur, *et hoc est nomen quod vocabunt eum, "Dominus iustus noster,"* exprimitur eius divinitas. Nam pro hoc nomine Dominus Hebraica veritas habet nomen Domini thetragrammaton, quod secundum Hebreos est nomen summi Dei creatoris omnium. Unde dicit Rabi Moyses in *Libro directionis dubiorum* parte prima capitulo sexagesimo quod hoc nomen Domini thetragrammaton significat divinam essentiam significatione perfecta et immixta. Cetera vero nomina videntur derivata ab operibus divinis, ut Creator, Dominus, Salvator et huiusmodi." *Postilla super Ezechielem*, Chapter 48.

46. "Dicunt expositores nostri quod ille angelus qui apparuit sibi sic apparebat in similitudine assumpta, quasi habens faciem ab ea aversam, quod autem sic videtur scilicet a dorso non manifeste et determinate cognoscitur, et per hoc designatur quod de angelis non habemus cognitionem nisi valde longinquam et remotam, non propriam et determinatam. Et simile habetur de Moyse Exod. 33 . . ." *Postilla super Genesim*, Chapter 16.

47. "Hebrei autem aliquid dicunt quod hic est verus textus: Hic vidi post videntem me. Et est sensus: Angelus vidit me hic, vocando et monendo, et postea vidi eum. Alii autem dicunt quod veritas textus est: Hic vidi post visum meum. Et est sensus: Hic vidi angelum Domini in hoc deserto: postquam videram eum ante in domo Abre, cuius ille angelus erat custos et visitator. Et propter ea non fuit territa ad visionem angeli, sicut Manue qui dixit, morte moriemur, quia vidimus angelum domini, Judicum xiii, quia fuerat assueta videre angelos domini in domo Abre." *Postilla super Genesim*, Chapter 16.

48. "Nec mirandum si in hoc loco et aliis pluribus locis veteris testamenti littera pluribus modis et sensibus accipiatur, etiam secundum Hebreos doctores, quia Hebrei non habent grammaticam ita distinctam et dearticulatam per declinationes nominum et verborum sicut Latini et Greci habent. Item apud eos sunt multe dictiones equivoce: et propter hoc eadem littera aliquando variis significationibus et sensibus accipitur." *Postilla super Genesim*, Chapter 16.

49. "Sciendum est etiam quod apud Hebreos verba sunt nomina equivoca etiam aliquando translatio nostra tenet unum sensum et Hebrei alium, sicut ostende in pluribus locis in operibus predictis. Variis doctores Hebreis Vetus Testamentum exponendo ideo equivocationem dictam inter se variantur. Ego in talibus consequenter secutus sum Rabi Salomonem cuius doctrina apud Iudeos modernos magis autentica reputatur." BAV Archivio S. Pietro D202, fol. 50r.

50. See Judah Rosenthal's edition of *Jacob ben Ruben: Milhamot Hashem* (Jerusalem: Mosad ha-Rav Kuk, 1963) and Joshua Levy, "Sefer Milhamot Hashem,

Chapter Eleven: The Earliest Jewish Critique of the New Testament" (Jacob ben Ruben, Nicholas de Lyra) (Ph.D. diss., New York University, 2004).

51. The alternative reading of innkeeper depends upon reading the Hebrew *zonah* as "one who nourishes," although the roots of the two words are not the same. Most Jewish authorities understood Rahab to be a prostitute and, like Christian authorities, saw in her a model of repentance and conversion to righteousness.

52. BAV Archivio S. Pietro D202, fol. 15r.

53. Rabbi Solomon ha-Levi (c. 1353–1435), a prominent member of the Jewish community in Burgos, was baptized in 1390. In 1394 he was ordained as a priest; by 1405 he was named bishop of Cartagena and in 1415 archbishop of Burgos. Heinz Schreckenberg, "Paulus von Burgos," in *Biographisch-Bibliographisches Kirchenlexikon* (Herzberg: Bautz, 1994) 7: 57–60.

54. It is important to note that Nicholas's genealogy does not take the form of the then-popular "tree of Jesse" motif, in which Christ's human ancestors provide the roots and Jesus emerges as a branch at the top of the tree in fulfillment of the prophecy in Jeremiah 23:5: *Behold the days come, saith the Lord, and I will raise up to David a just branch.*

55. "Dicit Ra. Sa. Hebreus quod iste psalmus loquitur ad litteram de rege messia, id est Christo, cuius adventus erit manifestus. Quid tunc fient multa mirabilia virtute divina interqua ut dicit erit unum, scilicet quod omnes Iudei per orbem dispersi quasi in momento congregabuntur ad ipsum in Hierusalem. Et secundum hoc exponit quod subditur, congregate illi sanctos eius. Et sic consequenter applicat litteram ad suum propositum prout potest. Omittatur igitur opinio eius quantum ad hoc quod continet falsitatem, scilicet quod Christus venturus sit in mundum et Iudei congregandi ad ipsum, et accipiatur id quod est veritatis, scilicet quod iste psalmus loquitur ad litteram de rege messia qui est Christus dominus noster." *Postilla super Psalmos*, Chapter 49.

56. Görge K. Hasselhoff, *Dicit Rabbi Moyses: Studien zum Bild von Moses Maimonides im lateinischen Westen vom 13. bis zum 15. Jahrhundert* (Würzburg: Königshausen & Neumann, 2004), 246–54. For a discussion of the various manuscript traditions, see Wolfgang Kluxen, "Literaturgeschichtliches zum lateinischen Moses Maimonides," *Recherches de théologie ancienne et médiévale* 21 (1954): 23–58, and Hasselhoff, *Dicit Rabbi Moyses*, and "The Reception of Maimonides in the Latin World: The Evidence of the Latin Translations in the Thirteenth–Fifteenth Century," *Materia giudaica* 6 (2001): 264–70. Thomas Aquinas famously cited the *Guide*, but a comparison of the passages mentioned by Nicholas with Aquinas' citations in the *Summa theologia* indicates that Thomas could not have been Nicholas's source.

57. Signer, "Nicholas of Lyra on the Prophet Ezechiel," 154–56.

58. MS Paris BNF lat. 16558, fols. 224v–230. The first part of the manuscript contains a thematic arrangement of extracts from the Talmud and Rashi's comentary on themes such as the authority of the Talmud, blasphemies, etc. The second part provides excerpts according to the order of tractates in the Talmud with Rashi's commentary at the end.

59. Gilbert Dahan, "Rashi, sujet de la controverse de 1240: Edition partielle du MS Paris, BN lat. 16558." *Archives juives* 4 (1978): 43–53; and Hailperin, *Rashi*

and the Christian Scholars, 116–29. On Nicholas's borrowing from Raymond, see Hailperin, *Rashi and the Christian Scholars*, 172–73; and Cohen, *The Friars and the Jews*, 188–89, 265–66.

60. Gruber, "What Happened to Rashi's Pictures?" See also Rosenau, "Architecture of Nicolaus de Lyra's Temple Illustrations," 300–303.

61. There are more illustrations in Nicholas's text than there would have been in Rashi's because Nicholas often presented two images of the same passage, one illustrating Christian interpretation and the other depicting Jewish opinion.

62. See, for example, the *Postilla litteralis* on Ezechiel 40:1 where Nicholas discusses the difficulty of comprehending Ezechiel's vision of the Temple and points out that not only do Latins and Hebrews disagree on interpretation, but also Hebrews among themselves, Rashi and Maimonides holding to different opinions here. "Et quia hec visio imaginaria ponitur hic satis obscure. Ideo circa descriptionem imaginarie visionis et eius expositionem, non solum variantur Hebrei et Latini, sed etiam Hebrei ab invicem, quia Ra. Moyses et Ra. Salomon ipsam varie describunt et exponunt."

63. "Sed ubi hoc sit ab eis traditum nescio. Maxime quia Ra. Sa. qui ordinavit glossas Hebraicas super totum Veterum Testamentum aliter dicit super locum istum." *Postilla litteralis super 2 Regum*, Chapter 4.

64. Hailperin, *Rashi and the Christian Scholars*.

65. Cf. Numbers Rabbah 13 and Babylonian Talmud Mas. Sotah 37a, both of which identify Nahshon, son of Amminadab as the first to enter the sea. According to Numbers Rabbah, Nahshon won by that act the privilege of bringing the first offering to God after the tabernacle was completed.

66. "Ubi translatio nostra habet ingressi sunt domum mulieris meretricis, translatio Chaldaica habet domum mulieris hospitalarie, et talis fuit Raab." *Postilla litteralis super Epistolam ad Hebraeos*, Chapter 11.

67. See Chapter 4 for further discussion of this passage.

68. Translation by Kaczynski in "Illustrations of Tabernacle and Temple Implements," 8.

69. "*Facies et propitiatorim de auro mundissimo*: Ra. Sa. et Hebrei dicunt quod istud propitiatorium erat operculum arche, tamen quia de alio operculo eius non sit mentio, tamen quia describitur eiusdem longitudinis et latitudinis sicut et archa. Aliqui alii doctores dicunt quod non erat operculum arche sed erat tabula aurea superius elevata, quasi portaretur ab ipsis cherubin qui erant in extremitatibus arche. Ita quod esset quasi sedile ipsius Dei, et arche operculum esset quasi scabellum illius sedis. Secundum illud Ps. 79, *Qui sedes super cherubin*, id est, super propitiatorium . . . *Ac de medio duorum cherubin qui erant super archam*: Ex hoc dicit Ra. Sa. quod duo cherubin stabant super operculum arche in extremitatibus eius. Alii autem doctores de quibus facta est mentio dicunt quod erant positi super pavimentum tabernaculi in extremitatibus arche. Dicuntur tamen hic esse super archam: quia elevabantur in altum ultra altitudenem arche. Ut autem predicta facilius capiantur descripsi ea in figura." *Postilla litteralis super Exodum*, Chapter 25.

70. "Figura arche propitiatorii et cherubin secundum alios doctores, et specialiter secundum Thomas de Aquino." Bibl. Mun. Reims MS 178, fol. 52v; Oxford, Bodl. MS 251, fol. 49r; Brit. Lib. Royal 3 D VII, fol. 65r, inter alia.

71. "[Apostolus] describit ea, quae erant in secundo tabernaculo, scilicet arca testamenti, de lignis sethin imputribilibus, circumtecta ex omni parte, id est, tam intus quam extra, auro. In arca autem erant tria, scilicet urna aurea habens manna, et hoc in memoriam illius beneficii eis praestiti, Ex. XVI, 32 ss., et virga Aaron quae fronduerat, Num. XVII, v. 8, in memoriam sacerdotii Aaron ne alius extraneus praesumeret accedere; et tabulae testamenti, Ex. XXV, 21, in memoriam legis. Item super arcam duo Cherubim qui tangebant se duabus alis, et tangebant alis duabus latera tabernaculi. Inter duas autem alas quibus tangebant se, erat tabula aurea eiusdem longitudinis et latitudinis, et arca, scilicet duorum cubitorum in longitudine, cubiti et semis in latitudine, et erat supereminens, quae dicebatur propitiatorium. Unde erat quasi sedes, de qua Deus exaudiret ad repropitiandum populo. Ps. LXXIX, 2: qui sedes super Cherubim, et cetera. Arca vero erat quasi scabellum pedum. Illi duo Cherubim versis vultibus ad se ipsos respiciebant in propitiatorium." Thomas Aquinas, *Super Epistolas S. Pauli lectura*, ed. Raffaele Cai (Turin: Marietti, 1953), 2: 428.

72. For a discussion of the question, see Chapter 4.

73. Nicholas was referring here to Simon Bar Kochba, leader of the failed Jewish revolt against Rome in 132–135 C.E.

74. See, for comparison, Beryl Smalley, "William of Auvergne, John of La Rochelle, and St. Thomas Aquinas on the Old Law," *Studies in Medieval Thought and Learning: From Abelard to Wyclif* (London: Hambledon Press, 1981), 121–36.

75. The *Quaestio de adventu Christi* will be treated extensively in Chapter 4.

Chapter 3. The Challenge of Unbelief: Knowing Christian Truth Through Jewish Scripture

1. Miri Rubin made this observation during comments on a panel considering Robert Lerner's *The Feast of Saint Abraham: Medieval Millenarians and the Jews* (Philadelphia: University of Pennsylvania Press, 2000) at the American Society for Church History annual meeting on January 9, 2004.

2. That theologians did so in ways that sometimes distorted the philosophy they employed does not negate the influence of philosophy on theology.

3. See Jeremy Cohen, *Friars and the Jews: The Evolution of Medieval Anti-Judaism* (Ithaca, N.Y.: Cornell University Press, 1982), and "The Jews as the Killers of Christ in the Latin Tradition, from Augustine to the Friars," *Traditio* 39 (1983): 1–27.

4. On the debate, see William Courtenay, *Schools and Scholars in Fourteenth-Century England* (Princeton, N.J.: Princeton University Press, 1987), 175–78; Katherine Tachau, *Vision and Certitude in the Age of Ockham: Optics, Epistemology, and the Foundations of Semantics, 1250–1345*, Studien und Texte zur Geistesgeschichte des Mittelalters 22 (Leiden: Brill, 1988); Bonnie Kent, *Virtues of the Will: The Transformation of Ethics in the Late Thirteenth Century* (Washington, D.C.: Catholic University Press, 1995); and Steven P. Marrone, *The Light of Thy Countenance: Science and Knowledge of God in the Thirteenth Century* (Leiden: Brill, 2001). Most of the schol-

arship focuses on Franciscan thinkers because, with the exception of the secular Henry of Ghent, the most important figures in the debate were Franciscans. Robert Pasnau focuses significant attention on Aquinas's theory of cognition as a representative synthesis of mid-thirteenth-century Aristotelian theories but acknowledges that Aquinas was not an innovator or a central figure in the debate. Pasnau, *Theories of Cognition in the Later Middle Ages* (Cambridge: Cambridge University Press, 1997), 12.

5. Steven Marrone, *Truth and Scientific Knowledge in the Thought of Henry of Ghent* (Cambridge, Mass.: Medieval Academy of America, 1985), 10.

6. Pasnau, *Theories of Cognition*, 9.

7. Nicholas of Lyra, "Whether the Jews recognized Christ at the time of his advent," BAV Vat. lat. 869 fol. 138r, also in *Postilla litteralis super Matthaeum*, chapter 21. "Quod illa notitia quam haberent de Christo per scripturas prophetarum non erat certa certitudine evidentie, tum quia talis certitudo habetur solum per demonstrationem et sensum, tum quia prophetie possunt aliquando varie exponi, et ideo erat vix notitia probabilis et verisimilis coniecture." John Baconthorpe's quotation of this passage in his commentary on Matthew (1336) has "parabolica" in place of "probabilis." Cambridge, Trinity College Library MS B.15.12 f. 169v. For more on Baconthorpe's use of Nicholas's work, see Chapter 5. I am indebted to Isaac Miller for first pointing out to me the relationship between Nicholas's line of reasoning here and larger philosophical discussions of proof and certitude. Nicholas's position runs directly counter to Thomas Aquinas's teaching in the *Summa theologia*, question 1, article 5, where he insists that the science of sacred doctrine exceeds all other sciences, not only because of its greater worth, but also because of its degree of certitude, which exceeds that of all other sciences because "other sciences gain their certainty through the light of natural reason, which can err, whereas this one gains its certainty through the light of divine wisdom, which cannot be deceived."

8. On the use of the term *verisimilitude*, see Tachau, *Vision and Certitude*, 17.

9. See, for example, A. Lukyn Williams, *Adversus Iudeos: A Bird's Eye View of Christian Apologiae Until the Renaissance* (Cambridge: Cambridge University Press, 1935); Cohen, *Friars and the Jews*.

10. I began to search for questions on the topic in the course of studying Nicholas of Lyra's 1309 *Quaestio de adventu Christi* for my doctoral dissertation. Palémon Glorieux's two-volume *Littérature quodlibétique* (Paris: Vrin, 1925–35) was very helpful as a starting point in locating related questions, and I included a survey of these questions in the dissertation. Gilbert Dahan has since put together a summary of quodlibetal questions on Jews and Judaism found in Glorieux, but he does not treat them in any depth. Dahan, "Juifs et judaïsme dans la littérature quodlibétique," *From Witness to Witchcraft: Jews and Judaism in Medieval Christian Thought*, ed. Jeremy Cohen, Wolfenbütteler Mittelalter-Studien 11 (Wiesbaden: Harrassowitz, 1996), 221–45. There are without a doubt still more questions of this sort to be found in unedited and unstudied quodlibetal collections. I have also found a number of similar questions in *Sentences* commentaries, including an anonymous thirteenth-century commentary on book 3, dist. 25 which asks, "whether the Jews could have known the time of the incarnation" and "whether the Jews recognized Christ to be the messiah promised in the law" (MS Paris BNF lat. 3237, fol. 34r); another

by an unknown but clearly Franciscan author, also in book 3, which asks "whether the one about whom the law and Scriptures speak and who was promised has already come, which the Jews demonstrate not to be the case" (MS BAV Vat. Chigi B.VI.95, fols. 3v–5v); and two by John Baconthorpe, O.Carm., in the prologue to book 4 of the *Sentences* asking "whether from the Scriptures of the Old Testament and the senses of those same Scriptures it is certain that Christ has already come since the Jews in this matter err through ignorance" (MS Paris Mazarine 900, fols. 1–4r) and "whether the Jews ought to have believed the preaching of the apostles according to the prophecies of the Old Law (fols. 4r–5v). Though the nature of the questions is closely related—note particularly the parallel between Roger Marston's and the later anonymous Franciscan's—I have decided to concentrate here on the quodlibetal precedents for Nicholas of Lyra's own important question. Nancy Turner dealt with *Sentences* commentary questions concerning Jews in *An Attack on the Acknowledged Truth: French, English, and German Theologians on the Jews in the Fourteenth Century* (Ph.D. diss., University of Iowa, 1996), parts of which have been published as "Robert Holcot on the Jews," in *Chaucer and the Jews: Sources, Contexts, Meanings*, ed. Sheila Delany (New York: Routledge, 2002), 133–44; "Jews and Judaism in Peter Aureol's *Sentences* Commentary," in *Friars and Jews in the Middle Ages and Renaissance*, ed. Steven J. McMichael and Susan E. Meyers (Leiden: Brill, 2004), 81–98; and "Jewish Witness, Forced Conversion, and Island Living: John Duns Scotus on Jews and Judaism," in *Christian Attitudes Toward the Jews in the Middle Ages: A Casebook*, ed. Michael Frassetto (New York: Routledge, 2006).

11. I do not mean to argue here that the debate over the role of divine illumination was directly relevant to these questions. The theory of divine illumination had to do with knowledge of natural things rather than divine things. The illuminative process suggested by Henry of Ghent and others was distinct from the illumination of grace that was necessary for knowledge of theological truths. Marrone, *Truth and Scientific Knowledge*, 14–15.) What I am suggesting here is a spillover from the debate, as part of the concern over certitude with respect to knowledge generally.

12. *Queritur utrum Iudei cognoverunt Jesum Nazarenum esset Christum sibi promissum; Utrum ex scripturis receptis a Iudeis possit efficaciter probari salvatorem nostrum fuisse hominem et Deum*, BAV Vat. lat. 869 fols. 130r, 130r–138r.

13. The same incorporation of polemic is found in related questions on faith and rationality where they address the problem of Jewish and Muslim unbelief. See, for example, question 3 in Matthew of Aquasparta, *Quaestiones disputatae: de fide et de cognitione*, 2nd ed. Bibliotheca Franciscana Scholastica Medii Aevi 1 (Florence, 1957), 70–99; and question 5 in Bartholomew of Bologna, *Die Quaestiones disputatae de fide des Bartholomäus von Bologna, O.F.M.*, ed. Meinolf Mückshoff, Beiträge zur Geschichte der Philosophie und Theologie des Mittelalters: Texte und Untersuchungen 24, no. 4 (Münster: Aschendorff, 1940), 77–104.

14. The text of the question *Utrum per prophetias possit probari Christum iam incarnatum fuisse* as found in MS Florence Bibl. Laurentiana, Conv. soppr. 123, has been published in *Fr. Rogeri Marston, O.F.M. Quodlibeta quatuor*, ed. Girard F. Etzkorn and Ignatius C. Brady, Bibliotheca Franciscana Scholastica Medii Aevi 26 (Florence: Quaracchi, 1968), 104–45. The introduction to their edition also contains a biography of Roger as well as a summary of his writing. Another copy of the ques-

tion is found in BAV Vat. lat. 1095 fols. 69r–74v under the incipit *Queritur utrum ille de quo lex et scriptura loquuntur possit probari per scripturam Veteris Testamenti iam venisse contra Iudeos.*

15. Etzkorn and Brady, *Fr. Rogeri Marston*, ix–xxiii.

16. Andrew G. Little and Franz Pelster, *Oxford Theology and Theologians, c. A.D. 1282–1302* (Oxford: Clarendon Press, 1934), 93–95.

17. Etzkorn and Brady assign the quodlibet containing the question on the advent of Christ to the Easter disputation of 1283 or 1284. Etzkorn and Brady, *Fr. Rogeri Marston*, lix–lxi.

18. Etzkorn and Brady, *Fr. Rogeri Marston*, 69–71.

19. With the exception of one other long question asking *Utrum creatura possit aliquid producere de nihilo*, in large part a refutation of Henry of Ghent's Quodlibet 4, q. 14, the other questions in the quodlibet are significantly shorter, running from two to nine pages in edited form with the overwhelming majority under five pages and many less than two.

20. "Exponunt eam Iudaei sic: Non auferetur sceptrum de Iuda, id est, ius sceptri, hoc est regendi et dominandi. Si enim de actuali dominio loquatur textus, planum est quod tempore captivitatis Babylonicae actuale dominium non habebant, nec etiam tempore Machabaeorum, quibus temporibus, etiam secundum fidem nostram, nondum venerat Christus. Necesse est ergo quod promissio sceptri non auferendi sit de iure et non de facto. Sed hoc ius dominandi sibi non fuisse ablatum, dicunt Iudaei, quamvis de facto illud amiserunt." Etzkorn and Brady, *Fr. Rogeri Marston*, 105.

21. Cf. Bonaventure, *Collationes de donis Spiritus sancti* 8, n. 12, as cited and discussed in Marrone, *Light of Thy Countenance*, 167ff.

22. "Sicut in acquisitione scientiae naturalis per doctrinam impossibile est hominem a lumine naturali aversum et conversum ad phantasmata, dum eisdem inhaeret, ipsa pro veris et intellectis approbans, non errare nec persuadibilem fore ad intelligentiam veritatis; phantasmata quippe quibus nimio inhaeretur amore, principia sunt erroris; sic omni homini non solum fidei lumine privato, sed pravitatis errore depravato, persuaderi non possunt ea quae sunt fidei christiane, et maxime de Christi incarnatione altissimum sacramentum. Unde sicut homini simplici, qualescumque demonstrationes mathematicae sibi fierent de solis quantitate, nunquam certitudo sibi fieret quod centies octogesies contineat quantitatem terrae, licet ita res se habeat in veritate, sic nec animus pravitatis errore distortus dirigi potest ad verae fidei rectitudinis lumen dum suis conceptionibus nimio conglutinatur amore. Omnem tamen intellectum indifferentem ad ea quae sunt veritatis, credo sufficienter posse captivari per Scripturam in obsequium Christi." For more on Roger's thinking on the necessity of eternal light in cognition of truth, see question 3 of *Quaestiones disputatae de anima* in Roger Marston, O.F.M., *Quaestiones disputatae de emanatione divina, de statu naturae lapsae, de anima*, Bibliotheca Franciscana Scholastica Medii Aevi 7 (Florence, 1932), 263.

23. "Et sumuntur hic quaedam ad ostendendum Christum venisse a parte synagogae desinentis, quaedam vero a parte ipsius Christi advenientis, et quaedam a parte Ecclesiae proficientis." Etzkorn and Brady, *Fr. Rogeri Marston*, 106.

24. "Secundum primam viam, quadrupliciter declaratur Christum iam ad-

venisse, videlicet ex evacuatione legalis sacrificii, ex translatione legalis sacerdotii, ex innovatione legalis eloquii, et ex exterminatione legalis populi." Etzkorn and Brady, *Fr. Rogeri Marston*, 106.

25. "Secundo convincitur Christum iamdum promissum nobis fuisse in carne exhibitum a parte ipsius Christi advenientis. Nam per prophetas nobis describitur, quantum ad humanitatis veritatem, quantum ad divinitatis sublimitatem, quantum ad conversationis sanctitatem, quantum ad passionis acerbitatem." Etzkorn and Brady, *Fr. Rogeri Marston*, 119.

26. "Tandem ex tertio principali iam convincitur Christum advenisse, videlicet ex parte Ecclesiae proficientis, in qua relucet credulitatis universalitas, conformitatis unitas, praedicationis prosperitas et informationis salubritas." Etzkorn and Brady, *Fr. Rogeri Marston*, 130–31.

27. See especially books 17 and 18 of Augustine's *City of God*, which Roger cites by name.

28. Roger drew particularly from Jerome's *Commentarius in Isaiam prophetam*, which he cited "in originali." Etzkorn and Brady, *Fr. Rogeri Marston*, 123.

29. Bede, *De temporum ratione liber*, in *Bedae Venerabilis Opera* 6, CCSL 123 B (Turnholt:Brepols, 1977).

30. Franz Pelster, "Roger Marston O.F.M. (d. 1303), ein englischer Vertreter des Augustinismus," *Scholastik* 3 (1928): 526–56, 548. Decima Douie was not so kind to Roger, accusing him of combining "extreme conservatism and devotion to St. Augustine, St. Anselm, and the Victorines with a narrow and second-rate intelligence, and [he] was provocative without being effective." Douie, *Archbishop Pecham*, 284.

31. Etienne Gilson, "Roger Marston: Un cas d'Augustinisme Avicennisant," *Archives d'histoire doctrinale et littéraire du Moyen Age* 8 (1933): 37–42.

32. On the dating of the *De cessatione legalium*, see the introduction to Robert Grosseteste's *De cessatione legalium*, ed. Richard C. Dales and Edward B. King, Auctores Britannici Medii Aevi 7 (London: Oxford University Press for the British Academy, 1986), xiv–xv. On contemporary discussions of the Old Law, see Beryl Smalley, "William of Auvergne, John of La Rochelle and St. Thomas Aquinas on the Old Law," in *Studies in Medieval Thought and Learning from Abelard to Wyclif* (London: Hambledon Press, 1981).

33. "Propter reverentiam magni doctoris domini Roberti Lincolniensis, qui ipsas studiose et solerti ingenio adinvenit." Quodlibet 2, question 5, Etzkorn and Brady, *Fr. Rogeri Marston*, 159.

34. Robert Grosseteste described the Jews as infidels in his *De cessatione legalium*, where he argued that to continue to observe the Law after Christ's Passion was to deny Christ and to expect the messiah in the future, "quemadmodum adhuc faciunt infideles Iudaei." Grosseteste, *De cessatione legalium*, 168. James Muldoon, in *Popes, Lawyers, and Infidels: The Church and the Non-Christian World 1250–1550* (Philadelphia: University of Pennsylvania Press, 1979), argued that medieval thinkers made a clear distinction between Jews and infidels, but that does not seem to be the case in these questions. Peter Olivi also described Jews as infidels when he spoke of the conversion of "universitas Iudaeorum et ceterorum infidelium" (below, n. 64) as did Nicholas of Lyra.

35. Cf. Grosseteste, *De cessatione legalium*, 118.

36. "Sanctitatem vero Christi qui iam advenit, legere potest et intueri qui credit Evangelio. Sed quia contra infideles agimus ad praesens, et praecipue contra Iudaeos, ex ipsorum historiis sumamus testimonium contra eos—Iosephus, in libro XVII Antiquitatum . . ." Etzkorn and Brady, *Fr. Rogeri Marston*, 128.

37. See, for example, the following: Roger's discussion of Isaiah 8 on 120–23; of Isaiah 9 on 126–27; of Isaiah 53 on 129, in Etzkorn and Brady, *Fr. Rogeri Marston*.

38. Etzkorn and Brady, *Fr. Rogeri Marston*, 109–11. Augustine, *City of God*, 724–28.

39. "Et si dicas quod in Hebraeo non scribitur becula, quod significat virginem, sed alma, quod significat adolescentulam, respondit Hieronymus in originali, dicens quod "alma non solum puella est vel virgo, sed virgo abscondita et secreta, quae nunquam virorum patuit aspectibus, sed magna parentum diligentia custodita est." Etzkorn and Brady, *Fr. Rogeri Marston*, 123. See Jerome, *Commentarius in Isaiam prophetam*, PL 24, 108.

40. "Firmiter igitur credo et nullatenus dubito quod Christum advenisse non tantum probabiliter sed sufficientissime probari potest per Scripturas." Etzkorn and Brady, *Fr. Rogeri Marston*, 144.

41. Etzkorn and Brady, *Fr. Rogeri Marston*, 145–46.

42. He has Josephus in mind here. Etzkorn and Brady, *Fr. Rogeri Marston*, 146.

43. *Utrum per Vetus Testamentum probari possit incarnatio Christi.* The question is found in Todi Biblioteca Comunale MS 98, fol. 20r. The titles of the questions from the nine quodlibeta and 29 ordinary questions found in the Todi MS have been published by Ferdinand Delorme, "Quodlibets et questions disputées de Raymond Rigaut, maître franciscain de Paris, d'après le Ms. 98 de la Bibl. Comm. de Todi," in *Aus der Geisteswelt des Mittelalters*, ed. Albert Lang, Joseph Lechner, and Michael Schmaus (Münster: Aschendorff, 1935), 2:826–41.

44. Glorieux, *Répertoires des maîtres de théologie*, 2:124.

45. Delorme, "Quodlibets et questions disputées," 826.

46. A marginal note on fol. 57v of the Todi MS connects the two men, and we know that Vital was familiar with Raymond's work. Vital summarizes Raymond's introduction to Quodlibet 8 in the prologue to his own Quodlibet 1 (edited in *La France franciscaine* 9 [1926]: 452–71). Delorme found that Vital's first question in that quodlibet drew upon Raymond's eighth question in Quodlibet 8. Delorme, "Quodlibets et questions disputées," 826. Stephano Defraia identifies parallel questions in the work of Peter Olivi, Raymond Rigauld, and Vital de Furno, in Peter Olivi, *Quodlibeta quinque: ad fidem codicum nunc primum edita cum introductione historico-critica*, ed. Stefano Defraia, Collectio Oliviana 7 (Grottaferrata (Rome): Editiones Collegii S. Bonaventurae ad Claras Aquas, 2002), 37, 41.

47. Marrone, *Light of Thy Countenance*, 392–93. Vital was interested enough in the theory of divine illumination to copy extensively from Henry of Ghent's work on the subject. Marrone, 268.

48. "Contra, Genesis 49, non auferetur sceptrum de Iuda, etc. Non conceditur quia sceptrum primo in captivitate cessavit." Todi Biblioteca Comunale MS 98, fol. 20r.

49. "Cum incarnatio Christi sit articulus fidei . . . sicut excedit naturalem perfectionem universi sic hec veritas non potest clare Iudei in lumine naturali sicut nec attingi plene nisi ab intellectu fideli nec per Vetus Testamentum probari ubi scripturam recipienti supposita cum notitia probatis et recipientis." Todi Biblioteca Comunale MS 98, fol. 20r.

50. "Et incarnatio et omnis articuli ex Veteris Testamento possit probari tantum quia novum clauditur in veteri sicut rota in medio rote." Todi Biblioteca Comunale MS 98, fol. 20r. Cf. Ezechiel 1:16.

51. "Unde sicut ex novo nunc probantur impleta sic ex veteri vere probantur predicta." Todi Biblioteca Comunale MS 98, fol. 20r.

52. *An ex Veteri Testamento possit probari Iudaeos in Christi adventu fuisse excecandos et a statu vere fidei excludendos; An tempus adventus messie possit per Vetus Testamentum probari.* The questions have recently been edited by Stefano Defraia in *Quodlibeta quinque*, 107–35. On Peter Olivi's life and work see David Burr, *The Persecution of Peter Olivi* (Philadelphia: American Philosophical Society, 1976); and Franz Ehrle, "Petrus Johannis Olivi, sein Leben und seine Schriften" in *Archiv für Literatur- und Kirchengeschichte des Mittelalters* (Berlin: Weidmannsche Buchhandlung, 1885–1900), 3:409–552.

53. Glorieux, *Répertoires des maîtres de théologie*, 2:127–34.

54. Kent, *Virtues of the Will*, 84.

55. On Olivi's place in the thirteenth-century discussion of epistemology and divine illumination specifically, see Pasnau, *Theories of Cognition*; and Kent, *Virtues of the Will*, 84–88.

56. Although the censures were not related to issues of poverty and the Franciscan mission, Ubertino da Casale thought that the attacks were motivated by hostility to Olivi's position on poverty. See E. Randolph Daniel, *The Franciscan Concept of Mission in the High Middle Ages* (Lexington: University Press of Kentucky, 1975), 82. See also Burr, *Persecution of Peter Olivi.*

57. Robert Lerner describes the move as punitive: "Censured in 1283, he was confined for awhile in Nîmes, where he was deprived of his books, and then, from 1287–1289 banished to teach theology to the friars in Florence." Lerner, *Feast of Saint Abraham*, 58.

58. "Dicendum quod ex Veteri Testamento probatur maiorem partem Iudeorum fuisse excecandam et reprobandam in primo Christi aduentu: non tamen totam: que quidem pars modica a prophetis reliquie uocantur: de quibus Isaie.x. dicitur: *Si fuerit populus Israel quasi arena maris: reliquie conuertentur ex eo.*" Defraia, *Quodlibeta quinque*, 108.

59. "Item capitulo VI, premissa solemni uisione maiestatis Dei, subdit se cum magno pondere missum a Deo ad predicandum populo suo: *Exceca cor populi huius*, et querente propheta usquequo duraret hec excecatio, dixit sibi Deus quod usque essent totaliter destructi, exceptis paucis reliquiis electorum." Defraia, *Quodlibeta quinque*, 110–111.

60. "Subdit immediate de generali conuersione gentium, *ita quod omnes ab occidente et ab oriente, timebunt nomen Domini, et gloriam eius.* Et ideo subdit: *Surge, et illuminare Hierusalem, quia uenit lumen tuum. Et ambulabunt gentes in lu-*

mine tuo etc.; ubi apertissime loquitur de fiendis sub Christo." Defraia, *Quodlibeta quinque*, 111.

61. For a discussion of Olivi's use of the term *status* and a discussion of the seven stages of history after the incarnation, see David Burr, "Olivi's Apocalyptic Timetable," *Journal of Medieval and Renaissance Studies* 11 (1981): 237–60.

62. This language is distinctively Olivi's, though of course he was hardly the first to emphasize Christ's poverty or to depict Christ specifically as a beggar. Bonaventure, in his *Apologia pauperum*, established many of these same arguments. On Olivi's place in the controversy over *usus pauper* and Christ's poverty, see David Burr, *Olivi and Franciscan Poverty: The Origins of the Usus Pauper Controversy* (Philadelphia: University of Pennsylvania Press, 1989).

63. "Hiis igitur prelibatis facile est ex secundo et tertio modo per prophetas probare quod Christus erat uenturus ad populum Iudeorum multiplici iniquitate tunc temporis plenum; et ab ipso arguendum et monendum ipsumque cum suis monitis ab eis deridendum et persequendum, ut sic omnino excecaretur in illo, et maxime quia uenturus erat ut pauper et ignotus et ut cerimoniarum legalium et superstitiosarum traditionum et temporalium diuitiarum euacuator et conculcator." Defraia, *Quodlibeta quinque*, 115.

64. "Nam ex hac conditione necessario probatur prophetas insimul et indistincte loqui de trino tempore Christi, in quorum primo maior pars Iudeorum erat excecanda et plenitudo gentium conuertenda. In secundo uero carnalis ecclesia quasi altera synagoga erat excecanda, et uniuersitas Iudeorum et ceterorum infidelium conuertenda. In tertio autem erat uniuersitas reproborum eternaliter in inferno damnanda, et uniuersitas electorum in celesti Hierusalem eternaliter glorificanda." Defraia, *Quodlibeta quinque*, 115–16.

65. Robert Lerner treats Peter's ideas about Jewish salvation as presented in this question extensively in *Feast of Saint Abraham*, 55–72.

66. On Olivi's apocalyptic vision, see David Burr, *Olivi's Peaceable Kingdom: A Reading of the Apocalypse Commentary* (Philadelphia: University of Pennsylvania Press, 1993).

67. "Contra: Quia Luc. XII, Christus increpat Iudeos . . . Sed irrationabiliter de hoc increparentur nisi potuissent hoc tempus probare, et per certas probationes cognoscere." Defraia, *Quodlibeta quinque*, 116–17.

68. ". . . quia non se disposuerunt ad Spiritum gratie et sue spiritualis illuminationis, per quem et internam uim littere et circumstantias sanctorum Christi et temporis in quo uenit intellexissent." Defraia, *Quodlibeta quinque*, 117.

69. ". . . secundo, obiectiones que contra ipsam a Iudeis uel a iudaizantibus dantur, et improbationem ipsarum." Defraia, *Quodlibeta quinque*, 119. He may have had in mind here Andrew of St. Victor's increasingly popular literal commentary on Daniel, which incorporated numerous Jewish interpretations of the text without critique. According to Smalley, Andrew's works were enjoying a renaissance in the last decades of the thirteenth century, and she found Olivi quoting from Andrew's commentaries on Kings, Isaiah, Ezechiel, and Ecclesiastes. Beryl Smalley, *The Study of the Bible in the Middle Ages*, 3rd ed. (Oxford: Blackwell, 1983), 182–85.

70. "Zacharie etiam primo capitulo et VI describuntur hic quattuor regna, et quarti et ultimi dicuntur esse robustissimi et perambulantes omnem terram, et

quod post ipsa tanquam post quattuor cornua ueniunt quattuor fabri, idest quattuor euangeliste uel apostoli, in quattuor partes orbis missi . . ." Defraia, *Quodlibeta quinque*, 118–19. In the appropriate passages from Zechariah, the four horns are said to be the horns of the nations that scattered Judah, Israel, and Jerusalem. God sends the smiths to cast down the horns of those nations that scattered Judah. In chapter 6, an angel explains to Zechariah his vision of four chariots drawn by different colored horses. These are said to represent "the four winds of the heaven, which go forth to stand before the Lord of all the earth . . . And they that were most strong, went out, and sought to go, and to run to and fro through all the earth. And he said: Go, walk throughout the earth: and they walked throughout the earth."

71. For example, Olivi cited Jerome's prologues to Haggai and Daniel for the calculation of years from the reign of Darius to Julius Caesar or to Vespasian. Defraia, *Quodlibeta quinque*, 122–23.

72. "Conueniunt tamen in summa, quia quod Beda minus ponit in regno Romanorum, superaddit priori regno Persarum; alter uero econuerso." Defraia, *Quodlibeta quinque*, 122.

73. ". . . Christi mors et reiectio ab eis facta fuit causa finalis destructionis eorum . . ." Defraia, *Quodlibeta quinque*, 120.

74. "Sed in hoc dicto unum absurdum cum multis aliis falsitatibus continetur." Defraia, *Quodlibeta quinque*, 131.

75. This midrash is found in the Babylonian Talmud, Sanhedrin 97a. It was well known in Christian circles and appears in Christian Bible commentaries and polemical tracts alike. Cf. Alan of Lille, *Summa Quadripartita*, book 3, PL 210, 399–422.

76. "Ab Adam usque ad primam promissionem factam Abrahe, Genesis XII, sunt precise duo milia anni. Ab illa autem promissione usque ad mortem Vespasiani imperatoris sub quo destructum est templum, sunt iterum duo milia anni . . . a prima promissione Abrahe, in quo lex quodammodo cepit, usque ad tempus in quo euidentissime euacuata fuit, sunt duo milia anni." Defraia, *Quodlibeta quinque*, 135. Olivi makes this point (about the ending of the age of the Law with the destruction of the Temple rather than with Christ's Passion) clearer in his Revelation commentary: " . . . dicimus legalia quantum ad obligationem necessariam fuisse mortificata in Christi passione et resurrectione et tandem sepulta et effecta mortifera in evangelii plena promulgatione et in templi legalis per Titum et Vespasianum destructione." Cited in David Burr, "Olivi's Apocalyptic Timetable," *Journal of Medieval and Renaissance Studies* 11 (1981): 241.

77. See Burr, "Olivi's Apocalyptic Timetable."

78. In his commentary on Revelation, Olivi accounted for Joachim's erroneous conclusions concerning the role of the Cathars by discussing layers of understanding resulting from both natural light and the light of grace. See Burr, "Olivi's Apocalyptic Timetable," 243.

79. Quodlibet 2, question 4, *Utrum Christus possit probari Iudeis iam venisse*, Florence Bibl. Naz. MS Conv. Sopp. D.6.359.

80. This dating of the text is based on the following passage on fol. 114v: ". . . ergo cum ipsi steterint 1296 annis sine sacrificiis, concedant nostrum sacrificium esse illud quo Deus petit honorari." Although the phrasing here might seem to suggest 1296 years had passed since the destruction of the Temple, i.e., around

1370, Peter was clearly dating the cessation of Jewish sacrifice to the advent of Christ. See n. 91 below. Peter Olivi had similarly fused the destruction of the cultic center with the career of Jesus, as in the following passage: "In the same way, we say that the Law was killed as far as obligation is concerned in the Passion and resurrection of Christ, yet was buried and made deadly in the full promulgation of the gospel and in the destruction of the Temple of the Law by Titus and Vespasian." Burr, "Olivi's Apocalyptic Timetable," 241. The manuscript itself can be dated by a list of ministers general of the Franciscan order on the first page of the manuscript. The original manuscript hand goes as far as the fourteenth minister general, Cardinal John de Murro. John was minister general from 1296 until 1304, but cardinal only after 1302. The scribe presumably completed his work during John's tenure, specifically during the period when he was both cardinal and minister general. Later hands continue the list of ministers up to the twenty-third, Louis of Venice. For a careful treatment of the manuscript, including its dating to 1302–1304 see Sylvain Piron, "Le poète et le théologien: Une rencontre dans le Studium de Santa Croce," *Picenum Seraphicum* 19 (2000), 87–134.

81. Hildebert A. Huning, *Die Stellung des Petrus de Trabibus zur Philosophie: Nach dem zweiten Prolog zum ersten Buch seines Sentenzenkommenatars, Ms. 154, Biblioteca Comunale, Assisi* (Werl/Westf.: Coelde, 1965), 19, 22.

82. Piron, "Le poète et le théologien," 95–97.

83. Bernard Jansen, "Petrus de Trabibus. Seine spekulative Eigenart oder sein Verhältnis zu Olivi," *Beiträge zur Geschichte der Philosophie und Theologie des Mittelalters. Texte und Untersuchungen*, Supplementband 2 (1923), 243–54. Piron challenges some long-held assumptions about Peter, most notably that he hailed from the south of France. Piron, "Le poète et le théologien," 93–95.

84. Ehrle, "Petrus Johannis Olivi," 459.

85. Jansen, "Petrus de Trabibus," 243–44.

86. Huning, *Die Stellung des Petrus de Trabibus*, 35–37, 39–43.

87. Huning, *Die Stellung des Petrus de Trabibus*, 21.

88. Cf. Matthew of Aquasparta's 1277/1278 question *Utrum ea de quibus est fides possint ratione probari*, Matthew of Aquasparta, *Quaestiones disputatae*, 119–41.

89. Here Peter is stating a position expressed by writers going back at least as far as Origen that there are passages within the Old Testament in which the literal sense has no validity of its own, except as a vehicle for the spiritual sense. See Smalley, "William of Auvergne," 121–24. Cf. Gilbert Crispin in Anna Sapir Abulafia, "Gilbert Crispin's Disputations: An Exercise in Hermeneutics," in *Les mutations socio-culturelles au tournant des XIe–XIIe siècles: Études Anselmiennes* (Paris, 1984), 511–20.

90. "Contra. Ad hoc nulla est ratio, quia eius adventus est articulis fidei, quia dominus et incarnatis est de Spiritu, scilicet omnis autem articulis est supra rationem. Nec potest probari per auctoritatem novi testamenti, quia non recipiunt . . . nec etiam per auctoritatem veteris testamenti, quam omnis auctoritas de preterito est falsa in sensu litterali, et nullis aliis sensus est argumentativis secundum dialecticos, nec de futuro quam ille adhuc fuerit vere secundum eos, nec probant aliud esse preteriter que dicunt aliud esse futurum." Florence Conv. Sopp. MS D.6.359, fol. 114r.

91. "Psalm 39 ubi volens dare signum sui adventus manifeste dicit esse quando oblationes pro peccato non fient nec sacrificia." Florence Conv. Sopp. MS D.6.359, Fol. 114v.

92. "Cum enim Deus numquam voluerit privari honore sibi debito per sacrificia, sicut patet in lege, semper enim voluit quibusdam sacrificiis coli a principio. Ergo cum tanto tempore fuerit privatus sacrificiis Iudeorum, oportet aliquam alia dari quibus honoretur quam plus acceptet quam illa legalia." Florence Conv. Sopp. MS D.6.359, Fol. 114v.

93. "Malachi 1 constat autem quod hoc non potest intelligi de sacrificio Iudeorum quia omnis oblatio erit immunda extra Ierusalem." Florence Conv. Sopp. MS D.6.359, Fol. 114v.

94. For Roger Marston's treatment of the same subject, see Etzkorn and Brady, *Fr. Rogeri Marston*, 108–10.

95. "Hoc atque dispersio diu duravit plus quam unquam aliquam alia, ergo oportet quod propter maius peccatum commisum per eos . . . non est atque aliquod maius ydolatria nisi peccatum mortis Christi invidiose et malitiose." Florence Conv. Sopp. MS D.6.359, Fol. 114v.

96. "Numquam cessavit quando aliqualiter haberent aliquod regimen dignitatis usque ad 5 annum ante natus Christi, et tunc fuit datus Herodi Ascalonite cui fuit data in uxorem ab Antonio Augusto quidam domina cui debebatur regimen et ex tunc devolutus est regnum ad alienigenam." Florence Conv. Sopp. MS D.6.359, Fol. 114^v.

97. "Et per hoc patet responsio ad argumentum procedit enim ab insufficienti, quia si una auctoritas precisa non sufficit, tamen cum alia ad iuncta bene convincit." Florence Conv. Sopp. MS D.6.359, Fol. 114^v.

98. Isaiah 7:9; Augustine, *Contra faustum manichaeum*, book 4, in *Sancti Aureli Augustini de utilitate credendi, De duabus animabus, Contra fortunatum, Contra adimantum, Contra epistulam fundamenti, Contra faustum*, ed. Joseph Zycha, Corpus Scriptorum Ecclesiasticorum Latinorum 25:1 (Vienna: Tempsky, 1891). On the afterlife of Augustine's notion of belief before understanding, see Edmund Hill, "Unless You Believe, You Shall Not Understand," *Augustinian Studies* 25 (1994): 51–64.

99. "Hanc questionem diffuse pertractat Augustinus 17 and 18 De civitate dei per totum." Florence Conv. Sopp. MS D.6.359, fol. 114v.

100. Augustine, *City of God*, book 17, chapter 35.

101. For example, Peter Alfonse addressed a point later taken up by both Roger Marston and Peter of Trabes, noting that since the duration of the current captivity was so much greater than that of the Babylonian Captivity, the sin that caused the second must have been far greater than the first. Peter Alfonse, *Dialogi contra Iudaeos*, PL 157, 567–81. On the use of Peter Alfonse's material by later medieval scholars, see John Victor Tolan, *Petrus Alfonsi and his Medieval Readers* (Gainesville: University Press of Florida, 1993), 110–15. On Andrew of St. Victor, see Mark Zier's introduction to *Expositio super Danielem: Andreae de Sancto Victore Opera 7*, CCCM 53F. (Turnhout: Brepols, 1990).

102. See Chapter 1.

103. Tachau, *Vision and Certitude*.

Chapter 4. Wrestling with Rashi: Nicholas of Lyra's Quodlibetal Questions and Anti-Jewish Polemic

1. There are well over one hundred extant manuscript copies of the second question on the advent of Christ, of which I have examined over fifty. To study the manuscript tradition thoroughly would be a project in itself and is beyond the scope of this work. I chose to use a single manuscript for all references in the present study because, beyond two variant incipits discussed in this chapter, the texts I have seen are quite uniform. I chose to use the fourteenth-century BAV MS Vat. lat. 869 here because it preserves two of the other questions from the quodlibet and is the only manuscript I've found with the quodlibetal version of the first question. In addition to Nicholas's two questions on the advent, the manuscript includes a third question asking "whether it is possible to prove the final salvation of King Solomon from the Old Testament." BAV Vat. lat. 869, fols. 130r–140v. The question on Solomon precedes the question on the advent of Christi in Assisi Bibl. Communale MS 172, fols. 189r–192r and a portion of the text follows the question on the advent of Christ in Paris BNF lat. 13781 71v–71bisv. Nicholas later incorporated this question into his *Postilla litteralis* on 2 Kings 7:15, "Ex hoc dicunt aliqui quod Salomon, licet peccaverit graviter, ut dictum est, tamen in fine penituerit et sic est salvatus . . . Sed hoc mihi valde dubium sicut diffusius tractavi in quadam questione de quolibet mihi super hoc proposita," and invoked it again at 22:51.

2. Although Scotus was expelled from Paris along with eighty other friars in 1303 for siding with Pope Boniface VIII in his struggle with the French king, Philip the Fair, he was readmitted within a year's time. See Richard Cross, *Duns Scotus* (New York: Oxford University Press, 1999), 4. BAV Vat. lat. 869 testifies to the contemporaneous reception of the two friars' work, as it preserved pieces of both men's Paris quodlibeta alongside each other. Stephen Brown's essay "Nicholas of Lyra's Critique of Scotus' Univocity" in *Historia Philosophia Medii Aevi: Studien zur Geschichte der Philosophie des Mittelalters*, ed. Burkhard Mojsisch and Olaf Pluta (Amsterdam: Grüner, 1991), 1:115–27, presumed Nicholas's authorship of the anonymous quodlibetal question found in BAV Vat. lat. 982 and Florence Laurentiana Cod. 3 Plut. 31 dextra (Santa Croce) based on Franz Pelster's attribution in "*Quodlibeta* und *Quaestiones* des Nikolaus von Lyra, O.F.M." in *Mélanges de Joseph de Ghellinck, S.J.* (Gembloux: Duculot, 1951), 2: 951–73, and "Nikolaus von Lyra und seine *Quaestio de usu paupere*," *AFH* 46 (1953): 211–50. As serious doubt has been cast on this attribution, we lack a direct response from Nicholas to Scotus. Nevertheless, the critique of Scotus described by Brown was disputed while Nicholas was in Paris, and he was quite likely present. On Pelster's attribution and arguments against it, see n. 7 below.

3. Katherine Tachau, *Vision and Certitude in the Age of Ockham: Optics, Epistemology, and the Foundations of Semantics, 1250–1345*. Studien und Texte zur Geistesgeschichte des Mittelalters 22 (Leiden: Brill, 1988), 55. Later Tachau calls Scotus' lectures on the *Sentences* the "most important . . . commentaries presented to Parisian theological students during the opening years of the fourteenth century" (86). Nicholas must have found himself profoundly at odds with Scotus on a range of

issues dealing with Jews, as Scotus's positions were markedly hostile to Jews. It would undoubtedly be worth exploring the extent to which some of Nicholas's questions on Jewish matters may have been directed in part against Scotus' opinions. See Nancy Turner, "Jewish Witness, Forced Conversion, and Island Living: John Duns Scotus on Jews and Judaism," in *Christian Attitudes Toward the Jews in the Middle Ages: A Casebook*, ed. Michael Frassetto (New York: Routledge, 2006).

4. "Explicit questiones abreviate de quolibet magister Enrici de Gandavo ordinate per fratrum Nicolaum de Lyra de ordine minorum magistrum Parisiensis. Paris Bibl. Mazarine MS 732, fols. 69r–168v.

5. Mark Zier has a helpful discussion of the question in "Nicholas of Lyra on the Book of Daniel," in *Nicholas of Lyra: The Senses of Scripture*, ed. Philip Krey and Lesley Smith (Leiden: Brill, 2000), 176–78.

6. Following the trial of the Talmud in Paris, twenty-four wagonloads of Jewish books were consigned to the flames in June 1242. Solomon Grayzel, *The Church and the Jews in the Thirteenth Century*, 2nd ed., rev. (New York: Hermon Press, 1966), 31–32, 250–53. Large numbers of Jewish books were confiscated during and after the 1306 expulsion of the Jews from France, and on December 7, 1309 three full wagonloads of Jewish books were burned publicly. *S. Martialis Chronicon*, in *Recueil des historiens des Gaules et de la France*, ed. Martin Bouquet, Léopold Delisle, et al. (Paris: Victor Palmé et al., 1738–1904), 21:813 C.

7. See n. 1 above on the third question, "whether it is possible to prove the final salvation of King Solomon from the Old Testament." Franz Pelster argued in "*Quodlibeta* und *Quaestiones* des Nikolaus von Lyra," and "Nikolaus von Lyra und seine *Quaestio de usu paupere*," that several anonymous quodlibeta preserved in BAV Vat. lat. 982 and Florence Laurentiana Cod. 3 Plut. 31 dextra (Santa Croce) were also disputed by Nicholas in a second round of disputations in 1310. The quodlibeta consider a number of controversial topics, including *usus pauper* and whether the time of Antichrist's arrival could be known. The question on the coming of Antichrist has been partially edited in Josep Perarnau, "Guiu Terrena Critica Arnau de Vilanova," *Arxiu de Textos Catalans Antics* 7/8 (1988–89): 221–22. The attribution is problematic in spite of Pelster's carefully argued thesis. Nowhere in Nicholas's extensive writings does he mention any of the questions presented in these quodlibeta, whereas he frequently refers to others of his known questions. Pelster writes that since the author of the quodlibeta debated the questions in Florence, we must assume that Nicholas spent some time teaching there. However, there is absolutely no evidence to indicate that Nicholas ever went to Florence, and he never mentions the region in his *Postilla litteralis*, whereas he frequently refers to places and events that took place in his native Normandy and his later city of residence, Paris. Rega Wood and Philip Krey have shown that the question on *usus pauper* is very much at odds with Nicholas's position in his *Postilla litteralis*, so much so that they question whether the same person could have written the two works, even allowing for an evolution of thought over the years. Krey convincingly argues that, for the present, the author of the quodlibeta must remain anonymous. For a discussion of Pelster's thesis and the problems inherent in it, see Rega Wood, "Church and Scripture in Franciscan Gospel Commentaries" (Ph.D. diss., Cornell University, 1975), and

Philip Krey, "Nicholas of Lyra: Apocalypse Commentary as Historiography" (Ph.D. diss., University of Chicago, 1990), 14–16, 37–47.

8. "Et in ea sit expressa mentio de eius divinitate sicut de humanitate et multe alie auctoritates consimilies in sequenti questione adducuntur . . ." BAV Vat. lat. 869, fol. 130r. The version of the question incorporated into the *Postilla litteralis* on Matthew 21 leaves out this reference.

9. The text twice indicates a composition date of 1309: "Ab illo tempore usque nunc fluxerunt mille trecenti novem anni scriptum est hoc opus"; and "Quia a principio mundi ipsi computant 5070 annos, usque ad annum domini 1309 in quo presens opus fuit scriptum," Paris BNF lat. 13781, fols. 64v, 67v. BAV Vat. lat. 869, which I use as the primary text here because of its preservation of the three quodlibetal questions as a group, records composition dates of 1314/15, fols. 134v; 136r. BAV Vat. lat. 869 is the only copy of the text I have encountered with those dates, and I take it to be a mistake. Perhaps a scribe confronted with the year 1314 (the number viiii could easily be misread as xiiii) as the date of composition decided to fix the number of years since the destruction of the Temple to correspond with that year. The two conflicting dates along with other minor errors in the text—missing or doubled words, for instance—indicate some carelessness on the part of the scribe. Some printed editions of the question, including the widely available Venice 1588 edition of the *Postilla*, which has the question at the end of the commentary, contain a variant in the first passage offering the year 1309 as that in which the work "coeptum est" rather than "scriptum est." Not one of the more than fifty fourteenth- and fifteenth-century MSS I consulted contained the word "coeptum" in place of "scriptum" and I have been unable to discover how this change entered the printed tradition. I do think it safe to dismiss this as a late mutation. As written quodlibeta grew into more lengthy treatises by the early fourteenth century, the time between the disputation itself and the writing of the master's final version also grew. Thus a quodlibet written and "published" by Nicholas in the year 1309 would probably have been disputed in the previous academic year (1308–9). Quodlibetal disputations were held only twice a year, at Advent and at Lent. Because the new year began at Easter in Paris, both disputation periods in a given academic year fell into the same calendar year. Both disputation periods in the academic year 1308–9 would have been held in the year 1308 (old style). Since only masters had the right to hold quodlibetal disputations, at least within a university setting, we know that the quodlibet could not have been disputed before this time. John Wippel, "Quodlibetal Questions Chiefly in Theology Faculties," in *Les questions disputées et les questions quodlibétique dans les facultés de théologie, de droit et de médecine*, ed. Bernardo C. Bazan et al., Typologie des sources du Moyen Age occidental, 44–45 (Turnhout: Brepols, 1985), 171–72; 186.

10. Henri Labrosse, "Oeuvres de Nicolas de Lyre," *Études Franciscaines* 35 (1923): 177–80. Examples of recent studies that depend upon Labrosse's dating schema in their discussion of Nicholas's text include Jeremy Cohen, *The Friars and the Jews: The Evolution of Medieval Anti-Judaism* (Ithaca, N.Y.: Cornell University Press, 1982); Gilbert Dahan, *L'exégèse chrétienne de la Bible en Occident médiéval: XIIe–XIVe siècle* (Paris: Cerf, 1999), and Michael Signer, "Vision and History: Nich-

olas of Lyra on the Prophet Ezechiel," in *Nicholas of Lyra: The Senses of Scripture*, ed. Philip Krey and Lesley Smith (Leiden: Brill, 2000), 147–71.

11. For a detailed treatment of the dating of the text (in both extant incipit forms) to 1309 see my "The Dating of Nicholas of Lyra's *Quaestio de Adventu Christi*," *AFH* 86 (1993): 297–312.

12. I am using here the quodlibetal version of the question as preserved in BAV Vat. lat. 869, fol. 130r. The earlier version differs only in small details from the later version presented in the *Postilla litteralis* on Matthew 21, but the details make clear the connection between this question and the one on proving the Advent from Jewish sources. Jeremy Cohen treated the *Postilla litteralis super Matthaeum* version of this question briefly in "The Jews As Killers of Christ in the Latin Tradition, from Augustine to the Friars," *Traditio* 39 (1983): 1–27. Nicholas's prooftexts here conform entirely to those long established in the Latin tradition.

13. "In populo Iudeorum aliqui erat minores, sicut layci et vulgares, tantummodo scientes illud quod est de necessitate salutis ut precepta decalogi et haec qui debent sciri ab omnibus sed subtilitates scriptarum et dicta prophetarum ignorantes." And a bit farther down, after introducing text proving that Scripture taught the common people to defer to the priests or elders on such matters: "Quod minores populi Iudeorum non cognoverunt Iesum esse Christum nec quantum ad divinitatem nec quantum ad humanitatem quia licet cognoscerent eum esse hominem verum tamen non cognoscebant illum hominem seu prophetam qui erat a deo promissus sicut Christum. Cuius ratio est quia ignorabant scripturas prophetarum qui locuntur de Christi divinitate et illas que locuntur determinatio temporis et de signis sui adventus." BAV Vat. lat. 869, fol. 130r. Cf. Cohen, "Jews as Killers of Christ," 3–8.

14. "Sed maiores cognoverunt eum esse verum prophetam a Deo promissum et missum quia sciebant scripturas loquentes de tempore sui adventus et de signis que omnia videbant in ipso impleri." BAV Vat. lat. 869, fol. 130r.

15. Bonnie Kent, *Virtues of the Will: The Transformation of Ethics in the Late Thirteenth Century* (Washington, D.C.: Catholic University of America Press, 1995); Risto Saarinen, *Weakness of the Will in Medieval Thought: From Augustine to Buridan* (Leiden: Brill, 1994).

16. Kent, *Virtues of the Will*, 152. See also Saarinen, *Weakness of the Will*. Thomas Aquinas had addressed the specific action of passion on the process of intellection and movement from habitual (universal) to actual (particular) knowledge in the *Summa theologia*, question 1, q. 77 and elsewhere. For a summary of his thought relevant to Nicholas's argument here, see Kent, *Virtues of the Will*, 156–74 and Saarinen, *Weakness of the Will*, 118–31. According to Aristotle and scholastic thinkers, passion works only on actual, not habitual knowledge. The incontinent man continues to perceive the moral good but fails to connect that universal sense with the particular situation at hand.

17. "Eodem modo dicendum est quod Iudei habent veram estimationem de Christo et in habitu et in actu in principio sed quando incepit contra eos praedicare excitati fuerunt contra eum passionibus ire rancoris et invidie quibus passionibus impediebantur ab actuali consideratione veritatis praehabite de Christo et ideo machinati sunt in eius mortem." BAV Vat. lat. 869, fol. 130r.

18. "Considerandum tamen quod illa notitia quam haberent de Christo per scripturas prophetarum non erat certa certitudine evidentie, tum quia talis certitudo habetur solum per demonstrationem et sensum, tum quia prophetie possunt aliquando varie exponi et ideo erat vix notitia probabilis et verisimilis coniecture." BAV Vat. lat. 869, fol. 130r.

19. Cohen, "Jews as Killers of Christ," 17–21.

20. Cohen writes, "The biblical evidence for the ignorance of the Jews, inasmuch as it concerns the *majores*, attests merely the failure of their knowledge to withstand their malice and ultimately to govern their actions." "Jews as Killers of Christ," 20–21.

21. In the quodlibetal version of the question, Matthew 21 is just one of several biblical passages invoked for and against the proposition. That Nicholas chose to place the question at this point in his *Postilla litteralis*, when it could have been placed in a number of other places equally well, suggests that he wanted to contribute a new layer of thought to the idea of Jewish culpability or malice in the Crucifixion.

22. "Quia non se disposuerunt ad spiritum gratie et sue spiritualis illuminationis per quem et internam vim littere et circumstantias sanctorum Christi et temporis in quo venit intellexissent." Peter Olivi, *Quodlibeta quinque: ad fidem codicum nunc primum edita cum introductione historico-critica*, ed. Stefano Defraia, Collectio Oliviana 7 (Grottaferrata (Rome): Editiones Collegii S. Bonaventurae ad Claras Aquas, 2002), 117.

23. See n. 25.

24. *Utrum ex scripturis a Iudeis receptis possit efficaciter probari salvatorem nostrum fuisse Deum et hominem.* BAV Vat. lat. 869, fol. 130r. The alternative incipit reads instead *Utrum per scripturas a Iudeis receptas possit probari misterium Christi in lege et prophetis promissi esse iam completum.*

25. "In contrarium arguebatur quia inter Iudeos fuerint et sunt ingeniosi et in scripturis legis et prophetarum valde studiosi igitur si predicta possent haberi efficaciter per scripturas ab eis receptas non est verisimile quod stetissent tamdiu in errore ergo etc." BAV Vat. lat. 869, fol. 130r.

26. *Queritur utrum per scripturas a Iudeis receptas possit probari mysterium Christi in lege et prophetis promissum esse iam completum.* BAV Archivio S. Pietro D202, fols. 62v–74r.

27. Although manuscripts with incipit 1 outnumber those with incipit 2 in the earliest copies of the text, numerous mid-fourteenth-century manuscripts with incipit 2 exist, including BAV Archivio S. Pietro D202, a collection of Lyra's works with a colophon dating it to 1343.

28. ". . . et maxime Ionathan filius Oziel cuius scriptura ita autentica est apud Hebreos quod nullus ausus fuit sibi contradicere, propter quod in libris notabilibus Iudeorum posuit Ebraicum purum in una columna et Chaldaicum scriptum ab isto Ionathan litteris Ebraicis in altera, et utuntur Iudei isto Chaldaico quasi pro expositione quia aliqua que erant multum obscura in Ebraico puro clarius ponuntur et quasi exponuntur in illo Chaldaico, ut infra patebit magis, et ideo translatio necessaria est ad disputandum cum iudeis in passibus multis." BAV Vat. lat. 869, fol. 130v. The Targum bearing Jonathan b. Uzziel's name was attributed to him erron-

eously; it was composed long after his death. For a general introduction to Targum literature, see Paul Virgil McCracken Flesher, "The Targumim," in *Judaism in Late Antiquity* 1, ed. Jacob Neusner (Leiden: Brill, 1995), 40–63. Contrary to Nicholas's suggestion that no Jew dared question the Targum, it could, in fact, be approached with considerable skepticism owing to the liberties it took in translating the Hebrew.

29. Compare Roger Marston, Raymond Rigauld, Peter Olivi and Peter Trabes in Chapter 3.

30. "Similiter dicta doctorum Hebraicorum qui glosaverunt vetus testamentus sunt autentica multa magis quam apud nos dicta Ieronymus vel Augustinus et aliorum doctorum catholicorum, et hoc potissime propter hoc quod scribitur Deut. 17, non declinabis a verbi eorum ad dextram sive ad sinistram ubi loquitur scriptura de sacerdotibus doctoribus, ad quos precepit scriptura in dubiis recurrere et eorum sententiam indiscusse tenere." BAV Vat. lat. 869, fol. 130v.

31. "Licet, autem, huiusmodi scripture per magna parte sint false, scilicet Thalmud et glose doctorum Hebraicorum, tantum per eas possumus eficaciter arguere ex quo sunt ab eis predicto modo recepte sicut econtrario argumentum quod facerent contra nos ex evangelio et scripturis apostolorum et huius esset eficax contra nos licet repugnent huius scripturas falsem continere." BAV Vat. lat. 869, fol. 130v.

32. Cohen, *Friars and the Jews*, 131–56.

33. "Si considerentur iste responsiones due sunt verissime . . . Similiter secunda responsio que dicit quod Asaph tripliter nominavit Deum, quia deus in tribus proprietatibus creavit mundum est verissima, quia tres proprietates constituentes personas et mundus creatus est in tribus proprietatibus istis quia indivisa sunt opera trinitatis. Patet etiam ex istis quod non est contra intentionem doctorum Ebraicorum quod aliqua pluralitas ponatur in divinis . . . Hanc autem responsionem ultimam que ut visum est continet veritate posteriores Iudei depravant dicentes quod iste tres proprietates in quibus deus creavit mundum sunt divina scilicet sapientia, bonitas, et potentia in quibus facit omnia, et ideo in principio quando dicitur 'creavit Heloym' ad denotandam istas tres proprietates sive atributa in deo in quibus omnia operatur, et eodem modo exponunt auctoritates alias. Sed ista responsio non est rationabilis. Primo quia sicut deus operatur per potentiam, sapientiam et amorem ita artifex creatus operatur per artem suam sicut per regulam directivam et per potentiam transmutandi materiam et per amorem lucri sicut propter finem. Si igitur propter predicta, scilicet propter potentiam, sapientiam, et bonitatem divinam, nomen divinum ponitur in plurali quando dicitur operari . . . Et confirmatur ratio quia sapientia, amor, et potentia plus diferunt in artifice creato quam in deo quia diferunt re abstracta quod non potest esse in deo. Modus loquendi in plurali magis conpetit in expressione operationis artificis quam ipsius domini." BAV Vat. lat. 869, fols. 131r–131v. Cf. Hugh of St. Victor and other earlier discussions of the Trinity in terms of wisdom, goodness, and power in Dominique Poirel, *Livre de la nature et débat trinitaire au XIIe siècle: Le De tribus diebus de Hughes de Saint-Victor* (Turnhout: Brepols, 2002).

34. "Item arguitur sic: intentio Moysi erat inducere populum ad cultum unius Dei et ipsum ab idolatria revocare ad quem iste populus erat pronus, ut patet

ex toto discursu veteris testamenti, cum igitur per modum predictum in plurali posset haberi aliqua occasio cogitandi pluralitatem Iudeis non est verisimile quod Moyses, qui cognoscebat pronitatem populi ad idolatriam, usus fuisset tali modo loquendi et in scripturis reliquisset nisi per hoc subtiliter sapientibus indicare voluisset quod cum unitate simplicis essentie in Deo sic pluralitas personarum, aliter suus modus scribendi esset contrarius sue intentione." BAV Vat. lat. 869, fol. 131v.

35. "Ista sunt que dixi de ista ratione quando hanc questionem determinavi. Sed postea venit ad manum meam quidam libellus Hebraice scriptus ubi predicta ratio aliter solvitur." BAV Vat. lat. 869, fol. 131v.

36. "Item non solum arguitur pluralitas personarum in divinis ex hoc nomine Heloym ut ipse supposito dicens quod innititur baculo arundineo confracto sed eandum pluralitatem clarius exprimunt prophete in multis locis." Vat. lat. 869, fol. 132r.

37. "Ista sunt verba Domini loquentis secundum quod patet ex textu immediate precedenti. Similiter ex hoc quod immediate subditur, hoc dicit 'redemptor tuus sanctus Israel' . . . Nunc autem ita est quod intermittentem et missum semper est distinctio personalis, ergo in trinitas personarum est in Deis scilicet Dei missi et Dei mittentis et spiritus eius. Deum autem missum dicimus Filium incarnatum, Deum autem mittentem et spiritum eius dicimus Patrem et Spiritum Sanctum." BAV Vat. lat. 869, fol. 132r.

38. "Ad evadendum autem istum dictum Rabbi Salomon advenit unum mendacium super locum istum dicens quod omnes prophete fuerunt in Monte Synai cum Moyse et ibi acciperunt prophetias denunciaverunt et publicaverunt populo tempore a deo determinato, et ideo dicit quod verba premissa sunt verba Isaia ab illo loco ex tempore ante quam fierent ibi ['ex tempore antequam fierent ibi eram'], id est a tempore datione legem de qua sit ibi sermo fui in Monte Synai et quod ibi subditur et nunc me misit dominus etc. referatur ad tempus quo Isaias missus [est] ad denunciandum populo ista que primus acceperat in Monte Synai a Deo." BAV Vat. lat. 869, fol. 132r.

39. "Et sic patet quod dictum Rabbi Salomonis non solum est contra prophetiam totam . . . sed etiam contra totam scripturam Veteris Testamenti ut patet ex predictis." BAV Vat. lat. 869, fol. 132v.

40. "Ad idem etiam facit quod habetur Ecclesiastes 4 funiculus tripliciter dificile rumpitur. Glossa Hebraica sensus videtur esse misterium trinitatis Dei non de facili discutitur. Sed glossam hanc antiquam pervertunt retorquentes hanc trinitatem ad tria attributa divina que sunt potentia, sapientia, et bonitas." BAV Vat. lat. 869, fol. 132v.

41. "Patet igitur primum principale, scilicet qualiter pluralitas personarum possit probari per scripturam a Iudeis receptam." BAV Vat. lat. 869, fol. 132v.

42. "Sed ista responsio nulla est, quia nullum predictorum nominatur proprio nomine Dei, quod est nomen Tetragrammaton, sed nominatur quodlibet predictorum a quodam effectu Dei, qui est Deus solus nominatur isto nomine. Et hoc non est inconveniens sicut aliquis homo bene vocatur Adeodatus vel Deusdedit vel aliud huius, non tamen vocatur deus absolute quia hoc esset impium, et hoc patet discurrendo per omnia predicta." BAV Vat. lat. 869, fol. 132v.

43. "Ezechiel ultimo non dicitur nomen civitatis Dominus ita quod nomine-

tur nomine Domini Tetragrammaton sed dicitur ibi 'nomen civitatis, Dominus ibidem,' id est, denominari debet a divina inhabitatione, et hoc patet per translationem Caldaicam, que sic habet: 'nomen civitatis expone [!] a die qua fecit Dominus descendere divinitatem suam ibidem.'" BAV Vat. lat. 869, fol. 132v. Paris BNF lat. 13781, fol. 60v, reads "exponent."

44. "Patet igitur ex predictis quod nomen Domini Tetragrammaton non dicitur de aliquo nisi de solo vero Deo." BAV Vat. lat. 869, fol 132v.

45. Maimonides' discussion of the names for God occurs in book 61 of the *Guide.*

46. On this charge, see Irven M. Resnick, "The Falsification of Scripture and Medieval Christian and Jewish Polemics," *Medieval Encounters* 2 (1996): 344–80.

47. "Contra istam solutionem non potest argui nisi ostendendo quod ipsi corrumpunt litteram ut negent Christi divinitatem. Hac autem optime posset fieri ex antiquis Bibliis que non essent corrumpte in passu isto et in aliis in quibus sit mentio de divinitate Christi, si possent haberi, et hoc modo illi qui precesserunt contra eos in isto passu et consimilibus arguebant. Licet autem ego non viderim aliquam Bibliam Hebraicam que non sit corrumpta in isto passu, tamen audivi a fide dignis ratione scientie et vite afirmantibus iuramento quod sic viderant in antiquis Bibliis sicut habet translatio Ieronymi superioribus adducta." BAV Vat. lat. 869, fol. 133r.

48. "Si autem non possent haberi biblie antique non corrumpte, recurrendendum est ad alias translationes quas iudei rationabiliter negare non possent et per hoc poterit dicta falsitas deprehendi." BAV Vat. lat. 869, fol. 133r.

49. Jeremiah 33:16, a rephrasing of the prophecy in Jeremiah 23:5, reads, *In those days shall Judah be saved, and Jerusalem shall dwell securely: and this is the name that they shall call him, The Lord our just one.*

50. "Item licet Iudei exspectent purum hominem futurum, tamen exspectant eum sicut prophetam sanctissimam et sanctiorem Moyse. Hoc autem esset impossibile si permitteret se vocari nomine Domini Tetragrammaton nisi sic esset secundum veritatem, immo incurreret peccatum blasphemie, et sic patet quod ista obiectio nulla esset." BAV Vat. lat. 869, fol. 133r.

51. "Item quod dicunt istam pacem debere intelligi de pace quam habuit populus Israel sub Ezechia interfecto exercitu Senacherib patet falsum per sequentem textum quia immediate subditur in auctoritate Isaia predicta, multiplicabitur eius imperium et pacis non erit finis, quia ista pax que fuit sub Ezechia fuit satis brevis, ut patet inspicienti quartum librum Regum. Item predicta responsio Iudeorum patet falsum per translationem Chaldaycam que sic habet 'infans datus est nobis et filius datus est nobis et reciperet super se legem ad servandam eam et vocabitur nomen eius de ante mirabilis consilio deus fortis permanens in secula seculorum messias in cuius deibus pax multiplicabitur.' Per hoc enim quod dicitur 'messias' patet quod haec auctoritas non est intelligenda de Ezechia sed de Christo. Per hoc autem quod hic dicitur 'et vocabitur nomen eius de ante mirabilis consilii Deus fortis, etc.' patet quod nomina divinitatem exprimentia referunt ad Christum, ita quod ipse est vere Deus." BAV Vat. lat. 869, fol. 133v.

52. "Quod autem ista determinatio 'de ante' que non est in Ebraico, hoc est ad denotandum quod hoc nomen Christus primus vocatum est a deo et etiam ab

angelo quam temporaliter nasceretur, secundum quod habetur Lucum 2 et Mattheum 1. Quod autem in translatione Chaldayca dicitur 'et recipiet super se legem ad servandam eam' loco cuius in Hebraico et in translatione Ieronymi habetur 'et factus est principatus super humerum eius,' hoc est ad denotandum quod Christus erat impleturus legem et servaturus secundum quod ipsemet dicit expresse Mattheus 5, 'non veni salvere legem sed ad implere.'" BAV Vat. lat. 869, fol. 133v.

53. "Item notandum quod in predicta auctoritate Isaia ubi de Christo dicitur multiplicabitur eius imperium in Ebraico positur 'lemarbe' quod sonat in latino 'ad multiplicandum.' Scribitur haec dictio Hebraicas [!] sic quod hec littera 'm' clausa ponitur in medio dictionis quod est contra naturam huius [littere] et modum scribendi Ebraicum, quia nusquam alibi positur nisi in fine dictionis, secundum quod tangit Ieronymus in Prologo Galeato ubi dicit quod apud Hebreos sunt 5 littere duplices quia per eas aliter scribuntur fines aliter media et principia, et de istis 5 litteris duplicibus una est littera men et men clausa et inest aperta, et inest clausa semper ponitur in fine dictionis, inest apertu in medio et principio dictionis. Hec autem ut dictum est ponitur inest clausa in medio dictionis contra naturam littere et modum scribendi ad denotandum quod Christus de quo loquitur propheta erat nascituus de virgine clausa contra modum nature, et quod misterium incarnationis erat clausum et secretum." BAV Vat. lat. 869, fol. 133v. Jerome's prologue discussed the Hebrew language but not this interpretation of Isaiah based upon the unusual placement of the final mem. See Jerome, *St. Eusebii Hieronymi, Prologus Galeatus*, PL 113.

54. Babylonian Talmud, Mas. Pesachim 54a; Nedarim 39b.

55. "Sed hoc dictum est ita irrationale quod non indiget improbatione. Lex enim non potuit per se creari sed in aliquo intellectu, hoc autem non potest esse in intellectu divino in quo non potest aliquid creari, nec in aliquo intellectu angelico vel humano potuit sic creari [nec in aliquo intellectu angelico vel humano potuit sic creari!] ante mundum, quia angelus vel homo non ponuntur in creata ante mundum secundum ipsos. [Similiter quod penitentia, que non est nisi de peccato preterito, fuerit ante mundum] et per consequens ante peccatum. Hoc etiam posset argui et de istis et de aliis consequentibus sed obmitto quia illa predicta frivola et absurda." BAV Vat. lat. 869, fol. 134r. The missing phrase about repentance in Vat. lat. 869 is present in other MSS, including Paris BNF lat. 13781, fol. 63r.

56. Raymond Martini, *Pugio fidei contra Mauros et Iudaeos*, fols. 516–17. Raymond's version lists (1) Throne of Glory, (2) Torah, (3) House of the Sanctuary, (4) Age of the Patriarchs, (5) Israel, (6) Name of the messiah, (7) Repentance. The text continues: "And there are those who say the Garden of Eden and *Gehenna*."

57. Chai Merchavia, *The Church Versus Talmudic and Midrashic Literature, 500–1248* (Jerusalem: Bialik, 1970) (Hebrew); Gilbert Dahan, "Rashi, sujet de la controverse de 1240: Edition partielle du MS. Paris, BN lat. 16558," *Archives juives* 4, no. 3 (1978): 43–53.

58. See Chapter 2.

59. "Patet igitur ex predictis secundum principale, scilicet qualiter ex scripturis a Iudeis receptis possit probari incarnatio divine persone." BAV Vat. lat. 869, fol. 134r.

60. "Postquam probatum est tempus Christi adventus preteritum per script-

uram canonicam veram, hoc idem probatur per glossa et dicta doctorum Hebreorum, apud eos autentica." BAV Vat. lat. 869, fol. 136r.

61. "Sed salva Bede reverentia utrumque dictum videtur falsum, quia in Hebraico non ponitur 'abreviate' prout sonat detruncationem seu diminutionem sed in Hebreo puro precise et notat temporis determinationem non plus nec minus." BAV Vat. lat. 869, fol. 135r.

62. See discussion in Chapter 3.

63. "Ad intellectum huius, sciendum quod Hebrei dicunt hoc fuisse dictum [a filio mulieris] Sarepte, quem suscitavit Helias, qui etiam habuit postea spiritum prophetie, et prophetavit de duratione mundi, quod duraret ut dictum est sex milibus annorum." BAV Vat. lat. 869, fol. 136r. This MS misreads "a filio mulieris" as "consilio intellectis." The midrash appears twice in the Babylonian Talmud: Sanhedrin 97a and Avodah Zarah 9a. Of the two Talmudic versions, only Avodah Zarah preserves the calculation of the age of Torah with Abraham's calling that Nicholas presents here. The midrash also appears in the *Tanna de-Vei Eliyahu*. See Meir Friedman, ed., *Tanna de-Vei Eliyahu* (reprint Jerusalem: Sifre Vahrman, 1969) (Hebrew); and William Braude and Israel Kapstein, *Tanna debe Eliyahu: The Lore of the School of Elijah* (Philadelphia: Jewish Publication Society of America, 1981). The story of Elijah's resuscitation of the woman's son is recounted in 3 Kings 17:9–16 (1 Kings 17:9–16 in the Hebrew Bible) and is referenced in Luke 4:25–26.

64. "Tamen illa captivitas non duravit nisi per 70 annos cum igitur captivitas inqua sunt modo per mille 240 annos, nec adhuc apereat eorum liberatio de proximo, eos oportet concedere quod peccatum illud propter quod tamdiu captivati sunt sic maius quam peccata precedentia captivitatem Babilonicam, cum pena debeat correspondere peccato, hoc autem non potest dici nisi propter illud peccatum gravissimum quo Christum eis in lege et prophetis promissum negantes et persequentes crudeliter occiderunt." BAV Vat. lat. 869, fol. 136v.

65. "Hoc etiam dicit Rabi Moyses in libro Iudicum Jesus Nazarenus visus est esse messias et interfectus est per domum iudicii, et ipse fuit causa et promeruit ut destrueretur Israel in gladio." BAV Vat. lat. 869, fol. 136v. Maimonides, *Mishneh Torah, Sefer Mishpatim*, chapter 11. See also the *Epistle to Yemen*, where he again decries Jesus' messianic pretensions and asserts that the Jewish court gave him "fitting punishment."

66. This notion of "first principles," derived from Aristotle's *Posterior Analytics*, referred to basic things that could be known without resorting to complex cognitive processes. The specific action by which such basic principles were known was understood differently by different medieval thinkers. See Steven Marrone, *The Light of Thy Countenance: Science and Knowledge of God in the Thirteenth Century* (Leiden: Brill, 2001), 332–34, 424–27.

67. "Item doctrina aliqua declaratur vera dupliciter. Uno modo per reductionem ad principia evidentia, et hoc modo declaratur veritas eorum que subiacent facultati naturali intellectus. Alio modo per divinum testimonium scilicet quando ad confirmationem alicuius doctrine sit tale miraculum de quo certum est quod non potest fieri nisi virtute divina, sicut est suscitatio mortui, illuminatio ceci nati et consimilia." BAV Vat. lat. 869, fol. 136v.

68. "Sacra autem scriptura predixit adventum Christi ut patet in multis locis

determinavit etiam tempus veniendi, videlicet quando fieret translatio regni, ut habetur Genesis 49 'non auferetur' etc., similiter locum nascendi, Michee 5 'et tu Betlehem Ephrata' etc. Similiter modum vivendi, scilicet quod Christus in paupertate viveret, Zacharia 9 'ecce rex tuus veniet tibi iustus et salvator et ipse pauper' etc. Similiter determinavit scriptura modum moriendi scilicet in humilitate patiencia ex parte ipsius Christi cum crudelitate maxima ex parte occidentium ipsum, ut habetur Isaia 53 sicut 'ovis ad occisionem ducetur' etc. Hec autem manifeste sunt impleta in Iesu Nazareno. Ex quo rationabiliter concluditur quod ipse fuit vere Christus." BAV Vat. lat. 869, fol. 136v.

69. "Multi litterati inter eos perceperunt etiam a tempore Christi sicut patet de Nathanaele et Nichodemo et Gamalieli qui fuerunt doctores et periti in lege. Similiter de Paulo apostolo et Apollo et multis aliis." BAV Vat. lat. 869, fol. 137v. Nathanael is named, along with Philip, as one of Jesus' first disciples in John 1:43–51. Nicodemus, understood to have been a Pharisee and member of the Sanhedrin, is portrayed in the Gospel According to John 7:50–52 and 19:39 as sympathetic to Jesus. Gamaliel was likewise a Pharisee and member of the Sanhedrin who is depicted coming to the apostles' defense in Acts 5:34–9. Apollos' preaching career is described in Acts 18:24–8.

70. "Multi tamen avertuntur a fide triplici de causa. Una est propter timorem penurie temporalis quia semper cupidi fuerunt et in lege eorum frequenter promittitur habundantia temporalium, ideo supra modum abhorrent contrarium." BAV Vat. lat. 869, fol. 137v.

71. See David Burr, *Olivi and Franciscan Poverty: The Origins of the Usus Pauper Controversy* (Philadelphia: University of Pennsylvania Press, 1989).

72. Expulsion was theologically problematic for many scholars and could only be justified by accusations of gross violations of Christian "benevolence" and "tolerance," such as usury. Nicholas was surprisingly quiet on the expulsion of the Jews in his writing, considering his presence in Paris during the event. King Philip IV's quick dispatch of those who sided against him in his conflict with the pope may have had much to do with Nicholas's reticence. On Jewish conversion, see Stacey, "The Conversion of Jews to Christianity in Thirteenth-Century England," *Speculum* 67 (1992): 263–83; Jonathan Elukin, "From Jew to Christian? Conversion and Immutability in Medieval Europe," in *Varieties of Religious Conversion in the Middle Ages*, ed. James Muldoon (Gainesville: University Press of Florida, 1997), 171–89.

73. "Alia causa est quia a cunabulis nutriuntur in odio Christi et legis Christiane et Christicolis maledicunt in synagogis omni die. Illa autem ad que sunt homines consueti a pueritia sunt quasi in naturam conversa et per consequens avertunt iudicium intellectis a veritate contraria." BAV Vat. lat. 869, fol. 137v.

74. "Tertia causa est propter dificultatem et altitudinem eorum que in fide catholica proponuntur, credenda sicut est trinitas personarum in una natura divina et due nature in una persona Christi, et sacramentum euchariste que nullo modo possunt capere, et ideo reputant nos tres deos colere. In ipsa etiam eucharistia reputant nos pessime ydolatrare, sicut per experientiam cognoverunt illi qui frequenter de istis cum eis contulerunt . . ." BAV Vat. lat. 869, fol. 137v.

75. ". . . et ideo a fide catholica avertuntur, et plures iam baptizati ad vomitum revertuntur." BAV Vat. lat. 869, fol. 137v.

76. Guillaume de Nangis, *Chronique latine de Guillaume de Nangis de 1113 à 1300 avec les continuations de cette chronique de 1300 à 1368*, ed. Hercule Geraud (Paris, 1843), 1:363–64, 380. On Nicholas's participation in Marguerite's trial, see Henri Labrosse, "Biographie de Nicolas de Lyre," *Études franciscaines* 17 (1907): 595.

77. On Christian anxiety over the sincerity of Jewish conversions, see Elukin, "From Jew to Christian?"

78. Deeana C. Klepper, "The Dating of Nicholas of Lyra's *Quaestio de adventu Christi*," *AFH* 86 (1993): 297–312.

79. Copies of the bull were sent to Franciscan and Dominican convents all across Europe. See Edward A. Synan, *The Popes and the Jews in the Middle Ages* (New York: Macmillan, 1965), 119–20 and Cohen, *Friars and the Jews*, 82–84.

Chapter 5. Christian Ownership of Jewish Text: Nicholas of Lyra as an Alternative Jewish Authority

1. Klaus Reinhardt, "Das Werk des Nikolaus von Lyra im Mittelalterlichen Spanien," *Traditio* 43 (1987): 321–58.

2. That we today recognize figures like Raymond Martini or Paul of Burgos to have been far more learned in Jewish tradition does not impinge on Nicholas's reputation in medieval Christendom.

3. Reinhardt, "Das Werk des Nikolaus von Lyre."

4. Philip Krey, "Many Readers But Few Followers: The Fate of Nicholas of Lyra's 'Apocalypse Commentary' in the Hands of His Late-Medieval Admirers," *Church History* 64 (1995): 185–201.

5. Christopher Ocker, *Biblical Poetics Before Humanism and Reformation* (Cambridge: Cambridge University Press, 2002), 181–83.

6. Paris Bibl. Mazarine MS 168, which dates to sometime in the fourteenth century, belonged to the Abbey of St. Victor, as written on the last folio.

7. This rubric is found in Munich Clm 5526, fol. 74r. The manuscript is clearly related to Paris BNF lat. 2384, which probably came first, and in which the identical rubric is found on fol. 193v.

8. On Nicholas's plagiarism, see Deeana C. Klepper, "The Dating of Nicholas of Lyra's *Quaestio de adventu Christi*." *AFH* 86 (1993): 297–312. A fourteenth-century manuscript of the Bibliothèque de St. Germain des Prés, now Paris BNF lat. 13781, contains all three texts preceded by the life of St. Anne and prophecies of St. Hildegard. Robert E. Lerner, in *The Powers of Prophecy: The Cedar of Lebanon Vision from the Mongol Onslaught to the Dawn of the Enlightenment* (Berkeley: University of California Press, 1983), 68, argues convincingly that Nicholas most likely copied from Paris BNF lat. 13781 (or its model) based on variants in one of the John of Paris texts, which Nicholas carries over. Patricia D. Stirnemann has generously examined the manuscript and states that in her view it is of Parisian production in the first half of the fourteenth century. Since, according to Hillenbrand, Nicholas of Strassburg was off at a provincial studium teaching philosophy between 1315 and 1320 and left Paris in 1323 to become lector at Cologne, he must have encountered

the Paris manuscript sometime between 1320 and 1323. For an outline of Nicholas of Strassburg's career, see the entry by Eugen Hillenbrand and Kurt Ruh in *Die deutsche Literatur des Mittelalters Verfasserlexikon*, ed. Karl Langosch and Kurt Ruh (Berlin: De Gruyter, 1987), 6:1154–62.

9. On Nicholas of Strassburg's work, see Eugen Hillenbrand, *Nikolaus von Strassburg: Religiöse Bewegung und Dominikanische Theologie im 14.Jahrhundert* (Freiburg/im Breisgau: Albert, 1968). See also the entry on Nicholas in *Die deutsche Literatur des Mittelalters Verfasserlexikon*. Heinrich Denifle was the first to identify Nicholas of Strassburg's plagiarism of parts 1 and 3 of the trilogy from John of Paris in "Der Plagiator Nicolaus von Strassburg," in *Archiv für Literatur- und Kirchengeschichte des Mittelalters* (Berlin: Weidmannsche Buchhandlung, 1885–1900), 4:312–329. Although Denifle suspected that Nicholas plagiarized part 2 as well, he was unable to identify the source. Ferdinand Delorme, "Un opuscule inédit de Roger Bacon O.F.M.," *AFH* 4 (1911): 209–12, correctly identified part 2 of the trilogy as Nicholas of Lyra's *Quaestio de adventu Christi*. Lerner independently suggested the plagiarism of part 2 from Nicholas of Lyra in *Powers of Prophecy*, 67–68. A thorough examination of the Nicholas of Strassburg text in Oxford Bodleian Library, MS Bodl. 140, fols. 60r–96r and Berlin Staatsbibliothek MS Theol. lat. quart. 175, fols. 62r–72v shows that it is, in fact, a direct plagiarism of the *Quaestio de adventu Christi*.

10. In some MSS 1323 and in others 1326. Three years after he dedicated the trilogy to the archbishop of Trier, Nicholas of Strassburg rededicated the work to Pope John XXII in thanks for having been granted a high position within the German Dominican order.

11. See Jürgen Miethke, ed., *Die Rektorbücher der Universität Heidelberg*, vol. 1, 1386–1410 (Heidelberg: Winter, 1990), 2:472. I am indebted to Robert E. Lerner for pointing out the entry.

12. BAV Archivio S. Pietro MS D202 was copied by Iohannes de Morreyo in 1343. The St. Victor MS is cited above, n. 6.

13. "Nota quomodo iste doctor de Lyra habuit in magnam reverentiam magistrum Hugonis de Sancto Victore." Paris Bibl. Mazarine MS 168, fol. 204r.

14. One very early example of this is Princeton MS y1937–266, described farther on in this chapter.

15. The text is extant in two manuscript copies, Bologna Biblioteca Universitaria MS 2725 and BAV Vat. Chigi A.V. 150. The two extant copies of George's work both date from the early fifteenth century and appear to have been copied from the same original source (the text is virtually identical). Both are single-text quarto volumes, written with care, extensively rubricated; both identify George as a Dominican master associated with the city of Siena. The Bologna manuscript also bears an elaborately illuminated initial author portrait. A colophon indicates that Iohannes Alzanus, O.P., "caused the manuscript to be made in Florence at a cost of 2 gold ducats," (fol. 128v). The payment in Venetian ducats (rather than in the gold florins of Florence) may (but does not necessarily) indicate a Venetian connection, especially since the Dominican order was establishing a strong presence in Venice during this period. Passages within the text identify the date of composition as 1388: BAV Vat. Chigi A.V. 150, fols. 9r, 13v. Apart from Gianfranco Fioravanti's very cur-

sory treatment of George as a source for later fifteenth-century anti-Jewish polemic in "Aspetti della polemica anti-giudaica nell'italia del quattrocento," in *Atti del secondo convegno tenuto a Idice, Bologna, nei giorni 4 e 5 Novembre 1981* (Rome: Fausto Parente e Daniela Piattelli, 1983), 35–57, the only modern study of George and his work is my own "Literal Versus Carnal: George of Siena's Christian Reading of Jewish Exegesis," in *Jewish Biblical Interpretation in Comparative Context*, ed. David Stern and Natalie Dohrmann (Philadelphia: University of Pennsylvania Press, forthcoming).

16. Augustine distinguished between literal and carnal reading in book 3 of *On Christian Doctrine* (especially chapters 5 and 9). For Augustine, the distinction between literal and carnal lies in the status of the passage relative to Christian theology: "when what is said figuratively is taken as if it were said literally, it is understood in a carnal manner" (book 3, chapter 9). In the later Middle Ages, Christian exegetes gave much greater weight to the value of the literal sense of passages that also contained future significance, relegating Augustine's figurative letter to the allegorical sense. On the use of and divergence from Augustine, see Margaret Gibson, "The *De doctrina christiana* in the School of St. Victor," in *Reading and Wisdom: The "De doctrina christiana" in the Middle Ages*, ed. Edward D. English (Notre Dame, Ind.: University of Notre Dame Press, 1995), 41–47; Beryl Smalley, *The Study of the Bible in the Middle Ages*, 3rd ed. (Oxford: Blackwell, 1983); and Ocker, *Biblical Poetics*.

17. BAV Vat. Chigi A.V. 150, fol. 14r.

18. BAV Vat. Chigi A.V. 150, fol. 41v.

19. For a summary of George's career, see Klepper, "Literal Versus Carnal."

20. Isidoro Ugurgieri Azzolini, *Fasti senesi, ossia vite di santi e beati senesi*, Biblioteca communale di Siena MS A.IV.22, fols. 351v–353v.

21. See the discussion in Chapter 2.

22. On the notion that George was reacting specifically against Nicholas of Lyra's approach to literal exegesis, see Klepper, "Literal Versus Carnal."

23. Hugo de Novocastro *De victoria Christi contra Antichristum*. Basel A V 39, fol. 140r. "Item magister Nicolaus de Lira ponit unam opinionem de eodem in quedam questionem contra Hebreos dictione Iudei per quedam transdictionem autenticam apud eos. Hunc est continentur in quodam libro apud eos qui vocatur liber Iudicum Ordinariorum traditum est a domo Helie id est a discipulis eius. Per sex milia erit mundus duo milia vanitatis duo milia legis et duo milia messie. Ad cuius intellectum sciendum quod Hebrei dicunt hoc factum a filio mulieris Sareptane qui fuit Ionas qui habuerit spiritum prophetie. Quod per duo milia annorum duravit tempus vanitatis scilicet ante legem ab origine mundi usque ad Abraham . . . Et duo milia legis et sic fuit quia a tempore Abrahe usque ad Christum fluxerunt duo milia annorum. Sed idem magister Nicolaus de Lira in eadem questione deducit et ostendit. Et duo milia ad finem. Utrum autem dies Christi durare debeant tamen per duo milia annorum plus vel minus de hiis me non intromitto." Robert Lerner brought to my attention the existence of two related manuscripts that contain Nicholas's text in the middle of citations from Hugh of Novocastro's work. They were copied at Carthusian charterhouses in Basel and Mainz. One is Basel MS

A V 39, fol. 140r; the other is Mainz Stadtbibl. MS 151, fol. 17r. The Mainz MS was copied in 1407; the Basel MS may have been copied earlier than this.

24. On the tradition of Nicholas of Lyra's works in print, see Edward A. Gosselin, "A Listing of the Printed Editions of Nicolaus de Lyra," *Traditio* 26 (1970): 399–426.

25. On the Paris book trade, see Richard Rouse and Mary Rouse, *Manuscripts and Their Makers: Commercial Book Producers in Medieval Paris, 1200–1500*, 2 vols. (Turnhout: Harvey Miller, 2000).

26. Louis Jacques Bataillon and Bertrand Guyot, eds., *La production du livre universitaire au Moyen Age: Exemplar et pecia* (Paris: Institut de Récherche et d'Histoire des Textes, 1991), 160–61.

27. Klaus Reinhardt, "Das Werk des Nikolaus von Lyra," 339.

28. Reinhardt, "Das Werk des Nikolaus von Lyra," 342–46. On Poncio's Apocalypse commentary and its relation to those of Nicholas and of Peter Aureol, O.F.M., see Bert Roest, "Reading the Book of History: Intellectual Contexts and Educational Functions of Franciscan Historiography 1226–1350" (Ph.D. diss., Rijksuniversiteit Groningen, 1996), 177–184.

29. Reinhardt, "Das Werk des Nikolaus von Lyra," 324–341.

30. Beryl Smalley, "John Baconthorpe's Postill on St. Matthew," *Medieval and Renaissance Studies* 4 (1958): 91–145. The essay was republished in Smalley's *Studies in Medieval Thought and Learning from Abelard to Wyclif* (London: Hambledon Press, 1981), 289–343, and that is the version I cite from here. See also Bartolomé Xiberta, *De scriptoribus scholasticis saeculi XIV ex Ordine Carmelitarum*, Bibliothèque de la Revue d'Histoire Ecclésiastique 6 (Louvain: Bureaux de la Revue, 1931) and Walter Ullman, "John Baconthorpe as Canonist," in *Church and Government in the Middle Ages: Essays Presented to C. R. Cheney on his 70th Birthday*, ed. Christopher N. L. Brooke, et al. (Cambridge: Cambridge University Press, 1976), 223–46.

31. Smalley, "John Baconthorpe's Postill," 291, 298–99. On John's political thought, see also Ullman, "John Baconthorpe as Canonist."

32. Smalley, "John Baconthorpe's Postill," 303.

33. Ocker, *Biblical Poetics*, 57.

34. Ocker, *Biblical Poetics*, 59.

35. "Notandum in genealogia salvatoris nullam sanctam mulierum assumi sed eas tamen quas scriptura reprehendit ut qui propter peccatores venerat de peccatoribus nascens omni peccata deleret. Unde et in consequentibus Raab meretrix et Ruth Moabitus ponitur et Bersabee uxor Urie. Hec Ieronimus. Sed Nicholaus de Lira dicit quod istud non videtur probabiliter." Cambridge Trinity College Library MS B.15.12, fol. 103r. Nicholas's own commentary at Matthew 1:1, *Liber generatione* reads: "Notandum in genealogia salvatoris nullam sanctam mulierum assumi sed eas tamen quas scriptura reprehendit ut qui propter peccatores venerat de peccatoribus nascens omni peccata deleret. Unde in consequentibus Raab meretrix et Ruth Moabitis ponitur et Bethsabee uxor Urie. Hec Ieronymus. Sed istud non videtur probabiliter dictum."

36. Smalley erroneously attributed the first part of this passage, "Nec debet aliquis moveri si ego recedo in hoc a dictis Ieronimi, quia dicta sanctorum non sunt tante auctoritatis quam liceat sentire contrarium in his que non sunt per sacram

scripturam determinata" to Baconthorpe, suggesting it demonstrated a preference for Lyra over Jerome. Smalley, "John Baconthorpe's Postill," 319. In fact, Baconthorpe was simply continuing his quotation of Nicholas in that line. See Chapter 2. John's own contribution begins: "Sed quia dictum Ieronimi non est faciliter respuendum et ideo contra Nicholaum potest sic argui." Cambridge Trinity College Library MS B.15.12, fol. 103v.

37. See Nicholas's discussion in Chapter 2.

38. "Nicholaus de Lira qui fuit multum instructus in Hebreo arguit contra eos . . ." Cambridge Trinity College Library MS B.15.12, fol. 109r.

39. "Nicholaus de Lyra concordat dicens . . . apud Iudeos omnes dies ebdomade denominantur a sabbato et ita dies immediate sequens sabbatum dicebatur prima sabbati id est prima a sabbato et secunda dies secunda sabbati et sic deinceps." Cambridge Trinity College Library MS B.15.12, fol. 189r.

40. "In hac Postilla per concordantiam prophetiarum et miraculorum Christi probatur quod Christus est messias in lege promissus quod negant Iudei." Cambridge Trinity College Library MS B.15.12, fol. 99v.

41. Cambridge Trinity College Library MS B.15.12, fols. 169v–170r. See Chapter 2.

42. Arduin Kleinhans. "Heinrich von Cossey, O.F.M. Ein Psalmen-Erklärer des 14. Jahrhunderts," in *Miscellanea Biblica et Orientalia, Athanasio Miller, completis LXX annis oblata*, ed. Adalbertus Metzinger, Studia Anselmiana, philosophica theologica 27–28 (Rome: Orbis Catholicus, 1951), 239–40. Only one copy of the Psalm commentary remains, Cambridge Christ College MS 11 (fifteenth century). An Apocalypse commentary has also been attributed to Henry. For problems with the attribution, see Kleinhans, 242.

43. Smalley, *Study of the Bible*, 348; Beryl Smalley, "Hebrew Scholarship Among Some Christians in Thirteenth-Century England, as Illustrated by Some Hebrew-Latin Psalters," in *Lectiones in Vetere Testamento Et in Rebus Judaicis*, no. 6 (London: Shapiro, Valentine, 1939), 5; Raphael Loewe, "Medieval Christian Hebraists of England: Herbert of Bosham and Earlier Scholars," *Transactions of the Jewish Historical Society of England* 17 (1953): 212; and Judith Olszowy-Schlanger, *Les manuscrits hébreux dans l'Angleterre médievale: Étude historique et paléographique*, Collection de la revue des études juives 29 (Paris: Peeters, 2003), 54–55. Henry included excerpts from the *Superscriptio Lincolniensis* (now Oxford MS Corpus Christi College 11) in his Psalm commentary. Olszowy-Schlanger cites Henry's comment that the *dominus Lincolniensis* (Robert Grosseteste) made the bilingual psalter.

44. Kleinhans, "Heinrich von Cossey, O.F.M.," 247–53. See especially Kleinhans' edition of Henry's commentary on Psalm 4, 249–253, which shows clearly the nature of Henry's dependence upon Nicholas.

45. "'Congregate illi sanctos eius' Dicit implendam sic quod in adventu messie omnes Iudei per orbem dispersi que in momento congregabuntur ad ipsum in Ierusalem. Unde mihi videtur sicut et Lira quod ad litteram prophetalis iste psalmus loquitur de Christo." Cambridge Christ College MS 11, fols. 86v–88v.

46. "Rabi Moyses Adarsan super illud Gen. 18 . . . dicit quod ista littera 'dixit dominus' etc. intellegitur de messia . . . sicut dicit Lira." Cambridge Christ College MS 11, fols. 183v–186r.

47. Henri Labrosse, "Sources de la biographie de Nicolas de Lyre," *Études franciscaines* 16 (1906): 394–96; Heinrich Rüthing, "Kritische Bemerkungen zu einer mittelalterlichen Biographie des Nikolaus von Lyra," *AFH* 60 (1967): 42–54.

48. Gilbert Dahan and Evencio Beltran, "Un hébraïsant à Paris vers 1400: Jacques Legrand," *Archives juives* 17 (1981): 41–49. On Jacques's use of Nicholas for Jewish interpretations, see 45–47.

49. John V. Tolan, *Petrus Alfonsi and His Medieval Readers* (Gainesville: University Press of Florida, 1993).

50. Martin Morard, "Entre mode et tradition: Les commentaires des Psaumes de 1160 à 1350," in *La Bibbia del XIII secole: Storia del testo, storia dell'esegesi. Atti del Convegno della Società Internazionale per lo Studio del Medioevo Latino* (SISMEL) (Florence, June 1–2 2001), ed. Giuseppe Cremascoli and Franco Santi (Florence: SISMEL, Edizioni del Galluzzo, 2004), 323–52. The essay is drawn from Morard's as yet unpublished thesis, *Le commentaire des Psaumes de saint Thomas d'Aquin: Edition critique partielle et introduction historique*, 5 vols. (diss. dactyl., Paris, École Nationale des Chartes, 2002).

51. Denys Turner, *Eros and Allegory: Medieval Exegesis of the Song of Songs*, Cistercian Studies Series 156 (Kalamazoo, MI: Cistercian Publications, 1995), 412.

52. Turner, *Eros and Allegory*, 415–18.

53. Turner, *Eros and Allegory*, 418.

54. Reinhardt, "Das Werk des Nikolaus von Lyra," 342–46.

55. Gareth Lloyd Jones, "Paul of Burgos and the Adversus Judaeos Tradition," *Henoch* 21 (1999): 313–29; Luciano Serrano, *Los Conversos Pablo de Santa Maria y Alfons de Cartagena* (Madrid: Consejo Superior de Investigaciones Científicas, 1942); Chai Merchavia, "The Talmud in the *Additiones* of Paul of Burgos," *Journal of Jewish Studies* 16 (1965): 115–134.

56. Gosselin, "A Listing of the Printed Editions of Nicolaus de Lyra," 399–426.

57. Jones, *Paul of Burgos*, 328.

58. William was the well-connected son of Hugh Courtenay, earl of Devon, and Margaret, daughter of the earl of Hereford. He was elected chancellor of the university at Oxford in 1367, bishop of Hereford in 1370, bishop of London 1375, and finally archbishop of Canterbury in 1381.

59. BAV Vat. lat. 162, fol. 89v, "Explicit Postillas super Librum Psalmorum edita a fratre Nicholao de Lyra de ordine fratrum minorum sacre theologie doctore. Anno domini M CCC XXVI. Iste liber scriptus, qui scripsit sit benedictus, anno domini millesimo ccc vicesimo nono a Gervasio Wallence apud Parisiis."

60. Adelaide Bennett, Jean F. Preston, and William P. Stoneman, *A Summary Guide to Western Medieval and Renaissance Manuscripts at Princeton University* (Princeton, N.J.: Princeton University Press, 1991). See also Princeton University Art Museum, *The Carl Otto von Kienbusch, Jr., Memorial Collection, Special Exhibition Catalogue, June 1956* (Princeton, N.J., 1956), no. 67. I am indebted to Adelaide Bennett for making the 1991 catalog entry available to me and to Jeffrey Hamburger for help in interpreting this and a number of other author portraits.

61. Rouse and Rouse, *Manuscripts and Their Makers*.

62. On fol. 48v there is a rare marginal note indicating *opinio Hebreorum* fol-

lowed immediately by the usual reference to *opinio Iudeorum*. Nicholas had used the term *Hebrei* on both occasions.

63. British Library Online Manuscripts Catalogue, "3 D, vii. Nicolaus de Lyra, *Postillae*: A Commentary, in Latin," http://www.bl.uk/catalogues/manuscripts/ HITS0001.ASP?VPath = c!/inetpub/wwwroot/mss/data/msscat/html/38202.htm& Search = 3 + D + VII&Highlight = F.

64. According to Bernice Kaczynski in "Illustrations of Tabernacle and Temple Implements in the *Postilla in Testamentum Vetus* of Nicolaus de Lyra," *Yale University Library Gazette* 48, no. 1 (1973): 2.

65. Gosselin, "A Listing of the Printed Editions of Nicolaus de Lyra."

66. Mary Dove, "Chaucer and the Translation of the Jewish Scriptures," in *Chaucer and the Jews: Sources, Contexts, Meanings,* ed. Sheila Delany, Multicultural Middle Ages Series (New York: Routledge, 2002), 89–107.

67. Mark Hazard, *The Literal Sense and the Gospel of John in Late-Medieval Commentary and Literature,* Studies in Medieval History and Culture 12 (New York: Routledge, 2002).

Bibliography

Unpublished Sources

Anonymous. *Quodlibeta.* Rome, Biblioteca Apostolica Vaticana, MS Vat. lat. 982.
Anonymous. *Quodlibeta.* Florence, Laurentiana dextra (Sancta Croce), Cod. 3 Plut. 31.
George Naddi of Siena. *Scrutamini Scripturas.* Bologna, University of Bologna, MS 2725; Rome, Biblioteca Apostolica Vaticana, Chigi MS A.V.150.
John Baconthorpe, O.Carm. *Postilla super Matthaeum.* Cambridge, Trinity College Library, MS B.15.12.
Hugh of Novocastro. *Victoria Christi contra Antichristum.* Basel, Universitätsbibliothek, Cod. A.V.39, fol. 140r.
Henry of Ghent. *Questiones abreviate de quolibet.* Paris, Bibliothèque Mazarine, MS 732, fols. 69r-168v.
Nicholas of Lyra. *De differentia nostrae translationis ab Hebraica littera Veteris Testamentis.* Rome, Biblioteca Apostolica Vaticana, Archivio di San Pietro MS D202, fols. 1r–49v.
Nicholas of Strassburg. Oxford Bodleian, MS Bodley 140, fols. 60r–96r.
Peter of Trabes. *Utrum Christus possit probari Iudeis iam venisse.* Florence, Biblioteca Nazionale, MS Conv. Sopp. D.6.359.
Raymond Rigauld. *Utrum per vetus testamentum probari possit incarnatio Christi.* Todi, Biblioteca Comunale, MS 98, fol. 20r.

Printed Primary Sources

Andrew of St. Victor. *Expositionem in Ezechielem. Andreas de Sancto Victore Opera* 6. CCCM 53E. Ed. Michael Signer. Turnhout: Brepols, 1991.
———. *Expositio super Danielem: Andreae de Sancto Victore Opera 7.* Ed. Mark Zier. CCCM 53F. Turnhout: Brepols, 1990.
Bartholomew of Bologna. *Die Quaestiones disputatae de fide des Bartholomäus von Bologna, O.F.M.* Ed. Meinolf Mückshoff. Beiträge zur Geschichte der Philosophie und Theologie des Mittelalters: Texte und Untersuchungen 24, no. 4. Münster: Aschendorff, 1940.
Bede. "De temporum ratione liber." In *Bedae Venerabilis Opera* 6. CCSL 123B. Turnhout: Brepols, 1977.
Berger, David. *From Crusades to Blood Libels to Expulsions: Some New Approaches to*

Medieval Antisemitism. Annual Lecture of the Victor J. Selmanowitz Chair of Jewish History 2. New York: Touro College Graduate School of Jewish Studies, 1997.

———, ed. *The Jewish-Christian Debate in the High Middle Ages: A Critical Edition of the Nizzahon Vetus with an Introduction, Translation, and Commentary.* Judaica, Texts and Translations. Philadelphia: Jewish Publication Society of America, 1979.

———. "Mission to the Jews and Jewish-Christian Contacts in the Polemical Literature of the High Middle Ages." *American Historical Review* 91 (June 1986): 576–91.

Brewer, John Sherren, ed. *Monumenta Franciscana* 1. London, 1858–82.

Denifle, Heinrich, and Emile Chatelaine, eds. *Chartularium Universitatis Parisiensis.* 4 vols. Paris, 1889–97.

Emden, Alfred B. *A Biographical Register of the University of Oxford to A.D. 1500.* Vol. 3. Oxford: Clarendon Press, 1959.

Glorieux, Palémon, ed. *La littérature quodlibétique.* 2 vols. Paris: Vrin, 1925–35.

Guillaume de Nangis. *Chronique latine de Guillaume de Nangis de 1113 à 1300 avec les continuations de cette chronique de 1300 à 1368.* Ed. Hercule Geraud. Paris, 1843.

Hieronymus de S. Fide. *Contra Iudaeorum perfidiam et Talmuth,* 1552.

Hugh of St. Victor. *The Didascalicon of Hugh of St. Victor: A Medieval Guide to the Arts.* Ed. Jerome Taylor. Records of Civilization, Sources and Studies 64. New York: Columbia University Press, 1961.

———. *Hugonis de Sancto Victore Didascalicon de studio legendi: A Critical Text.* Ed. Charles Henry Buttimer. Studies in Medieval and Renaissance Latin 10. Washington, D.C.: Catholic University Press, 1939.

Jacob ben Ruben. *Jacob ben Ruben: Milhamot ha-Shem.* Ed. Judah Rosenthal. Jerusalem: Mosad ha-Rav Kuk, 1963.

Laurière, Eusèbe de, et al., ed. *Ordonnances des roys de France de la troisième race, recueillies par ordre chronologique.* Paris: Imprimerie royale, 1723–1849.

Matthew of Aquasparta. *Quaestiones disputatae: de fide et de cognitione.* 2nd ed. Bibliotheca Franciscana Scholastica Medii Aevi 1. Florence, 1957.

Miethke, Jürgen, ed. *Die Rektorbücher der Universität Heidelberg.* Vol. 1, *1386–1410.* Heidelberg: Carl Winter, 1990.

Monumenta ordinis fratrum praedicatorum historica. Vol. 4. Rome, 1899.

Moses ha-Darshan. *Midrash Bereshit Rabbati.* Ed. Hanokh Albek. Jerusalem: Mekitse Nirdamim, 1966.

———. *Commentaire de la Genèse de R. Moïse le prédicateur.* Ed. and trans. Jean-Joseph Brierre-Narbonne. Paris: Guenther, 1939.

Nicholas of Lyra. *De visione divinae essentiae.* Ed. Michael Scott Woodward. *Franciscan Studies* 63 (2005): 325–407.

———. *The Postilla of Nicholas of Lyra on the Song of Songs.* Ed. and trans. James George Kiecker. Reformation Texts with Translation (1350–1650). Biblical Studies 3. Milwaukee: Marquette University Press, 1998.

———. *Textus biblie cum glosa ordinaria: Nicolai de Lyra postilla, moralitatibus eius-*

dem, Pauli Burgensis additionibus, Matthie Thoring replicis. Basel: Johannes Petri and Johannes Frobenius, 1506–1508.

Peter Olivi. Rome, Biblioteca Apostolica Vaticana, Prop. Fide IV 134. (Published without place, date or printer's marks.)

———. *Quodlibeta quinque: ad fidem codicum nunc primum edita cum introductione historico-critica.* Ed. Stefano Defraia. Collectio Oliviana 7. Grottaferrata (Rome): Editiones Collegii S. Bonaventurae ad Claras Aquas, 2002.

Porcheto Salvatici. *Victoria Porcheti adversus impios Hebreos in qua tum ex sacris litteris tum ex dictis Talmud ac Caballistarum et aliorum omnium authorum quos Hebraei recipunt, monstratur veritas catholicae fidei.* Paris: A. Justinianus, 1520.

Ramón Lull. *El "Liber Predicationis Contra Judeos" de Ramón Lull.* Ed. José M. Millás Vallicrosa. Madrid-Barcelona: Instituto Arias Montano, 1957.

Raymundus Martini. *Capistrum Iudaeorum.* Ed. and trans. Adolfo Robles Sierra. 2 vols. Würzburg: Echter Verlag, 1990.

Recueil des historiens des Gaules et de la France. 24 vols. Ed. Martin Bouquet, Léopold Delisle, et al. Paris: Victor Palmé et al., 1738–1904.

Robert Grosseteste. *De cessatione legalium.* Ed. Richard C. Dales and Edward B. King. Auctores Britannici Medii Aevi 7. London: Oxford University Press for the British Academy, 1986.

———. *Roberti Grosseteste Episcopi quondam Lincolniensis Epistolae.* Ed. Henry Richards Luard. Rolls Series 25. London: Longman, 1861.

Roger Bacon. *Compendium studii theologie.* Ed. Hastings Rashdall. Vol. 3, British Society of Franciscan Studies 3. Aberdeen: Typis Academicis, 1911.

———. *Compendium of the Study of Theology.* Ed. and trans. Thomas S. Maloney. Leiden: Brill, 1988.

———. *The Greek Grammar of Roger Bacon and a Fragment of His Hebrew Grammar.* Ed. Edmond Nolan and Samuel A. Hirsch. Cambridge: Cambridge University Press, 1902.

———. *Opera quaedam hactenus inedita.* Ed. John Sherren Brewer. Rolls Series 15. London: Longman, 1859.

———. *Opus maius.* 3 vols. Ed. John Henry Bridges. Oxford: Clarendon Press, 1897–1900. Reprint Frankfurt, 1964.

Roger Marston. *Quaestiones disputatae de emanatione divina, de statu naturae lapsae, de anima.* Bibliotheca Franciscana Scholastica Medii Aevi 7. Florence, 1932.

———.*Quodlibeta Quatuor.* Bibliotheca Franciscana Scholastica Medii Aevi 26. Ed. Girard F. Etzkorn and Ignatius C. Brady. Florence, Quaracci, 1968.

Salimbene de Adam. *The Chronicle of Salimbene de Adam.* Ed. Joseph L. Baird, Giuseppe Baglivi, and John Robert Kane. Binghamton, N.Y.: Medieval and Renaissance Texts and Studies, 1986.

Tanna de-Vei Eliyahu. Ed. Meir Friedmann. Reprint Jerusalem: Sifre Vahrman, 1969.

Thomas Aquinas. *Super Epistolas S. Pauli lectura.* 2 vols. Ed. Raffaele Cai. Turin: Marietti, 1953.

Vital de Furno. "Quodlibet I." Ed. Ferdinand Delorme. *La France franciscaine* 9 (1926): 452–71.

William Brito. *Summa Britonis sive Guillelmi Britonis Expositiones vocabulorum Biblie.* Ed. Lloyd W. Daley and Bernardine A. Daley. 2 vols. Padua: Antenoreis, 1975.

Secondary Sources

Ackroyd, Peter R., and C. F. Evans. *The Cambridge History of the Bible.* 3 vols. London: Cambridge University Press, 1970.

Allgeier, Arthur. "Eine unbekannte mittelalterliche Psalmenübersetzung." *Römische Quartalschrift* 37 (1939): 437–40.

Altaner, Berthold. "Die Fremdsprachliche Ausbildung der Dominikanermissionare während des 13. und 14. Jahrhunderts." *Zeitschrift für Missionswissenschaft* 23 (1933): 233–41.

———. "Zur Kenntnis des Hebräischen im Mittelalter." *Biblische Zeitschrift* 21 (1938): 288–308.

Anchel, Robert. "The Early History of the Jewish Quarters in Paris." *Jewish Social Studies* 2 (1940): 45–60.

Assis, Yom Tov. "Juifs de France réfugiés en Aragon (XIIIe–XIVe siècles)." *Revue des études juives* 142 (1983): 285–322.

Awerbuch, Marianne. *Christlich-Jüdische Begegnung im Zeitalter der Frühscholastik.* Munich: Chr. Kaiser, 1980.

Bacher, Wilhelm. *Die exegetische Terminologie der jüdischen Traditionsliteratur.* 2 vols. Leipzig, 1905.

Baldwin, John W. *Masters, Princes, and Merchants: The Social Views of Peter the Chanter and His Circle.* Princeton, N.J.: Princeton University Press, 1970.

———. *The Scholastic Culture of the Middle Ages, 1000–1300.* Civilization and Society: Studies in Social, Economic, and Cultural History. Lexington, Mass.: Heath, 1971.

Barber, Malcolm. *The New Knighthood: A History of the Order of the Temple.* Cambridge: Cambridge University Press, 1994.

———. *The Trial of the Templars.* Cambridge: Cambridge University Press, 1978.

Bataillon, Louis Jacques, and Bertrand Guyot, eds. *La production du livre universitaire au Moyen Age: Exemplar et pecia.* Paris: Institut de Récherche et d'Histoire des Textes, 1988.

Bazán, Bernardo C., "La Quaestio Disputata." In *Les genres littéraires dans les sources théologiques et philosophiques médiévales: Définition, critique et exploitation: Actes du Colloque International de Louvain-la-Neuve, 25–27 Mai 1981,* 31–41. Louvain-la-Neuve: Institut d'Études Médiévales de l'Université Catholique de Louvain, 1982.

Beaumont-Maillet, Laure. *Le Grand Couvent des Cordeliers de Paris: étude historiques et archéologique du XIIIᵉ siècle a nos jours.* Paris: H. Champion, 1975.

Bennett, Adelaide, Jean F. Preston, and William P. Stoneman. *A Summary Guide to Western Medieval and Renaissance Manuscripts at Princeton University.* Princeton, N.J.: Princeton University Press, 1991.

Berger, David, ed. *The Jewish-Christian Debate in the High Middle Ages: A Critical Edition of the Nizzahon Vetus with an Introduction, Translation, and Commentary.* Judaica, Texts and Translations 4. Philadelphia: Jewish Publication Society of America, 1979.

———. "Mission to the Jews and Jewish-Christian Contacts in the Polemical Literature of the High Middle Ages." *American Historical Review* 91 (1986): 576–91.

Berger, Samuel. *Quam notitiam linguae Hebraicae habuerint Christiani medii aevi temporibus in Gallia.* Nancy: Typis Berger-Levrault et sociorum, 1893.

———. *Histoire de la Vulgate pendant les premiers siècles du Moyen Age.* Paris: Hachette, 1893.

Berthier, André. "Les écoles de langues orientales fondées au XIII⁰ siècle par les Dominicains en Espagne et en Afrique." *Revue africaine* 73 (1932): 84–102.

———. "Un maître orientaliste du XIII⁰ siècle: Raymond Martin, O.P." *Archivum Fratrum Praedicatorum* 6 (1936): 267–311.

Biller, Peter. "Views of Jews From Paris Around 1300: Christian or Scientific?" In *Christianity and Judaism: Papers Read at the 1991 Summer Meeting and the 1992 Winter Meeting of the Ecclesiastical History Society,* ed. Diana Wood, 187–207. Oxford: Blackwell for the Ecclesiastical History Society, 1992.

Bischoff, Erich. *Kritische Geschichte der Thalmud-Übersetzungen Aller Zeiten und Zungen.* Frankfurt: J. Kauffmann, 1899.

Biver, Paul, and Marie-Louise Biver. *Abbayes, monastères, et couvents de Paris.* Paris: Éditions d'histoire et d'art, 1970.

Blumenkranz, Bernhard. "Anti-Jewish Polemics and Legislation in the Middle Ages: Literary Fiction or Reality?" *Journal of Jewish Studies* 15 (1964): 125–40.

———. *Les auteurs Chrétiens latins du Moyen Age sur les juifs et le Judaisme.* Paris: Mouton, 1963.

———. "Nicolas de Lyre et Jacob ben Reuben." *Journal of Jewish Studies* 16 (1965): 47–51.

Boulay, César Égasse du. *Historia Universitatis Parisiensis,* 976. Paris, 1665.

Boureau, Alain. "Un épisode central dans la construction de la magie noire du livre: De la rivalté des exégèses à la crémation du Talmud (1144–1242)." In *Das Buch als Magisches und als Repräsentationsobjekt,* ed. Peter Ganz, 137–57. Wiesbaden: Harrassowitz, 1992.

Braude, William, and Israel Kapstein. *Tanna debe Eliyahu: The Lore of the School of Elijah.* Philadelphia: Jewish Publication Society of America, 1981.

British Library Online Manuscripts Catalogue. "3 D, vii. Nicolaus de Lyra, *Postillae*: A commentary, in Latin." http://www.bl.uk/catalogues/manuscripts/HITS 0001.ASP?VPath = c!/inetpub/wwwroot/mss/data/msscat/html/38202.htm& Search = 3 + D + VII&Highlight = F

Browe, Peter. "Die Hostienschändungen der Juden im Mittelalter." *Römische Quartalschrift* 34 (1926): 167–198.

———. "Die eucharistischen Verwandlungswunder des Mittelalters." *Römische Quartalschrift* 37 (1929): 137–69.

Brown, Dennis. *Vir Trilinguis: A Study in the Biblical Exegesis of Saint Jerome.* Kampen: Kok, 1992.

Brown, Elizabeth A. R. "Philip V, Charles IV, and the Jews of France: The Alleged Expulsion of 1322." *Speculum* 66 (1991): 294–329.

Brown, Stephen F. "Nicholas of Lyra's Critique of Scotus' Univocity." In *Historia Philosophiae Medii Aevi: Studien zur Geschichte der Philosophie des Mittelalters*, ed. Burkhard Mojsisch and Olaf Pluta, 115–27. Amsterdam: Grüner, 1991.

———. "Richard Fishacre on the Need for 'Philosophy'." In *A Straight Path: Studies in Medieval Philosophy and Culture: Essays in Honor of Arthur Hyman*, ed. Ruth Link-Salinger, 23–36. Washington, D.C.: Catholic University of America Press, 1988.

Buc, Philippe. "The Book of Kings: Nicholas of Lyra's Mirror of Princes." In *Nicholas of Lyra: The Senses of Scripture*, ed. Philip Krey and Lesley Smith, 83–109. Leiden: Brill, 2000.

———. "Pouvoir royal et commentaires de la Bible (1150–1350)." *Annales: Economies, sociétés, civilisations* 44, 3 (1989): 691–713.

Bunte, Wolfgang. *Rabbinische Traditionen bei Nikolaus von Lyra: Ein Beitrag zur Schriftauslegung des Spätmittelalters*. Judentum und Umwelt 58. Berlin: Lang, 1994.

Burr, David. *The Persecution of Peter Olivi*. Philadelphia: American Philosophical Society, 1976.

———. "Olivi's Apocalyptic Timetable." *Journal of Medieval and Renaissance Studies* 11 (1981): 237–60.

———. *Olivi and Franciscan Poverty: The Origins of the Usus Pauper Controversy*. Philadelphia: University of Pennsylvania Press, 1989.

———. *Olivi's Peaceable Kingdom: A Reading of the Apocalypse Commentary*. Philadelphia: University of Pennsylvania Press, 1993.

———. *The Spiritual Franciscans: From Protest to Persecution in the Century After Saint Francis*. University Park: Pennsylvania State University Press, 2001.

Callus, Daniel A. P. "Robert Grosseteste as Scholar." In *Robert Grosseteste, Scholar and Bishop*, ed. Daniel A. P. Callus, 11–69. Oxford: Clarendon, 1955.

Chazan, Robert. *Medieval Jewry in Northern France: A Political and Social History*. Baltimore: Johns Hopkins University Press, 1973.

———. *Daggers of Faith: Thirteenth-Century Christian Missionizing and Jewish Response*. Berkeley: University of California Press, 1989.

———. *Barcelona and Beyond: The Disputation of 1263 and Its Aftermath*. Berkeley: University of California Press, 1992.

Chevalier, Ulysse. *Répertoire des sources historiques du Moyen Age*. Paris: Picard, 1905–7.

Cohen, Jeremy. *The Friars and the Jews: The Evolution of Medieval Anti-Judaism*. Ithaca, N.Y.: Cornell University Press, 1982.

———. "The Jews as the Killers of Christ in the Latin Tradition, from Augustine to the Friars." *Traditio* 39 (1983): 1–27.

———. *Living Letters of the Law: Ideas of the Jew in Medieval Christianity*. Berkeley: University of California Press, 1999.

———. "Raimundus Martini's *Capistrum Iudaeorum*" (Hebrew). In *Me'ah She'arim: Studies in Medieval Jewish Spiritual Life in Memory of Isadore Twer-*

sky, ed. Ezra Flaisher, Ya'akov Blidshtain, Karmi Horovits, and Dov Septimus, 279–96. Jerusalem: Hebrew University, 2001.

———. "Recent Historiography on the Medieval Church and the Decline of European Jewry." In *Popes, Teachers, and Canon Law in the Middle Ages: Essays in Honor of Brian Tierney*, ed. Stanley Chodorow and James Ross Sweeney, 251–262. Ithaca, N.Y.: Cornell University Press, 1989.

———. "Scholarship and Intolerance in the Medieval Academy." *American Historical Review* 91 (1986): 592–613.

Courtenay, William. "The Bible in the Fourteenth Century: Some Observations." *Church History* 54 (1985): 176–87.

———. *Schools and Scholars in Fourteenth-Century England*. Princeton, N.J.: Princeton University Press, 1987.

Cross, Richard. *Duns Scotus*. New York: Oxford University Press, 1999.

Dahan, Gilbert. *Le brûlement du Talmud à Paris: 1242–1244*. Paris: Cerf, 1999.

———. "Un dossier latin de textes de Rashi autour de la controverse de 1240." *Revue des études juives* 151 (1992): 321–336.

———. *L'exégèse chrétienne de la Bible en Occident médiéval, XIIᵉ–XIVᵉ siècle*. Paris: Cerf, 1999.

———. "Exégèse et polémique dans les commentaires de la Genèse d'Étienne Langton." In *Les juifs au regard de l'histoire: Mélanges en l'honneur de Bernhard Blumenkranz*, 129–48. Paris: Picard, 1985.

———. "Il y a sept cents ans à Paris (1290). L'affaire des billettes." *Communauté nouvelle* 58 (1991): 72–84.

———. *Les intellectuels chrétiens et les juifs au Moyen Age: Polémique et relations culturelles entre chrétiens et juifs en occident du XIIᵉ au XIVᵉ siècles*. Paris: Cerf, 1990.

———. "Les interprétations juives dans les commentaires du Pentateuque de Pierre la Chantre." In *The Bible in the Medieval World: Essays in Memory of Beryl Smalley*, ed. Katherine Walsh and Diana Wood, 131–55. Studies in Church History, Subsidia 4. Oxford: Blackwell, 1985.

———. "Juifs et judaïsme dans la littérature quodlibétique." In *From Witness to Witchcraft: Jews and Judaism in Medieval Christian Thought*, ed. Jeremy Cohen, 221–45. Wolfenbütteler Mittelalter-Studien 11. Wiesbaden: Harrassowitz, 1996.

———. *La Polémique chrétienne contre le judaïsme au Moyen Age*. Paris: Albin Michel, 1991.

———. "Rashi, sujet de la controverse de 1240: Edition partielle du Ms. Paris, BN Lat. 16558." *Archives juives* 4, no. 3 (1978): 43–53.

———. "Saint Bonaventure et les Juifs." *Archivum Franciscanum Historicum* (hereafter *AFH*) 77 (1984): 369–405.

Dahan, Gilbert, and Evencio Beltran. "Un hébraïsant à Paris vers 1400: Jacques Legrand." *Archives juives* 17 (1981): 41–49.

Daniel, E. Randolph. *The Franciscan Concept of Mission in the High Middle Ages*. Lexington: University Press of Kentucky, 1975.

Delègue, Yves. *Les machines du sens: Fragments d'une sémiologie médiévale*. Paris: Editions des Cendres, 1987.

Delorme, Ferdinand. "Un opuscule inédit de Roger Bacon O.F.M." *AFH* 4 (1911): 209–12.

———. "Quodlibets et questions disputées de Raymond Rigaut, maître franciscain de Paris, d'après le MS. 98 de la Bibl. Comm. de Todi." In *Aus der Geisteswelt des Mittelalters* 2, ed. Albert Lang, Joseph Lechner, and Michael Schmaus, 826–41. Münster: Aschendorff, 1935.

Denifle, Heinrich. "Der Plagiator Nicolaus von Strassburg." In *Archiv für Literatur- und Kirchengeschichte des Mittelalters*. 7 vols. vol. 4, 312–29. Berlin: Weidmann-sche Buchhandlung, 1885–1900.

———. "Die Handschriften der Bibel-Correctorien des 13. Jahrhunderts." In *Archiv für Literatur- und Kirchengeschichte des Mittelalters*. 7 vols. vol. 4, 277–78. Berlin: Weidmannsche Buchhandlung, 1885–1900.

Destrez, Jean. *La pecia dans les manuscrits universitares du XIIIe et du XIVe siècle.* Paris: Éditions Jacques Vautrain, 1935.

Doucet, Victorin. "Maîtres franciscains de Paris: Supplément au répertoires des maîtres en théologie." *AFH* 27 (1934): 531–64.

Douie, Decima. *Archbishop Pecham.* Oxford: Clarendon Press, 1952.

Dove, Mary. "Chaucer and the Translation of the Jewish Scriptures." In *Chaucer and the Jews: Sources, Contexts, Meanings,* ed. Sheila Delany, 89–107. Multicultural Middle Ages Series. New York: Routledge, 2002.

———. "Nicholas of Lyra and the Literal Senses of the Song of Songs." In *Nicholas of Lyra: The Senses of Scripture,* ed. Philip Krey and Leslie Smith, 129–46. Leiden: Brill, 2000.

Ehrle, Franz. "Der Kampf um die Lehre des hl. Thomas von Aquin." *Zeitschrift für katholische Theologie* 37 (1913): 266–318.

———. "Petrus Johannis Olivi, sein Leben und seine Schriften." In vol. 3, 409–552. *Archiv für Literatur- und Kirchengeschichte des Mittelalters.* 7 vols. Berlin: Weidmannsche Buchhandlung, 1885–1900.

Elukin, Jonathan. "From Jew to Christian? Conversion and Immutability in Medieval Europe." In *Varieties of Religious Conversion in the Middle Ages,* ed. James Muldoon, 171–89. Gainesville: University Press of Florida, 1997.

Felder, Hilarin. *Geschichte der Wissenschaftlichen Studien im Franziskanerorden bis um die Mitte des 13. Jahrhunderts.* Freiburg/im Breisgau: Herder, 1904.

Félibien, Michel, and Gui Alexis Lobineau. *Histoire de la ville de Paris, composée par Dom Michel Félibien, revue, augmentée et mise au jour par Dom Gui Alexis Lobineau, justifée par des preuves autentiques.* 5 vols. Paris, 1725.

Feret, Pierre. *La faculté de théologie de Paris au Moyen Age.* 3 vols. Paris: Picard, 1895.

Finke, Heinrich P. *Papsttum und Untergang des Templeordens.* 2 vols. Münster: Aschendorff, 1907.

Fioravanti, Gianfranco. "Aspetti della polemica anti-giudaica nell'italia del quattrocento." In *Atti del secondo convegno tenuto a Idice, Bologna, nei giorni 4 e 5 Novembre 1981,* 35–57. Associazione italiana per lo studio del giudaismo. Rome: Fausto Parente e Daniela Piattelli, 1983.

Franklin, Alfred. *Les anciennes bibliothèques de Paris.* 3 vols. Paris: Imprimerie impériale, 1867–70; Imprimerie nationale, 1873.

Frassetto, Michael, ed. *Christian Attitudes Toward the Jews in the Middle Ages: A Casebook*. New York: Routledge, 2006.

Fredborg, K. M., Lauge Nielsen, and Jan Pinborg. "An Unedited Part of Roger Bacon's *Opus Maius: De Signis*." *Traditio* 34 (1978): 75–136.

Funkenstein, Amos. "Basic Types of Christian Anti-Jewish Polemics in the Later Middle Ages." *Viator* 2 (1971): 373–82.

———. "Changes in the Patterns of Christian Anti-Jewish Polemic in the Twelfth Century" (Hebrew). *Zion* 33 (1968): 125–144.

Gelles, Benjamin J. *Peshat and Derash in the Exegesis of Rashi*. Leiden: Brill, 1981.

Gibson, Margaret. "The *De doctrina christiana* in the School of St. Victor." In *Reading and Wisdom: The De doctrina christiana in the Middle Ages*, ed. Edward D. English. Notre Dame, Ind.: University of Notre Dame Press, 1995.

Gilson, Etienne. "Roger Marston: Un cas d'Augustinisme Avicennisant." *Archives d'histoire doctrinale et littéraire du Moyen Age* 8 (1933): 37–42.

Glorieux, Palémon. "Discussiones: D'Alexandre de Hales à Pierre Auriol, la suite des maîtres franciscains de Paris au XIIIᵉ siècle." *AFH* 26 (1933): 264.

———. *Répertoire des maîtres en théologie de Paris au XIIIᵉ siècle*. 2 vols. Paris: Vrin, 1933–34.

Golb, Norman. *The Jews in Medieval Normandy: A Social and Intellectual History*. Cambridge: Cambridge University Press, 1998.

Goldschmidt, Lazarus. *Eine Talmudische Realkonkordanz*. Berlin: Verlag von M. Poppelauer, 1909.

Gonzague, François-Scipion de. *De Origine seraphicae religionis franciscanae eiusque progressibus de regularis observantias institutione forma adminstrationis ac legibus, ad mirabilique eius proprogatione*. Rome, 1587.

Goodwin, Deborah. *"Take Hold of the Robe of a Jew": Herbert of Bosham's Christian Hebraism*. Leiden: Brill, 2006.

Gosselin, Edward A. "A Listing of the Printed Editions of Nicholas of Lyra." *Traditio* 26 (1970): 399–426.

Graboïs, Aryeh. "The Hebraica Veritas and Jewish-Christian Intellectual Relations in the Twelfth Century." *Speculum* 50 (1975): 613–34.

Grayzel, Solomon. *The Church and the Jews in the Thirteenth Century*. 2nd ed. rev. New York: Hermon Press, 1966.

Gross, Henri. *Gallia Judaica*. Paris: Cerf, 1897.

Gross-Diaz, Theresa. "What's a Good Soldier to Do? Nicholas of Lyra on the Psalms." In *Nicholas of Lyra: The Senses of Scripture*, ed. Philip Krey and Lesley Smith, 111–28. Leiden: Brill, 2000.

Gruber, Mayer I. "What Happened to Rashi's Pictures?" *Bodleian Library Record* 14 (1992): 111–24.

Guttmann, Jacob. "Alexandre de Hales et le Judaïsme." *Revue des études juives* 19 (1989): 224–34.

———. *Die Scholastik des dreizehnten Jahrhunderts in ihren Beziehungen zum Judenthum und zur Jüdischen Literatur*. Breslau: Marcus, 1902. Breslau: M. and H. Marcus, 1970.

Hailperin, Herman. *Rashi and the Christian Scholars*. Pittsburgh: University of Pittsburgh Press, 1963.

Hasselhoff, Görge K. *Dicit Rabbi Moyses: Studien zum Bild von Moses Maimonides im lateinischen Westen vom 13. bis zum 15. Jahrhundert.* Würzburg: Königshausen & Neumann, 2004.

———. "The Reception of Maimonides in the Latin World: The Evidence of the Latin Translations in the Thirteenth–Fifteenth Century." *Materia giudaica* 6 (2001): 264–70.

Hazard, Mark. *The Literal Sense and the Gospel of John in Late-Medieval Commentary and Literature.* Studies in Medieval History and Culture 12. New York: Routledge, 2002.

Hill, Edmund, "Unless You Believe, You Shall Not Understand." *Augustinian Studies* 25 (1994): 51–64.

Hillenbrand, Eugen. *Nikolaus von Strassburg: Religiöse Bewegung und Dominikanische Theologie im 14. Jahrhundert.* Freiburg/im Breisgau: Albert, 1968.

Hillenbrand, Eugen, and Kurt Ruh. "Nicholas of Lyra." In *Die Deutsche Literatur des Mittelalters Verfasserlexikon,* ed. Karl Langosch and Kurt Ruh, vol. 6, 1154–62. Berlin: De Gruyter, 1978–.

Hood, John Y. B. *Aquinas and the Jews.* Philadelphia: University of Pennsylvania Press, 1995.

Hsia, R. Po-chia. *The Myth of Ritual Murder: Jews and Magic in Reformation Germany.* New Haven, Conn.: Yale University Press, 1988.

Hülsen-Esch, Andrea von. "Kleider Machen Leute: Zur Gruppenrepräsentation von Gelehrten im Spätmittelalter." In *Die Repräsentation der Gruppen: Texte—Bilder—Objekte,* ed. Otto Gerhard Oexle and Andrea von Hülsen-Esch, 225–57. Göttingen: Vandenhoeck & Ruprecht, 1998.

Huning, Hildebert A. *Die Stellung des Petrus de Trabibus zur Philosophie: Nach dem zweiten Prolog zum ersten Buch seines Sentenzenkommenatars, MS. 154, Biblioteca Comunale, Assisi.* Werl/Westf.: Coelde, 1965.

Jansen, Bernard. "Petrus de Trabibus: Seine spekulative Eigenart oder Sein Verhältnis zu Olivi." *Beiträge zur Geschichte der Philosophie und Theologie des Mittelalters: Texte und Untersuchungen Supplementband* 2 (1923): 243–54.

Jones, Gareth Lloyd. "Paul of Burgos and the Adversus Judaeos Tradition." *Henoch* 21 (1999): 314–29.

Jordan, William C. *The French Monarchy and the Jews: From Philip Augustus to the Last Capetians.* Middle Ages Series. Philadelphia: University of Pennsylvania Press, 1989.

———. "Home Again: The Jews in the Kingdom of France, 1315–1322." In *The Stranger in Medieval Society,* ed. F. R. P. Akehurst and Stephanie Cain Van D'Elden, 27–45. Minneapolis: University of Minnesota Press, 1997.

———. "Princely Identity and the Jews." In *From Witness to Witchcraft: Jews and Judaism in Medieval Christian Thought,* ed. Jeremy Cohen, 257–73. Wolfenbütteler Mittelalter-Studien 11. Wiesbaden: Harrassowitz, 1996.

Kaczynski, Bernice. "Illustrations of Tabernacle and Temple Implements in the *Postilla in Testamentum Vetus* of Nicolaus de Lyra." *Yale University Library Gazette* 48 (1973): 1–11.

Kamesar, Adam. *Jerome, Greek Scholarship, and the Hebrew Bible.* Oxford: Clarendon Press, 1993.

Kamin, Sarah. *Rashi's Exegetical Categorization in Respect to the Distinction Between Peshat and Derash.* Jerusalem: Hebrew University, 1986.

———. "The Relation of Nicolas de Lyre to Rashi in his Commentary on Song of Songs." In *Jews and Christians Interpret the Bible*, 62–72. Hebrew. Jerusalem: Magnes Press, Hebrew University, 1991.

Kamin, Sarah, and Avrom Saltman, eds. *Secundum Salomonem: A Thirteenth-Century Latin Commentary on the Song of Solomon.* Ramat Gan: Bar-Ilan University Press, 1989.

Kent, Bonnie. *Virtues of the Will: The Transformation of Ethics in the Late Thirteenth Century.* Washington, D.C.: Catholic University of America Press, 1995.

Klauck, Hans-Josef. "Theorie der Exegese bei Bonaventura." In vol. 4, 71–128. *Bonaventura, 1274–1974*, ed. Jacques Guy Bougerol and Etienne Gilson. Grottaferrata: Collegio San Bonaventura, 1974.

Kleinhans, Arduin. "Heinrich von Cossey, O.F.M. Ein Psalmen-Erklärer des 14. Jahrhunderts." In *Miscellanea Biblica et Orientalia, Athanasio Miller, completis LXX annis oblata*, ed. Adalbertus Metzinger, 239–53. Studia Anselmiana, philosophica theologica 27–28. Rome: Orbis Catholicus, 1951.

———. "De studio sacrae Scripturae in ordine fratrum minorum saeculo XIII." *Antonianum* 7 (1932): 413–440.

Klepper, Deeana C. "The Dating of Nicholas of Lyra's *Quaestio de adventu Christi.*" *AFH* 86 (1993): 297–312.

———. "'First in Knowledge of Divine Law': The Jews and the Old Law in Nicholas of Lyra's Romans Commentary." In *Reading Romans in the Middle Ages*, ed. Charles Cosgrove, Peter Hawkins, and Brenda Schildgen. London: T&T Clark/Continuum, forthcoming.

———. "Literal Versus Carnal: George of Siena's Christian Reading of Jewish Exegesis." In *Jewish Biblical Interpretation in Comparative Context*, ed. David Stern and Natalie Dohrmann. Philadelphia: University of Pennsylvania Press, forthcoming.

Kluxen, Wolfgang. "Literaturgeschichtliches zum lateinischen Moses Maimonides," *Recherches de théologie ancienne et médiévale* 21 (1954): 23–58

Kraus, Samuel. *Das Leben Jesu nach Jüdischen Quellen.* Berlin: S. Calvary, 1902.

Krey, Philip. "The Apocalypse Commentary of 1329: Problems in Church History." In *Nicholas of Lyra: The Senses of Scripture*, ed. Philip Krey and Lesley Smith, 267–88. Leiden: Brill, 2000.

———. "Many Readers But Few Followers: The Fate of Nicholas of Lyra's 'Apocalypse Commentary' in the Hands of His Late-Medieval Admirers." *Church History* 64 (1995): 185–201.

———. "Nicholas of Lyra: Apocalypse Commentary as Historiography." Ph.D. diss., University of Chicago, 1990.

———. "'The Old Law Prohibits the Hand and Not the Spirit': The Law and the Jews in Nicholas of Lyra's Romans Commentary of 1329." In *Nicholas of Lyra: The Senses of Scripture*, ed. by Philip Krey and Lesley Smith, 251–66. Leiden: Brill, 2000.

Kriegel, Maurice. "Mobilisation politique et modernisation organique: Les expulsions des juifs au bas Moyen Ages." *Archives des sciences sociales de religions* 46, no. 1 (1978): 5–11.

———. "La juridiction inquisitoriale sur les juifs à l'époque de Philippe le Hardi et Philippe le Bel." In *Les juifs dans l'histoire de France*, ed. Myriam Yardeni, 70–77. Leiden: Brill, 1980.

Labrosse, Henri. "Sources de la biographie de Nicolas de Lyre." *Études franciscaines* 16 (1906): 383–404.

———. "Biographie de Nicolas de Lyre." *Études franciscaines* 17 (1907): 488–505, 593–608.

———. "Oeuvres de Nicolas de Lyre." *Études franciscaines* 19 (1908): 41–52, 153–75, 368–79; 35 (1923): 171–87, 400–432.

Laguna Paúl, Teresa. *Postillae in vetus et novum testamentum de Nicolás de Lyra.* Seville: Universidad de Sevilla, 1979.

Langlois, Charles-Victor. "Nicolas de Lyre, Frère Mineur." In *Histoire littéraire de la France*, vol. 36, 355–401. Paris, 1927.

Lavin, Marilyn Aronberg. "The Altar of Corpus Domini in Urbino." *Art Bulletin* 49 (1967): 1–24.

Lazard, L. "Note sur la légende du juif de la rue des Billetes." *Annuaire des archives Israélites* 4 (1887–88): 56–60.

Leff, Gordon. *Paris and Oxford Universities in the Thirteenth and Fourteenth Centuries.* New York: Wiley, 1968.

Lerner, Robert. *The Heresy of the Free Spirit in the Later Middle Ages.* Berkeley: University of California Press, 1972.

———. "An 'Angel of Philadelphia' in the Reign of Philip the Fair: The Case of Guiard of Cressonessart." In *Order and Innovation in the Middle Ages*, ed. William C. Jordan et al., 343–64, 529–40. Princeton, N.J.: Princeton University Press, 1976.

———. *The Powers of Prophecy: The Cedar of Lebanon Vision from the Mongol Onslaught to the Dawn of the Enlightenment.* Berkeley: University of California Press, 1983.

———. *The Feast of Saint Abraham: Medieval Millenarians and the Jews.* Philadelphia: University of Pennsylvania Press, 2000.

Lesnick, Daniel R. *Preaching in Medieval Florence: The Social World of Franciscan and Dominican Spirituality.* Athens: University of Georgia Press, 1989.

Levy, Joshua. "Sefer Milhamot ha-Shem, Chapter Eleven: The Earliest Jewish Critique of the New Testament." Ph.D. diss., New York University, 2004.

Lieberman, Saul. *Shkiin: A Few Words on Some Jewish Legends, Customs, and Literary Sources Found in Karaite and Christian Works.* 2nd ed. Jerusalem: Sifre Vahrman, 1970.

Liere, Frans van. "The Literal Sense of the Books of Samuel and Kings: From Andrew of St. Victor to Nicholas of Lyra." In *Nicholas of Lyra: The Senses of Scripture*, ed. Philip Krey and Lesley Smith, 59–81. Leiden: Brill, 2000.

Little, Andrew G. *The Grey Friars in Oxford.* Oxford: Clarendon Press, 1892.

———. "The Franciscan School at Oxford in the Thirteenth Century." *AFH* 19 (1926): 803–74.

Little, Andrew G., and Franz Pelster. *Oxford Theology and Theologians, c. A.D. 1282–1302.* Oxford: Clarendon Press, 1934.

Little, Lester. *Religious Poverty and the Profit Economy in Medieval Europe.* Ithaca, N.Y.: Cornell University Press, 1983.

Loeb, Isidore. "La controverse sur le Talmud sous St. Louis." *Revue des études juives* 1, 2, 3 (1880): 247–61; 48–70; 39–57.

———. "Les expulsions des juifs de France au XIVᵉ siècle." In *Jubelschrift zum Siebszigsten Geburtstag des Prof. Dr. H. Graetz,* 39–56. Breslau: Schottlaender, 1887. Reprint Hildesheim, 1973.

Loewe, Raphael. "Herbert of Bosham's Commentary on Jerome's Hebrew Psalter. A Preliminary Investigation into Its Sources." *Biblica* 34 (1953): 44–77, 159–92, 275–98.

———. "The Medieval Christian Hebraists of England: Herbert of Bosham and Earlier Scholars." *Transactions of the Jewish Historical Society of England* 17 (1953): 225–49.

———. "The Medieval Christian Hebraists of England: The *Superscriptio Lincolniensis.*" *Hebrew Union College Annual* 28 (1957): 205–52.

———. "Alexander Neckam's Knowledge of Hebrew." *Medieval and Renaissance Studies* 4 (1958): 17–34.

———. "Latin *Superscriptio* Manuscripts on Portions of the Hebrew Bible Other Than the Psalter." *Journal of Jewish Studies* 9 (1958): 63–71.

Long, James R. "On the Usefulness Of 'Augustinianism' as a Historical Construct: Two Test Cases from Oxford." *Medieval Perspectives* 16 (2001): 74–83.

———. "Richard Fishacre." In *A Companion to Philosophy in the Middle Ages,* ed. Jorge J. E. Gracia and Timothy B. Noone, 563–68. Oxford: Blackwell, 2003.

Longpré, Ephrem. "Guillaume de la Mare." In *Dictionnaire de théologie catholique,* vol. 8, 2467–70. Paris: Letouzey et Ané, 1925.

———. "Le quodlibet de Nicolas de Lyre, O.F.M." *AFH* 23 (1930): 42–56.

Lubac, Henri. *Exégèse médiévale: Les quatre sens de l'écriture.* 4 vols. Paris, 1959.

Maccoby, Hyam, ed. and trans. *Judaism on Trial: Jewish-Christian Disputations in the Middle Ages.* Rutherford, N.J.: Fairleigh Dickinson University Press, 1982.

Madigan, Kevin. "Lyra on the Gospel of Matthew." In *Nicholas of Lyra: The Senses of Scripture,* ed. Philip Krey and Lesley Smith, 195–221. Leiden: Brill, 2000.

Mailloux, Benoit. "St. Thomas et les juifs: Essais et belans." *Journées thomistes* 1 (1935): 217–35.

Mandonnet, Pierre F. "Premiers travaux de polémique thomiste." *Revue des sciences philosophiques et théologique* 7 (1913): 46–70, 245–62.

Marenbon, John. *Later Medieval Philosophy (1150–1350): An Introduction.* London: Routledge & Kegan Paul, 1987.

Marrone, Steven. *Truth and Scientific Knowledge in the Thought of Henry of Ghent.* Cambridge, Mass.: Medieval Academy of America, 1985.

———. *The Light of Thy Countenance: Science and Knowledge of God in the Thirteenth Century.* Leiden: Brill, 2001.

McEvoy, James. *Robert Grosseteste.* Oxford: Oxford University Press, 2000.

McGinn, Bernard. "Bonaventure's Apocalyptic Theology of History." In McGinn,

Visions of the End: Apocalyptic Traditions in the Middle Ages. New York: Columbia University Press, 1979.

McVaugh, Michael. "Further Documents for the Biography of Arnau De Vilanova." *Acta hispanica ad medicinae scientiarumque historiam illustrandam* 2 (1982): 363–72.

Menache, Sophia. "Faith, Myth and Politics: The Stereotype of the Jews and Their Expulsion from England and France." *Jewish Quarterly Review* 75 (1985): 351–74.

Merchavia, Chai. "The Talmud in the *Additiones* of Paul of Burgos," *Journal of Jewish Studies* 16 (1965): 115–134.

———. *The Church Versus Talmudic and Midrashic Literature.* Hebrew. Jerusalem: Bialik, 1970.

Merrill, Eugene H. "Rashi, Nicholas De Lyra, and Christian Exegesis." *Westminster Theological Journal* 38, no. 1 (1975): 66–79.

Michalski, A. J. "Raschis Einfluss auf Nikolaus von Lyra in der Auslegung der Bücher Leviticus, Numeri, und Deuteronimum." *Zeitschrift für alttestamentliche Wissenschaft* 35 (1915): 218–45; (1916): 29–63.

———. "Raschis Einfluss auf Nikolaus von Lyra in der Auslegung des Buches Josua." *Zeitschrift für alttestamentliche Wissenschaft* 39 (1921): 300–307.

Minnis, Alastair J. *Medieval Theory of Authorship.* Philadephia: University of Pennsylvania Press, 1984.

Mollat, Guillaume, ed. *Bernard Gui: Manuel de l'inquisiteur.* Paris: Champion, 1927.

Moore, Rebecca. *Jews and Christians in the Life and Thought of Hugh of St. Victor.* South Florida Studies in the History of Judaism. Atlanta: Scholars Press, 1998.

Morard, Martin. *Le commentaire des Psaumes de saint Thomas d'Aquin: Édition critique partielle et introduction historique.* 5 vols. Thèse pour l'obtention du titre d'archiviste paléographe, diss. dactyl., Paris, École nationale des Chartes, 2002.

———. "Entre Mode et Tradition: Les Commentaires des Psaumes de 1160 à 1350." In *La Bibbia del XIII Secolo: Storia del testo, Storia dell'esegesi. Atti del Convegno della Società Internazionale per lo Studio del Medioevo Latino* (SISMEL) (Florence, June 1–2, 2001), ed. Giuseppe Cremascoli and Francesco Santi, 323–52. Florence: SISMEL, Edizioni del Galluzzo, 2004.

Muldoon, James. *Popes, Lawyers, and Infidels: The Church and the Non-Christian World, 1250–1550.* Philadelphia: University of Pennsylvania Press, 1979.

Mundill, Robin R. *England's Jewish Solution: Experiment and Expulsion, 1262–1290.* Cambridge: Cambridge University Press, 1998.

Mutius, Hans Georg von. *Die Christiliche-Jüdische Zwangsdisputation zu Barcelona: Nach dem Hebraischen Protokoll des Moses Nachmanides.* Frankfurt: Peter Lang, 1982.

McMichael, Steven J. and Susan E. Myers, eds. *Friars and Jews in the Middle Ages and Renaissance.* Leiden: Brill, 2004.

Neumann, J. "Influence de Raschi et d'autres commentateurs juifs sur les *Postillae Perpetuae* de Nicolas de Lyre." *Revue des études juives* 26, 27 (1893): 172–82; 250–62.

Nisse, Ruth. *Defining Acts: Drama and the Politics of Interpretation in Medieval England.* Notre Dame, Ind.: University of Notre Dame Press, 2005.

Ocker, Christopher. *Biblical Poetics Before Humanism and Reformation*. Cambridge: Cambridge University Press, 2002.

Olszowy-Schlanger, Judith. "The Knowledge and Practice of Hebrew Grammar Among Christian Scholars in Pre-Expulsion England: The Evidence of 'Bilingual' Hebrew-Latin Manuscripts." In *Hebrew Scholarship in the Medieval World*, ed. Nicholas de Lange, 107–28. Cambridge: Cambridge University Press, 2001.

———. *Les manuscrits hébreux dans l'Angleterre médievale: Étude historique et paléographique*. Collection de la revue des études juives 29. Paris: Peeters, 2003.

Osana, J. "Doctrina apologetica magistri Nicolai de Lyra." Ph.D. diss., Gregorian University, 1953.

Pasnau, Robert. *Theories of Cognition in the Later Middle Ages*. Cambridge: Cambridge University Press, 1997.

Patschovsky, Alexander. "Der 'Talmudjude':Vom mittelalterlichen Ursprung eines neuzeitlichen Themas." In *Juden in der christlichen Umwelt während des späten Mittelalters*, ed. Alfred Haverkamp and Franz-Josef Ziwes, 13–27. Berlin: Duncker & Humblot, 1992.

Patton, Corinne. "Creation, Fall, and Salvation: Lyra's Commentary on Genesis 1–3." In *Nicholas of Lyra: The Senses of Scripture*, ed. Philip Krey and Lesley Smith, 19–43. Leiden: Brill, 2000.

Pelster, Franz. "Roger Marston O.F.M. (d. 1303), ein englischer Vertreter des Augustinismus." *Scholastik* 3 (1928): 526–56.

———. "*Quodlibeta* und *Quaestiones* des Nikolaus von Lyra O.F.M. (d. 1349)." In *Mélanges Joseph de Ghellinck, S.J.*, vol. 2, *Moyen Age, époques moderne et contemporaine*, 951–73. Gembloux: Duculot, 1951.

———. "Nikolaus von Lyra und seine *Quaestio de usu paupere*." *AFH* 46 (1953): 211–50.

Perarnau, Josep. "Guiu Terrena Critica Arnau de Vilanova." *Arxiu de Textos Catalans Antics* 7/8 (1988–89): 221–22.

Piganiol de la Force, Jean Aimar. *Description Historique de la Ville de Paris et des environs*. Paris: Chez les Libraires Associés, 1765.

Piron, Sylvain. "The Formation of Olivi's Intellectual Project: 'Petrus Ioannis Olivi and the Philosophers' Thirty Years Later." In *Oliviana: Recherches sur Petrus Ioannis Olivi et les courants spirituels, XIIIe–XVe siècles*, vol. 1. 2003. http://www.oliviana.org/document6.html (accessed July 7, 2005)

———. "Parcours d'un intellectuel franciscain. D'une théologie vers une pensée sociale: L'oeuvre de Pierre de Jean Olivi (Ca. 1248–1298) et son traité de contractibus." Ph.D. diss. École des Hautes Études en Sciences Sociales, 1999.

———. "Le poète et le théologien: Une rencontre dans le Studium de Santa Croce." *Picenum Seraphicum* 19 (2000): 87–134.

Poirel, Dominique . *Livre de la nature et débat trinitaire au XIIe siècle: Le De tribus diebus de Hughes de Saint-Victor*. Turnhout: Brepols, 2002.

Popper, William. *The Censorship of Hebrew Books*. New York: Knickerbocker Press, 1899.

Princeton University Art Museum. *The Carl Otto von Kienbusch, Jr., Memorial Collection, *Special Exhibition Catalogue, June 1956. No. 67.* Princeton, N.J.: Princeton University Press, 1956.

Raedts, Peter. *Richard Rufus of Cornwall and the Tradition of Oxford Theology.* Oxford: Clarendon Press, 1987.

Raunie, Emile. *Epitaphier du Vieux Paris: Recueil genéral des inscriptions funéraires des églises, couvents, collèges, hospices, cimitières, et charniers depuis le Moyen Age jusqu'à la fin du XVIIIᵉ siècle.* 4 vols. Paris: Paris Couvent de Cordeliers, 1893–1914.

Reinhardt, Klaus. "Das Werk des Nikolaus von Lyra im Mittelalterlichen Spanien." *Traditio* 43 (1987): 321–58.

Rembaum, Joel. "The Talmud and the Popes: Reflections on the Talmud Trials of the 1240s." *Viator* 13 (1982): 203–23.

———. "The Development of a Jewish Exegetical Tradition Regarding Isaiah 53." *Harvard Theological Review* 75, no. 3 (1982): 289–311.

Renan, Ernest. *Les rabbins français du commencement du quatorzième siècle.* Paris, 1877.

Resnick, Irven M. "The Falsification of Scripture and Medieval Christian and Jewish Polemics." *Medieval Encounters* 2 (1996): 344–80.

Riché, Pierre, and Guy Lobrichon, eds. *Le Moyen Age et la Bible.* Paris: Beauchesne, 1984.

Roest, Bert. Reading the Book of History: Intellectual Contexts and Educational Functions of Franciscan Historiography 1226–1350. Ph.D. diss., Rijksuniversiteit Groningen, 1996.

Rosenau, Helen. "The Architecture of Nicolaus de Lyra's Temple Illustrations and the Jewish Tradition." *Journal of Jewish Studies* 25 (1974): 294–304.

Rosenthal, Judah M. "The Talmud on Trial: The Disputation at Paris in the Year 1240." *Jewish Quarterly Review* 47 (1956–57): 58–76; 145–69.

Rouse, Richard H., and Mary A. Rouse. *Manuscripts and Their Makers: Commercial Book Producers in Medieval Paris, 1200–1500.* 2 vols. Turnhout: Harvey Miller, 2000.

Rubin, Miri. *Gentile Tales: The Narrative Assault on Late Medieval Jews.* 1999. Reprint Philadelphia: University of Pennsylvania Press, 2004.

Ruh, Karl. "Nikolaus Von Lyra." In *Die Deutsche Literatur des Mittelalters. Verfasserlexikon,* ed. Wolfgang Stammler and Karl Langosch, et al., vol. 5, 1117–22. Berlin: de Gruyter, 1987.

Rüthing, Heinrich. "Kritische Bemerkungen zu einer mittelalterlichen Biographie des Nikolaus von Lyra." *AFH* 60 (1967): 42–54.

Saarinen, Risto. *Weakness of the Will in Medieval Thought: From Augustine to Buridan.* Leiden: Brill, 1994.

Sapir Abulafia, Anna. "Gilbert Crispin's Disputations: An Exercise in Hermeneutics." In *Les mutations socio-culturelles au tournant des XIᵉ–XIIᵉ siècles: Études anselmiennes.* Ed. Raymonde Foreville, 511–20. Paris: Editions du Centre national de la recherche scientifique, 1984.

———. *Christians and Jews in Dispute: Disputational Literature and the Rise of Anti-Judaism in the West (c. 1000–1150).* Variorum Collected Studies Series Cs621. Aldershot: Variorum, 1998.

Sbaraglia, Giovanni Giacinto. *Supplementum et castigatio ad scriptores trium ordinum Sancti Francisci*. 3 vols. Rome: A. Nardecchia, 1906.

Shatzmiller, Joseph. *Shylock Reconsidered: Jews, Moneylending, and Medieval Society*. Berkeley: University of California Press, 1990.

Schmitt, Jean-Claude. "Le miroir du canoniste: Les images et le texte dans un manuscrit médiéval." *Annales ESC* 48, no. 6 (1993): 1471–95.

Schreckenberg, Heinz. *Die Flavius-Josephus-Tradition in Antike und Mittelalter*. Arbeiten zur Literatur und Geschichte des Hellenistischen Judentums. Leiden: Brill, 1972.

———. *Die Christlichen Adversus-Judaeos Texte und ihr Literarisches und Historisches Umfeld* (1.–11. Jh.). Frankfurt am Main: Peter Lang, 1982.

———. *Jewish Historiography and Iconography in Early and Medieval Christianity*. Assen: Van Gorcum; Minneapolis: Fortress Press, 1992.

———. "Paulus von Burgos." In *Biographisch-Bibliographisches Kirchenlexikon*, 57–60. Herzberg: Bautz, 1994.

Schwarzfuchs, S. "The Expulsion of the Jews from France, 1306." In *The Seventy-fifth Anniversary Volume of the Jewish Quarterly Review*, ed. Abraham A. Neuman and Solomon Zeitlin, 482–89. Philadelphia: Jewish Quarterly Review, 1967.

Serrano, Luciano. *Los Conversos Pablo de Santa Maria y Alfons de Cartagena*. Madrid: Consejo Superior de Investigaciones Científicas, 1942.

Shailor, Barbara. "A New MS of Nicolaus de Lyra." *Yale University Library Gazette* 58 (1983): 9–16.

Shank, Michael H. *"Unless You Believe You Shall Not Understand": Logic, University, and Society in Late Medieval Vienna*. Princeton, N.J.: Princeton University Press, 1988.

Schatzmiller, Joseph. "Converts and Judaizers in the Early Fourteenth Century." *Harvard Theological Review* 74 (1981): 63–77.

———. *Shylock Reconsidered: Jews, Moneylending, and the Medieval Society*. Berkeley: University of California Press, 1990.

Shereshevsky, Esra. "Hebrew Traditions in Peter Comestor's Historia Scholastica." *Jewish Quarterly Review* (1968–69): 268–89.

Signer, Michael. "St. Jerome and Andrew of St. Victor: Some Observations." *Studia Patristica* 18 (1982): 333–37.

———. "Thirteenth-Century Christian Hebraism: The *Expositio* on Canticles in MS Vat. lat. 1053." In vol. 3, *Approaches to Judaism in Medieval Times*, ed. David R. Blumenthal, 98–100. Atlanta: Scholars Press, 1988.

———. "Peshat, Sensus Literalis, and Sequential Narrative: Jewish Exegesis and the School of St. Victor in the Twelfth Century." In *The Frank Talmage Memorial Volume*, ed. Barry Walfish, 203–16. Haifa: University of Haifa, 1993.

———. "Vision and History: Nicholas of Lyra on the Prophet Ezechiel." In *Nicholas of Lyra: The Senses of Scripture*, ed. Philip Krey and Lesley Smith, 147–71. Leiden: Brill, 2000.

Singer, Charles. "Hebrew Scholarship in the Middle Ages among Latin Christians." In *The Legacy of Israel*, ed. Edwyn R. Bevan and Charles Singer, 283–314. Oxford: Clarendon Press, 1927.

Smalley, Beryl. "Hebrew Scholarship Among Christians in Thirteenth-Century England, as Illustrated by Some Hebrew-Latin Psalters." In *Lectiones in Vetere Testamento Et in Rebus Judaicis*, no. 6, 1–18. London: Shapiro, Valentine, 1939.

———. "A Commentary on the Hebraica by Herbert of Bosham." *Recherche de théologie ancienne et medievale* 18 (1951): 29–65.

———. "The Biblical Scholar." In *Robert Grosseteste, Scholar and Bishop*, ed. Daniel A. P. Callus, 70–97. Oxford: Clarendon Press, 1955.

———. *English Friars and Antiquity in the Early Fourteenth Century*. Oxford: Blackwell, 1960.

———. "William of Auvergne, John of La Rochelle, and St. Thomas Aquinas on the Old Law." In *Studies in Medieval Thought and Learning from Abelard to Wyclif*. London: Hambledon Press, 1981.

———. "John Baconthorpe's Postill on St. Matthew." *Medieval and Renaissance Studies* 4 (1958): 91–145.

———. *The Study of the Bible in the Middle Ages*. 3rd ed. Oxford: Blackwell, 1983.

Smith, Lesley. "The Rewards of Faith: Nicholas of Lyra on Ruth." In *Nicholas of Lyra: The Senses of Scripture*, ed. Philip Krey and Lesley Smith, 45–58. Leiden: Brill, 2000.

Southern, Richard W. "The Place of England in the Twelfth Century Renaissance." In *Medieval Humanism and Other Studies*, 158–80. Oxford: Blackwell, 1970.

———. *Robert Grosseteste: The Growth of an English Mind in Medieval Europe*. Oxford: Clarendon Press, 1986.

Stacey, Robert. "The Conversion of Jews to Christianity in Thirteenth-Century England." *Speculum* 67 (1992): 263–83.

Stadler, Herbert. "Textual and Literary Criticism and Hebrew Learning in English Old Testament Scholarship, as Exhibited by Nicholas Trevet's *Expositio Litteralis Psalterii* and by MS Corpus Christi College (Oxford) 11." Master's thesis, Corpus Christi College, Oxford, 1989.

Stowe, Kenneth. *Alienated Minority: The Jews of Medieval Latin Europe*. Cambridge, Mass.: Harvard University Press, 1992.

Strack, Hermann L., and Paul Billerbeck. *Kommentar zum Neuen Testament aus Talmud und Midrasch*. Munich: Beck, 1922–61.

Stuehrenberg, Paul F. "The Medieval Commentary Tradition: The Glossa Ordinaria, Hugh of St. Cher, and Nicholas of Lyra and the Study of the Bible in the Middle Ages." *Journal of Religious and Theological Information* 1, no. 2 (1993): 91–101.

Synan, Edward A. *The Popes and the Jews in the Middle Ages*. New York: Macmillan, 1965.

Tachau, Katherine. *Vision and Certitude in the Age of Ockham: Optics, Epistemology, and the Foundations of Semantics, 1250–1345*. Studien und Texte zur Geistesgeschichte des Mittelalters 22. Leiden: Brill, 1988.

Tolan, John Victor. *Petrus Alfonsi and His Medieval Readers*. Gainesville: University Press of Florida, 1993.

Turner, Denys. *Eros and Allegory: Medieval Exegesis of the Song of Songs*. Cistercian Studies Series 156. Kalamazoo, Mich.: Cistercian Publications, 1995.

Turner, Nancy. "An Attack on the Acknowledged Truth: French, English, and German Theologians on the Jews in the Fourteenth Century." Ph.D. diss., University of Iowa, 1996.

———. "Robert Holcot on the Jews." In *Chaucer and the Jews: Sources, Contexts, Meanings*, ed. Sheila Delany, 133–44. New York: Routledge, 2002.

———. "Jews and Judaism in Peter Aureol's *Sentences* Commentary." In *Friars and Jews in the Middle Ages and Renaissance*, ed. Steven J. McMichael and Susan E. Myers, 81- 98. Leiden: Brill, 2004.

———. "Jewish Witness, Forced Conversion, and Island Living: John Duns Scotus on Jews and Judaism." In *Christian Attitudes Toward the Jews in the Middle Ages: A Casebook*, ed. Michael Frassetto. New York: Routledge, 2006.

Ullman, Walter. "John Baconthorpe as Canonist." In *Church and Government in the Middle Ages: Essays Presented to C. R. Cheney on his 70th Birthday*, ed. Christopher N. L. Brooke, et al., 223–46. Cambridge: Cambridge University Press, 1976.

Valli, E. "Das Verhältnis des Claus Cranc zu Nicolaus von Lyre." *Neuphilologische Mitteilungen* 53 (1952): 331–38.

Verdeyen, P. "Le procés d'inquisition contre Marguerite Porete et Guiard de Cressonessart (1309–1310)." *Revue d'histoire ecclésiastique* 81 (1986): 41–94.

Vernet, Félix. "Nicolas de Lyre." In *Dictionnaire de théologie catholique*, 1410–22. Paris: Letouzey & Ané, 1926.

Viard, Jules. "Date de la mort de Nicolas de Lyre." *Bibliothèque de l'Ecole des Chartes* 56 (1895): 141–143.

Vidal, Jean-Marie. *Bullaire de l'inquisition française au XIVe siècle et jusqu'à la fin du grand schisme*: Paris: Librairie Letouzey & Ané, 1913.

Visscher, Eva de. "The Jewish-Christian Dialogue in 12th-Century Western Europe: The Hebrew and Latin Sources of Bosham's Commentary on the Psalms." Ph.D. diss., University of Leeds, 2003.

Walde, Bernhard. *Christliche Hebraisten Deutschlands am Ausgang des Mittelalters*. Münster: Aschendorffsche Verlagsbuchhandlung, 1916.

Walfish, Barry. *The Frank Talmage Memorial Volume*. Haifa: Haifa University Press; Hanover, N.H.: University Press of New England, 1993.

Walsh, Katherine, and Diana Wood. *The Bible in the Medieval World: Essays in Memory of Beryl Smalley*. Studies in Church History Subsidia 4. Oxford: Published for the Ecclesiastical History Society by Blackwell, 1985.

Wauhkonen, Rhonda. "The Authority of Text: Nicholas of Lyra's Judaeo-Christian Hermeneutic and the Canterbury Tales." *Florilegium: Carleton University Annual Papers on Classical Antiquity and the Middle Ages* 11 (1992): 141–59.

Williams, A. Lukyn. *Adversus Iudeos: A Bird's Eye View of Christian Apologiae Until the Renaissance*. Cambridge: Cambridge University Press, 1935.

Wilpert, Paul, ed. *Judentum im Mittelalter: Beiträge zum christlich-jüdischen Gespräch*. Berlin: De Gruyter, 1966.

Wippel, John. "The Condemnations of 1270 and 1277 at Paris." *Journal of Medieval and Renaissance Studies* 7 (Fall 1977): 169–201.

———. "Quodlibetal Questions Chiefly in Theology Faculties." In *Les questions disputées et les questions quodlibétique dans les facultés de théologie, de droit et de médecine*, ed. Bernardo C. Bazán et al., 153–222. Typologie des sources du Moyen Age occidental 44–45. Turnhout: Brepols, 1985.

Wood, Rega. "Church and Scripture in Franciscan Gospel Commentaries." Ph.D. diss., Cornell University, 1975.

———. "Nicholas of Lyra and Lutheran Views of Ecclesiastical Office." *Journal of Ecclesiastical History* 29, 4 (1978): 451–62.

———. "Richard Rufus of Cornwall." In *A Companion to Philosophy in the Middle Ages*, ed. Jorge J. E. Gracia and Timothy B. Noone, 579–87. Oxford: Blackwell, 2003.

Xiberta, Bartolomé. *De scriptoribus scholasticis saeculi XIV ex Ordine Carmelitarum.* Bibliothèque de la Revue d'Histoire Ecclésiastique 6. Louvain: Bureaux de la Revue, 1931.

———. *Analecta ordinis Carmelitarum* 6 (1929): 3–128; 516–26.

Yardeni, Myriam, ed. *Les juifs dans l'histoire de France: Premier colloque international de Haifa.* Leiden: Brill, 1980.

Yerushalmi, Yosef H. "The Inquisition and the Jews of France in the Time of Bernard Gui." *Harvard Theological Review* 63 (1970): 317–76.

Zier, Mark. "Nicholas of Lyra on the Book of Daniel." In *Nicholas of Lyra: The Senses of Scripture*, ed. Philip Krey and Lesley Smith, 173–93. Leiden: Brill, 2000.

Index

Acknowledgments

I have experienced such generosity over the many years I have been at work on this project that I could not possibly name all of those who have played a role in bringing the book to fruition. Some of the work for this book was begun many years ago while I was a fellow at the American Academy in Rome, and I remain grateful for the support I enjoyed then. Williams College was extraordinarily generous during the time I served as a visiting professor of history there, funding a trip to consult Italian manuscripts and archival materials. Boston University has since supported my research in a number of ways. A fellowship at the University of Pennsylvania's Center for Advanced Judaic Studies allowed me to spend a semester of uninterrupted time on the project in the stimulating company of colleagues working on related issues in Jewish, Christian, and Islamic exegesis; much of my thinking on Nicholas of Lyra's role as Hebraist emerged during that time. The Boston University Humanities Foundation has borne the cost of Harvard University library borrowing privileges for me for the past several years, an invaluable contribution. Librarians at Boston University, Harvard University, the University of Pennsylvania, the British Library, the Bodleian Library, the Bayerische Staatsbibliothek, the Bibliothèque Nationale de France, and the Biblioteca Apostolica Vaticana were particularly helpful at various stages; the head librarian at St. John's Seminary in Brighton, Massachusetts, graciously allowed me access to the library's collection while it was closed for the summer. Laura Giles, of the Princeton University Art Museum, went out of her way to make a valuable manuscript in the museum's collection available to me, including providing digitized images for study. Adelaide Bennett, of Princeton University's Index of Christian Art, came through with helpful information on the manuscript at just the right time. My work was also facilitated by the generosity of book collector David Wells, who gave to me his copy of the first volume of the 1506 Basel edition of Nicholas of Lyra's *Postilla litteralis super Bibliam*, just for the pleasure of seeing the book used.

John Clayton was chair of the Department of Religion at Boston University when I first arrived. His enthusiasm for my research and his conviction that a historian could and should feel at home in a religion department made the transition to a new disciplinary environment a positive experience. Sadly, he did not live to see this work brought to completion; he is missed. My students and my colleagues in the departments of both Religion and History at Boston University have contributed to a stimulating environment in which to work; special thanks are due to Peter Hawkins, Michael Zank, and Jon Roberts for their encouragement. Stephen Prothero, my department chair, helped to bring the manuscript to completion by providing me with a research assistant during the final stages of preparation. Emily Taylor Merriman has been the most wonderful research assistant imaginable, chasing books, manuscripts, and illuminations, providing editorial feedback, proofreading, and being generally indispensable. Thanks also to Cristine Hutchison-Jones for technical assistance with the manuscript in various versions.

I am sincerely grateful to Jerome Singerman, Mariana Martinez, Alison Anderson, and the staff at the University of Pennsylvania Press for their help in bringing the book to print. I would also like to thank the Press's anonymous readers and the copy editor for their helpful comments, as well as Matthew Reidsma, who took great care in proofreading the Latin. I owe special thanks to David Ruderman, series editor, for his encouragement and help moving the manuscript toward publication. I would like to thank Koninklijke Brill N.V. for permission to reprint material in Chapter 1 that appeared originally in a volume edited by Philip Krey and Lesley Smith entitled *Nicholas of Lyra: The Senses of Scripture* (2000), and the British Library, the Bibliothèque Nationale de France, the Princeton University Art Museum, the Bibliothèque Municipale de Reims, and the Bibliothèque Municipale de Tours for permission to reproduce images.

I am grateful to many individuals whose conversation at critical moments forwarded the work in different ways, including Jeremy Cohen, Michael Signer, Philip Krey, Lesley Smith, Kevin Madigan, Christopher Ocker, Stephen McMichael, Ruth Nisse, Miri Rubin, Gilbert Dahan, Alexander Patschovsky, Nina Caputo, Nancy Turner, Jeffrey Hamburger, Deborah Goodwin, and above all Robert E. Lerner, with whom I had the privilege of studying at Northwestern University and whose influence is evident in my work. I am grateful beyond words for his encouragement and guidance over the years. Any remaining faults in the current work are my own responsibility entirely.

My personal debts are as great as my intellectual ones. Deborah Steiner and Abigail Gillman both provided a level of encouragement and support without which I could not have navigated the challenges I faced along the academic path. My husband, Jeff, has traveled along with me and has been a steadfast partner and companion; thanks do not suffice. My children, Rachel and Liora, give meaning to it all, and I am grateful to them for trying to understand the value of this work. I thank the rest of my family, too, for their love and support. Finally, I owe a tremendous debt to Patricia and Kent Shifferd, first inspiring undergraduate professors, then mentors, now friends; they opened windows onto worlds that I could not have imagined and transformed my life. I dedicate this book to them in small repayment for the riches they have given me.